PREFACES TO SHAKESPEARE

Books *by* Harley Granville-Barker

Plays.

The Marrying of Ann Leete.
The Voysey Inheritance. (Revised 1913.)
Waste. (Rewritten 1926.)
The Madras House. (Revised 1925.)
Rococo : Vote by Ballot : Farewell to the Theatre. (Three
    one-act plays.) 1917.
The Secret Life. 1923.
His Majesty. 1928.

With LAURENCE HOUSMAN.

Prunella : or, Love in a Dutch Garden. 1906.

With DION CLAYTON CALTHROP.

The Harlequinade. 1918.

English Versions of Foreign Plays.

Anatol : *by* Arthur Schnitzler. 1911.
Deburau : *by* Sacha Guitry. 1921.
Doctor Knock : *by* Jules Romains. 1925.
Six Gentlemen in a Row : *by* Jules Romains. 1927.

With HELEN GRANVILLE-BARKER.

The Kingdom of God : *by* Gregorio Martínez Sierra. 1927.
The Romantic Young Lady : *by* the same. 1929.
Take Two from One : *by* G. and M. Martínez Sierra. 1931.
The Women have their Way: A Hundred Years Old :
    Fortunato : The Lady from Alfaqueque : *by* Serafín and
    Joaquín Alvarez Quintero. 1927.
Love Passes by : Don Abel wrote a Tragedy : Peace and
    Quiet : Doña Clarines : *by* Serafín and Joaquín Alvarez
    Quintero. 1932.

Criticism.

The Exemplary Theatre. 1922.
From Henry V. to Hamlet.
Prefaces to Shakespeare : First Series. 1927.
Prefaces to Shakespeare : Second Series. 1930.
A National Theatre. 1930.
On Dramatic Method. 1931.

SIDGWICK & JACKSON, LTD.

PREFACES TO SHAKESPEARE

BY
HARLEY
GRANVILLE-BARKER

Second Series

LONDON : SIDGWICK & JACKSON, LTD.
44 MUSEUM STREET
1935

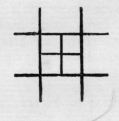

First published . . . 1930
Second impression . . 1935

G. 2887.

Richard Clay & Sons, Ltd., Printers, Bungay, Suffolk.

THE substance (or some of it) of the prefaces to *Romeo and Juliet* and *Antony and Cleopatra* was delivered in lectures at University College, Aberystwith; and my thanks are due, and are warmly paid, to that foundation and to the audiences who patiently listened to me. Prefaces to *The Merchant of Venice* and *Cymbeline* made part of my share in The Player's Shakespeare, but these that follow bear small relation to them. Coming back to the plays, and re-reading those prefaces, I was not, on the whole, astonished to find how much I had had to learn; the study of Shakespeare's stage and his stagecraft is by no means a simple business. And I have been able to profit, I hope, from such considered criticism as the companion volume to this present one (published two years ago) has received.

But some of it served to show me that I did not, perhaps, make the aim of the work and—I am tempted to add, for this I believe—the need for it very clear, nor the method adopted clear enough. Upon a minor point of method, for instance, I find one critic (otherwise most kindly) reproaching me with my use of the word playwright. It is in itself a good word, surely, and has ample sanction. But I should have pointed out, I suppose—since this he did not see—that I was carefully using it in a particular sense, for the craftsman, the playmaker as distinct from the completer dramatist, the artist. This may seem finicky, and the distinction will not, of course, be exact. But one is constantly needing to make this distinction and others like it, and qualification as constant becomes tiresome. All æsthetic discussion suffers, in its very nature, from inexact thought, doubly by the confusion and by a poverty of current terms. Both the art and the craft of the Shakespearean stage are the harder to discuss because one must so continually use words that have no agreed meaning, and often be held up by lack of any word at all that will not smack too aggravatingly of the twelve-volume Oxford Dictionary and Torquemada. Such confusion as comes from main stage, front stage and outer stage, inner stage and alcove, upper stage and balcony being used to express, not seven things, but three, a reader can fairly easily resolve. But take the word ' scene,' which may well be wanted on every other page, and then in every paragraph. It has more nearly a dozen meanings than one, and it actively breeds confusion. Will it be too much to say that half our modern misunderstandings of Shakespeare's stagecraft are due to the shifting (over three centuries) and varied meanings of ' scene '? *Antony and Cleopatra* with its crowd of ' scenes,' which Shakespeare never named scenes at all, which, if he had, would still have been quite unlike the ' scene ' that the reader of to-day will have in mind, is our most distinguished victim— as I have now tried to show. But the confusion dogs us all the time. It is, however, one inevitable part of the rediscovery of Shakespeare the playwright, and evidence that a rediscovery there has to be. As to poverty of vocabulary, that trouble can be trusted to cure itself. One is chary of drastic remedies. Sir Mark Hunter (to whom I owe much

PREFACE

more than this) gave me the excellent word ' ana-
topism ' for a convenient complement to anachronism, which I was using too loosely. Coleridge
fathered it, apparently, and de Quincey found it
useful. But after dallying with it a little I felt I
had better let it alone till it came back into commoner currency. Somehow, when Shakespeare's
art is the topic, one does not want to have to pull
up short and ask: Now what does *this* mean?

Another kindly critic visited me with a subtler
reproach. He could not quite make out what was
wrong. He thought it might be that '. . . some
of us like our Shakespeare neat, or, shall we say,
prefer a direct communion with him. . . .' I
sympathise. But if a play is to be treated as a play,
we cannot have it so; the actors and their acting
intervene. But if these prefaces, continues my
critic, are for the producer, in that they are redundant too. ' For there are as many ways of producing Shakespeare capably as there have been
or ever will be producers capable of producing his
plays, and no other artist will be content with any
other way than his own.' Not quite so many, I
think; and I rather distrust that artist who will
not be content with any other way than his own.
After all, there was once Shakespeare's. We cannot
reproduce this exactly, I agree, because too much
that was topical would always be lacking; nor,
therefore, should we try to. But his stagecraft had
its essentials, and until the producer has mastered
these his own inspired way is neither here nor there.
Much of Shakespeare's stagecraft—and the best of
it, no doubt—is fundamental to all drama. Show
it on what sort of stage you will, it cannot fail of its
effect. But more than we have thought is framed

vii

to the stage for which he wrote it (why we never thought it would be is a mystery!) and, lacking the belongings of this—the essential, not the incidental and accidental belongings—it will fail of its full effect, and often of any. No one will deny, at least, that if we crush it without more consideration into the conditions of the modern theatre we stifle the life out of it.

All I have set out to do is to rediscover as much as I can of this lost stagecraft. One must, I think, make the attempt play by play. Shakespeare's stage changed a little, perhaps more than a little, during his working lifetime, and he himself enlarged its artistic resources to the limits of recognition. We have generalised far too freely upon the matter. I should have made this aim clear to my critic. But, looking back, I find I did make it clear; I am now repeating myself. However, there is no great harm in that. One remembers the Bellman's 'What I tell you three times is true.' He might have made it thirty.

One difficulty—and fault—I must own to. It is impossible to study Shakespeare as a craftsman only; for his craft is the lesser part of his art, and the two are inextricably woven together. I cannot do other than try to interpret each play as a whole; and, as with all art, it must be largely a personal interpretation. But if Shakespeare's duality is not to be disentangled, mine certainly is; and the artist who cannot ' be content with any other way than his own ' should be able to separate the useful metal from the dross. That, at least, is my hope. For these books have quite a practical aim. I want to see Shakespeare made fully effective on the English stage. This is the best sort of help I can lend.

Let my kindly critic forgive me then—but if he cannot, and this catches his eye, he had better read no further—when he finds that these prefaces, and, in particular, those to *Antony and Cleopatra* and *Cymbeline*, leave him his Shakespeare by no means neat, but deep drowned in interpretation. I have done this deliberately to show how much and how intensive a study needs to be given to the masterpieces (the minor plays do not need it) if all their secrets, their dramatic secrets merely, are to be revealed. I could have found lots more to say. Others will find other things to say. The sooner they say them and put them to the proof the better; and the more I shall, at any rate, try to be pleased. This sort of work finds its best reward in being forgotten because the need for it has gone.

I am in debt, as one likes to be, to my fellow-students; most particularly to Sir Mark Hunter, who has read my proofs and saved me from many a blunder, would have saved me from many more, perhaps, had I let him. I ought to add that we are at daggers drawn on the question of act division, and that he likes Mark Antony better than I do. The text for my quotations and their punctuation in the main is taken from the Arden Shakespeare. The altogether admirable Nonesuch edition now appearing tempted me to use the Folio text for them: one should read the plays in it, undoubtedly. But wedged in among modern spelling, the effect would have been spotty and distracting. There are other difficulties too. I have found (who does not?) the Furness Variorum most valuable.

H. G.-B.

October 1929.

CONTENTS

xi

CONTENTS

ROMEO AND JULIET

ROMEO AND JULIET is lyric tragedy, and this must be the key to its interpreting. It seems to have been Shakespeare's first unquestionable success, proof positive of his quality and token that he was bringing to the theatre something no one else could bring. If marred by one or two clumsy turns, its stagecraft is simple and sufficient; and the command of dramatic effect is masterly already. It is immature work still, but it is not crude. The writing shows us a Shakespeare skilled in devices that he is soon to reject or adapt to new purpose. This, which to the critic is one of the most interesting things about the play, is a stumbling block to its acting. But the passion and poignant beaut of it all, when we surrender ourselves to them, m e such reservations of small enough account.

Whether we have the play as Shakespeare fir wrote it may be doubted; we probably have it in the second Quarto as it last left his hands. But signs, as they may seem to be, of re-writing and re-touching at one time or another, must always, in this or any of his plays, be warily viewed. They may, of course, be so obvious as to ask no proof; but when they depend on nice calculation one must remember that the critical foot rule is poor measure for genius—and the very poorest for genius in its springtime.

ii. 2

The Mercutio of the Queen Mab speech is not, it can be argued, the Mercutio of

> No, 'tis not so deep as a well, nor so wide as a church door; but 'tis enough, 'twill serve.

Did the Juliet, one asks, of

> Hath Romeo slain himself? Say thou but " I "
> And that bare vowel " I " shall poison more
> Than the death-darting eye of cockatrice:
> I am not I, if there be such an " I " . . .

and the rest of the fantasia, turn within a sitting or so into the Juliet of

> Ancient damnation! Oh most wicked fiend!
> Is it more sin to wish me thus forsworn,
> Or to dispraise my lord with that same tongue,
> Which she hath praised him with above compare
> So many thousand times?

and the Romeo of

> . . . more courtship lives
> In carrion flies than Romeo: they may seize
> On the white wonder of dear Juliet's hand. . . .
> This may flies do, when I from this must fly. . . .

into the stark figure of the scene in Mantua, meeting the news of her death with

> Is it even so? Then I defy you, stars! . . .

—into the Romeo who pays the apothecary with

> There is thy gold; worse poison to men's souls,
> Doing more murder in this loathsome world
> Than these poor compounds that thou mayest not sell;
> I sell thee poison, thou hast sold me none.

By all the rules, no doubt, there should be two Shakespeares at work here. But in such a a ferment as we now find him (himself, in

2

some sort, a young Romeo on the turn from a Rosaline of phrase-making to a deeper-welling love) he may well have been capable of working on Tuesday in one fashion, on Wednesday in another, capable of couplet, sonnet, word-juggling, straight sober verse, or hard-bitten prose, often as the popular story he was turning to account and the need of the actors for the thing they and he were so apt at seemed to demand, at times out of the new strength breeding in him. Our present concern, however, is with the play as we have it, and its interpreting in the theatre.

THE CONDUCT OF THE ACTION

The dominating merit of this is that Shakespeare takes Brooke's tale, and at once doubles its dramatic value by turning its months to days.

These violent delights have violent ends. . . .

and a sense of swiftness belongs to them, too. A Hamlet may wait and wait for his revenge; but it accords with this love and its tragedy that four days should see its birth, consummation and end. Incidentally we can here see the ' double-time '— which has so exercised the ingenuity of commentators, who will credit him with their own— slipping naturally and easily into existence.[1] He makes dramatic use of time when he needs to.

Capulet. But soft, what day is this?
Paris. Monday, my lord.
Capulet. Monday! Ha! ha! Well, Wednesday is too soon;
O' Thursday let it be:—o' Thursday, tell her,
She shall be married to this noble earl . . .

[1] In the preface to the *Merchant of Venice* this discussion is raised again.

This sense of the marriage looming but three days ahead is dramatically important; later, to intensify it, he even lessens the interval by a day. But (his mind reverting now and then to Brooke's story as he read it, possibly before he saw that he must weave it closer) he will carelessly drop in phrases that are quite contradictory when we examine them. But what audience will examine them as they flash by?

I anger her sometimes (says the Nurse to Romeo) and tell her that Paris is the properer man . . .

(when neither Paris nor Romeo has been in the field for four and twenty hours.)

Is it more sin to wish me thus forsworn,
Or to dispraise my lord with that same tongue
Which she hath praised him with above compare
So many thousand times? . . .

(when, all allowance made for Juliet's exaggeration, the Nurse has not had twice twenty-four hours in which to praise or dispraise). But notice that this suggestion of the casual slackness of normal life conveniently loosens the tension of the tragedy a ✦ little. There is, indeed, less of carelessness than a sort of instinctive artistry about it; and the method is a natural by-product of the freedom of Shakespeare's theatre.

But he marshals his main action to very definite purpose. He begins it, not with the star-crossed lovers (though a prologue warns us of them), but with a clash of the two houses; and there is far more significance in this than lies in the fighting. The servants, not the masters, start the quarrel. If Tybalt is a firebrand Benvolio is a peacemaker; and though Montague and Capulet themselves are drawn in, they have the grace to be a little ashamed after. The hate is cankered; it is an ancient quarrel set new abroach; and even the tetchy Capulet owns that it should not be so hard for men of their age to keep the peace. If it were not for the servants, then, who fight because they always have fought, and the Tybalts, who will quarrel about nothing sooner than not quarrel at all, it is a feud ripe for settling; everyone is weary of it; and no one more weary, more impatient with it than Romeo;

> O me! What fray was here?
> Yet tell me not—for I have heard it all. . . .

We are not launching, then, into a tragedy of fated disaster, but—for a more poignant if less highly heroic theme—of opportunity muddled away and marred by ill-luck. As a man of affairs, poor Friar Laurence proved deplorable; but he had imagination. Nothing was likelier than that the Montagues and Capulets, waking one morning to find Romeo and Juliet married, would have been only too thankful for the excuse to stop killing each other.

> And the continuance of their parents' rage,
> Which, but their children's end, nought could remove . . .

says the Prologue. Nought in such a world as this, surmises the young Shakespeare; in a world where

> I thought all for the best.—

avails a hero little; for on the heels of it comes

> O, I am fortune's fool!

Some other consolation than callous oblivion there must be for us, one would hope; but he is to

5

finish his dramatist's course without finding very much.

Having stated his theme, he develops it, as his habit already is (and was to remain; the method so obviously suits the continuities of the Elizabethan stage), by episodes of immediate contrast in character and treatment. Thus, after the bracing rattle of the fight and the clarion of the Prince's judgment, we have our first sight of Romeo, fantastic, rueful, self-absorbed. His coming is preluded by a long passage of word music; and, that its relevance may be plain, the verse slips into the tune of it at the first mention of his name. Benvolio's brisk story of the quarrel, dashed with irony, is finishing—

> . . . While we were interchanging thrusts and blows,
> Came more and more, and fought on part and part
> Till the Prince came, who parted either part.

—when Lady Montague interposes with

> O, where is Romeo? Saw you him to-day?
> Right glad am I he was not in this fray.

and promptly, like a change from wood wind, brass and tympani to an andante on the strings, comes Benvolio's

> Madam, an hour before the worshipped sun
> Peered forth the golden window of the east . . . .

Montague echoes him; and to the wooing smoothness of

> But he, his own affections' counsellor,
> Is to himself—I will not say, how true,
> But to himself so secret and so close,
> So far from sounding and discovery
> As is the bud bit with an envious worm,
> Ere he can spread his sweet leaves to the air,
> Or dedicate his beauty to the sun.
> Could we but learn from whence his sorrows grow,
> We would as willingly give cure as know.

6

Romeo appears; moody, oblivious of them all three. It is a piece of technique that belongs both to Shakespeare's stage in its simplicity and to the play's own lyrical cast.

Then (for contrasts of character and subject), close upon Romeo's mordant thought-play and word play with Benvolio come Capulet and Paris, the sugary old tyrant and the man of wax, match-making —and such a good match for Juliet as it is to be! Close upon this comes Benvolio's wager that he'll show Romeo at the feast beauties to put Rosaline in the shade; and upon that, our first sight of Juliet, when she is bid take a liking to Paris at the feast if she can.

The scene of the procession of the maskers to Capulet's house (with Romeo a spoil-sport as befits his mood) is unduly lengthened by the bravura of the Queen Mab speech, which is as much and as little to be dramatically justified as a song in an opera is.[1] But Shakespeare makes it serve to quicken the temper of the action to a pitch against which—as against the dance, too, and Tybalt's rage—Romeo's first encounter with Juliet will show with a quiet beauty all its own. Did he wonder for a moment how to make this stand out from every-

---

[1] The young gentlemen are gate-crashers, we perceive; there are few novelties in the social world! But Capulet is delighted; he even, when the unlooked-for fun is over and the recalcitrant regular guests have been coaxed to dance, presses a 'trifling foolish banquet' upon the strangers; cake and wine upon the sideboard, that is to say, and not, as the word now implies, a substantial sit-down affair. But etiquette, it seems, is against this. Having measured them a measure and so wound up the occasion very merrily, the 'strangers' do begone. Seriously, the conduct of this scene, when it is staged, needs attention. It is generally quite misunderstood and misinterpreted.

7

thing else in the play? They share the speaking of a sonnet between them, and it is a charming device. One must picture them there. The dance is over, the guests and the maskers are in a little chattering, receding crowd, and the two find themselves alone.[1] Juliet would be for joining the others; but Romeo, his mask doffed, moves towards her, as a pilgrim towards a shrine.

If I profane with my unworthiest hand. . . :

It is hard to see what better first encounter could have been devised. To have lit mutual passion in them at once would have been commonplace; the cheapest of love tragedies might begin like that. But there is something sacramental in this ceremony, something shy and grave and sweet; it is a marriage made already. And she is such a child; touched to earnestness by his trembling earnestness, but breaking into fun at last (her defence when the granted kiss lights passion in him) as the last quatrain's metre breaks for its ending into

You kiss by the book.

The tragedy to come will be deepened when we remember the innocence of its beginning. The encounter's ending has significance too. They are not left to live in a fool's paradise for long. Romeo hears who she is and faces his fate. An hour ago he was affecting melancholy while Mercutio and his fellows laughed round him. Now, with the sport at

[1] The company, that is to say, drift up towards the inner stage, from which, as from the withdrawing rooms beyond the great hall, Capulet and the guests had come to welcome the masked invasion, and as they all move away the guessing at who the strangers are dies down.

its best, he braces to desperate reality. Then, as the guests and maskers depart and the laughter dies, Juliet grows fearful. She hears her fate and must face it, too.

> My only love sprung from my only hate,
> Too early seen unknown, and known too late,
> Prodigious birth of love it is in me
> That I must love a loathed enemy.

The child is no more a child.

A chorus follows. This may have some further function than to fill up time while furniture is shifted or stage fittings are adjusted; it is of no dramatic use.[1] Then Romeo appears alone.

And now, with his finest stroke yet, all prepared and pending (the love duet that is to be spoken from balcony to garden), Shakespeare pauses to do still better by it; and at the same time fits Mercutio to his true place in the character scheme.[2] To appreciate the device we must first forget the obliging editors with their *Scene 1, a lane by the wall of Capulet's orchard. Enter Romeo. . . . He Climbs the wall and leaps down within it. . . . Scene 2, Capulet's Orchard. Enter Romeo*—for all this has simply obliterated the effect.[3] The *Enter Romeo alone* of the Quartos

[1] But for more argument about the question of act division that is involved see p. 32.

[2] The Bodleian has recently recovered its original First Folio, and the pages of the balcony scene are the best thumbed of all.

[3] Rowe is responsible for this. A few of the later editors scented something wrong, but only half-heartedly tried to put it right. Grant White was an honourable exception; but he places Mercutio and Benvolio in the orchard too. Juliet's line

The orchard walls are high and hard to climb. . . .

discounts that.

and Folio is the only authentic stage direction con-
cerning him. What happens when Mercutio and
Benvolio arrive in pursuit? He hides somewhere
about the stage. He has, they say, 'leapt this
orchard wall '; but no wall is there, and—more
importantly—there is no break in the continuity
of the scene, now or later ; it should be proof enough
that to make one we must cut a rhymed couplet in
two. The confusion of whereabouts, such as it is,
that is involved, would not trouble the Elizabethans
in the least; would certainly not trouble an audience that later on was to see Juliet play half a scene
on the upper stage and half on the lower, with
no particular change of place implied. The effect,
so carefully contrived, lies in Romeo's being well
within hearing of all the bawdry now to follow,
which has no other dramatic point; and that the
chaff is about the chaste Rosaline makes it doubly
effective.

Dominating the stage with his lusty presence,
vomiting his jolly indecencies, we see the sensual
man, Mercutio ; while in the background lurks
Romeo, a-quiver at them, youth marked for
tragedy.[1] His heart's agonising after Rosaline had
been real enough. He has forgotten that! But
what awaits him now, with another heart, passionate
as his own, to encounter? This is the eloquence of
the picture, which is summed up in Romeo's
rhyming end to the whole dithyramb as he steals
out, looking after the two of them:

He jests at scars that never felt a wound. . . .

---

[1] The effect will, of course, be intensified if he never leaves
our sight, but the mere continuity of the scene, and our sense
of him there, produces it.

The discord thus struck is perfect preparation for the harmony to come ; and Mercutio's ribaldry has hardly died from our ears before Juliet is at her window.

Throughout the famous scene Shakespeare varies and strengthens its harmony and sustains its drama by one small device after another. We must return to more careful study of it. At its finish, with the brisk couplet

> Hence will I to my ghostly father's cell,
> His help to crave, and my dear hap to tell.

to bring us to earth again ; and the action speeds on, to find a new helmsman in Friar Laurence. His importance to the play is made manifest by the length of his first soliloquy, and Shakespeare is looking forward already, we find, to the potion for Juliet. All goes smoothly and happily; the Friar is sententious, the lovers are ecstatic, Mercutio, Benvolio and the nurse make a merry work-a-day chorus. Only that one note of warning is struck, lightly, casually:

> Tybalt, the kinsman of old Capulet,
> Hath sent a letter to his father's house. . . .

The marriage scene brings this ' movement ' to its close.

The Friar. So smile the heavens upon this holy act
That after-hours with sorrow chide us not!
Romeo. Amen, amen! But come what sorrow can,
It cannot countervail the exchange of joy
That one short minute gives me in her sight.
Do thou but close our hands with holy words,
Then love-devouring death do what he dare,
It is enough I may but call her mine.
The Friar. These violent delights have violent ends,
And in their triumph die. . . .

Youth triumphant and defiant, age sadly wise; a
scene of quiet consummation, stillness before the
storm. We are just half-way through the play.

> Come, come with me, and we will make short work.
> For, by your leaves, you shall not stay alone,
> Till holy church incorporate two in one.

But upon this, in immediate, most significant contrast, there stride along Mercutio and Benvolio,
swords on hip, armed servants following them,
Mercutio with mischief enough a-bubble in him for
the prudent Benvolio to be begging:

> I pray thee, good Mercutio, let's retire;
> The day is hot, the Capulets abroad,
> And if we meet we scarce shall 'scape a brawl,
> For now, these hot days, is the mad blood stirring.

—and (with one turn of the dramatist's wrist)
tragedy is in train.[1]

The scene that follows is the most strikingly
effective thing in the play. It comes quickly to its
crisis when Romeo enters to encounter Tybalt face
to face. For this moment the whole action has been
preparing. Consider the constituents of the situation. Tybalt has seen Romeo eyeing his cousin
Juliet from behind a mask and its privilege, and to
no good purpose, be sure. But in Benvolio's and
Mercutio's eyes he is still the lackadaisical adorer of
Rosaline, a scoffer at the famous family quarrel
suddenly put to the proof of manhood by a Capulet's
insult. We know—we only—that he has even now
come from his marriage to Juliet, from the marriage
which is to turn these

> . . . households' rancour to pure love.

---

[1] One cannot too strongly insist upon the effect Shakespeare
gains by this vivid contrast between scene and scene, swiftly
succeeding each other. It is his chief technical resource.

The moment is made eloquent by a silence. For what is Romeo's answer to be to an insult so complete in its sarcastic courtesy?

> Romeo, the love I bear thee can afford
> No better term than this: Thou art a villain.

Benvolio and Mercutio, Tybalt himself, have no doubt of it; but to us the silence that follows—its lengthening by one pulse-beat mere amazement to them—is all suspense. We know what is in the balance. The moment is, for Romeo, so packed with emotions that the actor may interpret it in half a dozen ways, each legitimate (and by such an endowment we may value a dramatic situation). Does he come from his 'one short minute' with Juliet so rapt in happiness that the sting of the insult cannot pierce him, that he finds himself contemplating this Tybalt and his inconsequent folly unmoved? Does he flash into passion and check it, and count the cost to his pride and the scorn of his friends, and count them as nothing, all in an instant? Whatever the effect on him, we, as we watch, can interpret it, no one else guessing. And when he does answer:

> Tybalt, the reason that I have to love thee
> Does much excuse the appertaining rage
> To such a greeting: villain am I none;
> Therefore, farewell; I see thou know'st me not.

the riddle of it is plain only to us. Note that it is the old riddling Romeo that answers, but how changed! We can enjoy, too, the perplexity of those other onlookers and wonder if no one of them will jump to the meaning of the

> . . . good Capulet, which name I tender
> As dearly as my own. . . .

But they stand stupent and Romeo passes on.

13

Upon each character concerned the situation tells differently; yet another test of its dramatic quality. Benvolio stands mute.. He is all for peace, but such forbearance who can defend?[1] For Tybalt it is an all but comic let down. The turning of the cheek makes the smiter look not brave, but ridiculous; and this ' courageous captain of compliments' takes ridicule very ill, is the readier, therefore, to recover his fire-eating dignity when Mercutio gives him the chance. And Mercutio, so doing, adds that most important ingredient to the situation, the unforeseen.

Why the devil came you between us? (he gasps out to Romeo a short minute later) I was hurt under your arm.

But what the devil had he to do with a Capulet–Montague quarrel? The fact is (if one looks back) that he has been itching to read fashion-monger Tybalt a lesson; to show him that ' *alla stoccata* ' could not carry it away. But ' *alla stoccata* ' does; and, before we well know where we are, this arbitrary catastrophe gives the sharpest turn yet to the play's action, the liveliest of its figures crumples to impotence before us, the charming rhetoric of the Queen Mab speech has petered out in a savage growl.

The unexpected has its place in drama as well as the plotted and prepared. But observe that Shakespeare uses Mercutio's death to precipitate an essential change in Romeo; and it is this change,

[1] He had been forced to a bout himself with Tybalt the day before; and his description a little later of Romeo,

With gentle breath, calm look, knees humbly bowed. . . .

has exasperation, as well, perhaps, as some politic exaggeration in it.

not anything extrinsic, that determines the main tragedy. After a parenthesis of scuffle and harsh prose he is left alone on the stage, and a simpler, graver, sterner emotion than any we have known in him yet begins to throb through measured verse.

> This gentleman, the prince's near ally,
> My very friend, hath got this mortal hurt
> In my behalf; my reputation stained
> With Tybalt's slander—Tybalt, that an hour
> Hath been my cousin. O sweet Juliet,
> Thy beauty hath made me effeminate,
> And in my temper softened valour's steel.

Then he hears that his friend is dead, accepts his destiny—

> This day's black fate on more days doth depend;
> This but begins the woe others must end.

—and so to astonish the blood-intoxicated Tybalt! With a hundred words, but with expression and action transcending them, Shakespeare has tied the central knot of his play and brought his hero from height to depth.

We are sped on with little relaxation; returning, though, after these close-woven excitements, to declamation with Benvolio's diplomatic apologies (to the play's normal method, that is to say), while a second massed confronting of Montagues and Capulets marks, for reminder, this apex of the action.

We are sped on; and Juliet's ecstasy of expectation, the—

> Gallop apace, you fiery-footed steeds. . . .

—makes the best of contrasts, in matter and manner, to the sternness of Romeo's banishing. A yet sharper contrast follows quickly with the Nurse's coming, carrying the ladder of cords (the highway

15

to the marriage bed, for emphasis of irony), standing mute a minute while Juliet stares, then breaking
incontinently into her

> . . . he's dead, he's dead, he's dead.

From now—with hardly a lapse to quiet—one
scene will compete with the next in distraction till
Friar Laurence comes to still the outcry of mourning over the drugged Juliet on her bed. The lovers
compete in despair and desperate hope; Capulet
precipitates confusion; the Friar himself turns fool-
hardy. All the action is shot through with haste and
violence, and with one streak at least of gratuitous
savagery besides. For if the plot demands Capulet's
capricious tyrannies it does not need Lady Capulet's
impulse to send a man after Romeo to poison him.
But the freshly kindled virus of hatred (does Shakespeare feel?) must now spend itself even to exhaustion. From this point to the play's end, indeed,
the one reposeful moment is when Romeo's

> . . . dreams presage some joyful news at hand.

But the next is only the more shattering; and from
then to the last tragic accidents it is a tale of yet
worse violence, yet more reckless haste.[1]

[1] The slaughtering of Paris is wanton and serves little
dramatic purpose. Lady Montague is dead also by the end
of the play (though no one gives much heed to that) and Q1
even informs us that

> . . . young Benvolio is deceased too.

Here, however, the slaughter is probably less arbitrary—from
one point of view. The actors had other parts to play. By
the time Q 2 has come into being Shakespeare knows better
than to call attention to Benvolio's absence. Who notices
it? But his audiences—a proportion of them—no doubt
loved a holocaust for its own sake, and he was not above
indulging them now and then.

16

It is, of course, in the end a tragedy of mischance.
Shakespeare was bound by his story, was doubtless
content to be; and how make it otherwise? Nevertheless, we discern his deeper dramatic sense, which
was to shape the maturer tragedies, already in revolt.
Accidents make good incidents, but tragedy determined by them has no significance. So he sets out,
we see, in the shaping of his characters, to give all
likelihood to the outcome. It is by pure ill-luck
that Friar John's speed to Mantua is stayed while
Balthasar reaches Romeo with the news of Juliet's
death; but it is Romeo's headlong recklessness that
leaves Friar Laurence no time to retrieve the mistake.
It is, by a more subtle turn, Juliet's over-acted
repentance of her 'disobedient opposition,' which
prompts the delighted Capulet to

> . . . have this knot knit up to-morrow morning.

And this difference of a day proves also to be the
difference between life and death.

Before ever the play begins, the chorus foretells
its ending. The star-crossed lovers must, we are
warned,

> . . . with their death bury their parents' strife.

But Shakespeare is not content with the plain
theme of an innocent happiness foredoomed. He
makes good dramatic use of it. Our memory of
the prologue, echoing through the first scenes of
happy encounter, lends them a poignancy which
makes their beauties doubly beautiful. The sacrament of the marriage, with Romeo's invocation—

> Do thou but close our hands with holy words,
> Then love-devouring death do what he dare,
> It is enough I may but call her mine.

—read into it, stands as symbol of the sacrifice that

ii. 3

all love and happiness must make to death. But
character also is fate; it is, at any rate, the more
dramatic part of it, and the life of Shakespeare's art
is to lie in the manifesting of this. These two lovers,
then, must in themselves be prone to disaster. They
are never so freed from the accidents of their story
as his later touch would probably have made them.
But by the time he has brought them to their full
dramatic stature we cannot—accidents or no—
imagine a happy ending, or a Romeo and Juliet   +
married and settled as anything but a burlesque.

So, the turning point of Mercutio's death and
Tybalt's and Romeo's banishing being past, Shakespeare brings all his powers to bear upon the
moulding of the two figures to inevitable tragedy;
and the producer of the play must note with care
how the thing is done. To begin with, over a succession of scenes—in all but one of which either
Romeo or Juliet is concerned—there is no relaxing of tension, vehemence or speed; for every
flagging moment in them there is some fresh spur,
they reinforce each other too, the common practice
of contrast between scene and scene is more or less
foregone.[1] And the play's declamatory method is
heightened, now into rhapsody, now into a veritable
dervish-whirling of words.

Shakespeare's practical ability—while he still
hesitates to discard it—to turn verbal conventions to
lively account is shown to the full in the scene
between Juliet and the Nurse, with which this stretch
of the action begins—his success, also his failure.
The passage in which Juliet's bewildered dread finds
expression in a cascade of puns is almost invari-

[1] I say deliberately ' in all but one,' not two, for the reason
I give later.

18

ably cut on the modern stage, and one may sympathise with the actress who shirks it. But it is, in
fact, word-play perfectly adapted to dramatic use;
and to the Elizabethans puns were not necessarily
comic things.

> Hath Romeo slain himself? Say thou but " I,"
> And that bare vowel " I " shall poison more
> Than the death-dealing eye of cockatrice:
> I am not I, if there be such an " I,"
> Or those eyes shut that make thee answer " I."
> If he be slain say " I "; or if not, no:
> Brief sounds determine of my weal or woe.

Shut our minds to its present absurdity (but it is
no more absurd than any other bygone fashion),
allow for the rhetorical method, and consider the
emotional effect of the word-music alone—what a
vivid expression of the girl's agonised mind it makes,
this intoxicated confusion of words and meanings!
The whole scene is written in terms of conventional
rhetoric. We pass from play upon words to play
upon phrase, paradox, antithesis.

> O serpent heart, hid with a flowering face!
> Did ever dragon keep so fair a cave?
> Beautiful tyrant! fiend angelical!
> Dove-feathered raven! wolvish ravening lamb!
> Despised substance of divinest show!
> Just opposite to what thou justly seem'st;
> A damned saint, an honourable villain! . . . .

The boy-Juliet was here evidently expected to give
a display of virtuosity comparable to the singing of
a *scena* in a mid-nineteenth century opera. That
there was no danger of the audience finding it
ridiculous we may judge by Shakespeare's letting the
Nurse burlesque the outcry with her

> There's no trust,
> No faith, no honesty in men; all perjured,
> All forsworn, all naught, all dissemblers!

19

For it is always a daring thing to sandwich farce with tragedy; and though Shakespeare was fond of doing it, obviously he would not if the tragedy itself were trembling on the edge of farce.

The weakness of the expedient shows later, when, after bringing us from rhetoric to pure drama with the Nurse's

> Will you speak well of him that killed your cousin?

and Juliet's flashing answer

> Shall I speak ill of him that is my husband?

—one of those master touches that clarify and consummate a whole situation—Shakespeare must needs take us back to another screed of the sort which now shows meretricious by comparison. For a finish, though, we have the fine simplicity, set in formality, of

> *Juliet.* Where is my father and my mother, Nurse?
> *Nurse.* Weeping and wailing over Tybalt's corse.
> Will you go to them? I will bring you thither.
> *Juliet.* Wash they his wounds with tears! Mine shall be spent
> When theirs are dry, for Romeo's banishment.
> Take up those cords. Poor ropes, you are beguiled,
> Both you and I, for Romeo is exiled.
> He made you for a highway to my bed,
> But I, a maid, die maiden-widowed.

By one means and another, he has now given us a new and a passionate and desperate Juliet, more fitted to her tragic end.

In the scene that follows we have desperate Romeo in place of desperate Juliet, with the Friar to lift it to dignity at the finish and to push the story a short step forward. The maturer Shakespeare would not, perhaps, have coupled such similar scenes so closely; but both likeness and repetition serve his present purpose.

To appraise the value of the next effect he makes we must again visualise the Elizabethan stage.[1] Below

Enter Capulet, Lady Capulet and Paris.

With Tybalt hardly buried, Juliet weeping for him, it has been no time for urging Paris' suit.

> 'Tis very late (says Capulet), she'll not come down to-night:
> I promise you, but for your company,
> I should have been a-bed an hour ago.

Paris takes his leave, asks Lady Capulet to commend him to her daughter. She answers him:

> I will, and know her mind early to-morrow;
> To-night she's mewed up to her heaviness.

But *we* know that, at this very moment, Romeo and Juliet, bride and bridegroom, are in each other's arms.

Paris is actually at the door, when, with a sudden impulse, Capulet recalls him.[2]

> Sir Paris, I will make a desperate tender
> Of my child's love. I think she will be ruled
> In all respects by me; nay, more, I doubt it not.
> Wife, go you to her ere you go to bed;
> Acquaint her here of my son Paris' love,
> And bid her, mark you me, on Wednesday next. . . .

And by that sudden impulse, so lightly obeyed, the

---

[1] But we must do this throughout.

[2] And we may rely on this as one of the very few authenticated pieces of Shakespearean ' business.' For Q1 says

> *Paris offers to go in, and Capolet calls him again.*

If the presumed reporter watching the performance thought it important and had the time to note this down, it must have been markedly done.

tragedy is precipitated. Capulet, bitten by an idea, is in a ferment.

> . . . Well, Wednesday is too soon:
> O' Thursday let it be:—o' Thursday, tell her,
> She shall be married to this noble earl.
> Will you be ready? Do you like this haste? . . . .

(In a trice he has shaken off the mourning uncle and turned jovial, roguish father-in-law.)

> Well, get you gone! O' Thursday be it then—
> Go you to Juliet ere you go to bed,
> Prepare her, wife, against this wedding day. . . .

(What, we are asking, will Lady Capulet find if she does go?)

> Farewell, my lord. Light to my chamber, ho!
> Afore me, it's so very late
> That we may call it early by and by:—
> Good-night.

Now comes the well-prepared effect. Hardly have ⅟ the three vanished below, bustling and happy; when with

> Wilt thou begone? It is not yet near day. . . .

Juliet and Romeo appear at the window above, clinging together, agonised in the very joy of their union, but all ignorant of this new and deadly blow which (again) *we* know is to fall on them.

Only the unlocalised stage is capable of just such an effect as this. Delay in the shifting of scenery may be overcome by the simple lifting of a front scene to discover Romeo and Juliet in her chamber behind it; but Shakespeare's audience had not even to shift their imaginations from one place to another. The lower stage was anywhere downstairs in Capulet's house. The upper stage was

22

associated with Juliet; it had served for her balcony and had been put to no other use.[1] So while Capulet is planning the marriage with Paris not only will our thoughts have been travelling to her, but our eyes may have rested speculatively, too, on those closed curtains above.

Shakespeare speeds his action all he can. Capulet, itching with his new idea, gives invaluable help. Romeo has hardly dropped from the balcony before Lady Capulet is in her daughter's room.[2] Capulet himself comes on her heels. It is barely daybreak and he has not been to bed. (The night is given just that confused chronology such feverish nights seem to have.) With morning Juliet flies to the Friar, to find Paris already with him, the news already agitating him ; she herself is the more agitated by the unlooked-for meeting with Paris. The encounter between them, with its equivoque, oddly echoes her first encounter with Romeo; but it is another Juliet that now plays a suitor with words. It is a more deeply passionate Juliet, too, that turns from Paris' formal kiss with

> Oh, shut the door, and when thou hast done so
> Come weep with me ; past hope, past cure, past help.

than so passionately greeted the news of Tybalt's death and Romeo's banishment. Child she may still be, but she is now a wife.

We should count the Friar's long speech with which he gives her the potion, in which he tells her his plan, as a sort of strong pillar of rhetoric,

[1] The musicians at Capulet's supper would probably have sat in it; but this is hardly a dramatic use. Nor does the mere association with Juliet *localise* it. There is no such scientific precision in the matter.

[2] For the stage business involved here, see p. 33.

from which the play's action is to be swung to the next strong pillar, the speech (in some ways its counterpart), in which Juliet nerves herself to the drinking it. For, with Romeo removed for the moment, the alternating scene falls to Capulet and his bustlings; these are admirable as contrast, but of no dramatic power, and the action at this juncture must be well braced and sustained.

We come now to another and still more important effect, that is (yet again) only to be realised in the theatre for which it was designed. The curtains of the inner stage are drawn back to show us Juliet's bed. Her nurse and her mother leave her, she drinks the potion, and—says that note-taker at the performance, whose business it was, presumably, to let his employers know exactly how all the doubtful bits were done—

She falls upon the bed within the curtains.

There has been argument upon argument whether this means the curtains of the bed or of the inner-stage—which would then close on her. The difference in dramatic effect will be of degree and not kind. What Shakespeare aims at in the episodes that follow is to keep us conscious of the bed and its burden; while in front of it, Capulet and the servants, Lady Capulet and the nurse pass hither and thither, laughing and joking over their preparation for the wedding, till the bridal music is playing, till, to the very sound of this, the Nurse bustles up to draw back the curtains and disclose the girl there stark and still.[1]

[1] To Shakespeare's audience it would make little matter which sort of curtains they were. A closed bed standing shadowed on the inner stage is at once to be ignored and

This is one of the chief dramatic effects of the play; and it can only be gained by preserving the continuity of the action, with its agonies and absurdities cheek by jowl, with that bridal music sharpening the irony at the last. It is a comprehensive effect, extending from the drinking of the potion to the Nurse's parrot scream when she finds Juliet stiff and cold; and even beyond, to the coming of the bridegroom and his train, through the long-spoken threnody, to the farce of the ending—which helps to remind us that, after all, Juliet is not dead. It is one scene, one integral stretch of action; and its common mutilation by *Scene IV. Hall in Capulet's house*. . . . *Scene V. Juliet's chamber. Enter Nurse* . . . with the consequences involved, is sheer editorial murder.

Modern producers, as a rule, do even worse by it than the editors. They bring down a curtain upon a display of virtuosity in a ' potion-scene,' long drawn out, worried to bits, and leave us to recover till they are ready with Romeo in Mantua and the apothecary. And even faithful Shakespeareans have little good to say of that competition in mourning between Paris and Capulet, Lady Capulet and the Nurse. It has been branded as deliberate burlesque. It is assuredly no more so than was Juliet's outbreak against Romeo upon Tybalt's

---

recognised. We also, with a little practice, can ignore it, with Capulet; though to our more privileged gaze there it significantly is, in suspended animation, as it were, till the Nurse, fingering its curtains, brings it back to dramatic life, as we have known she must, as we have been waiting breathlessly for her to do. Whether they should be bed curtains or stage curtains is a matter of convention, a question of more imagination or less.

death; to each, we notice, the Nurse provides a comic, characteristic echo, which would have little point if it did not contrast, rather absurdly, with the rest. Burlesque, of a sort, comes later with Peter and the musicians; Shakespeare would not anticipate this effect, and so equivocally! The passage does jar a little; but we must remember that he is working here in a convention that has gone somewhat stale with him, and constrainedly; and that he can call now on no such youthful, extravagant passion as Juliet's or Romeo's to make the set phrases live. The situation is dramatically awkward, besides; in itself it mocks at the mourners, and Friar Laurence's reproof of them, which comes unhappily near to cant, hardly clarifies it. Shakespeare comes lamely out; but he went sincerely in. Nor does the farce of Peter and the musicians, conventional as it is, stray wholly beyond likelihood. Peter is comic in his grief; but many people are. Will Kempe, it may be, had to have his fling; but this part of the scene has its dramatic value, too. It develops and broadens—vulgarises, if you will—the irony of the bridal music brought to the death-bed; and, the traditional riddle-me-ree business done with (and Will Kempe having 'brought off an exit' amid cheers), there is true sting in the tail of it:

First Musician. What a pestilent knave is this same!
Second Musician. Hang him, Jack! Come, we'll in here; tarry for the mourners, and stay dinner.

And, of course, it eases the strain before tragedy gets its final grip of us.

We find Romeo in Mantua poised upon happiness before his last sudden plunge to despair and death.

Shakespeare has now achieved simplicity in his treatment of him, brought the character to maturity and his own present method to something like perfection. What can be simpler, more obvious yet more effective than the dream with its flattering presage of good news—

> I dreamt my lady came and found me dead—
> Strange dream, that gives a dead man leave to think !—
> And breathed such life with kisses in my lips,
> That I revived, and was an emperor. . . .

—followed incontinently by Balthasar's

> Her body sleeps in Capels' monument,
> And her immortal part with angels lives . . .

So much for dreams ! So much for life and its flatteries ! And the buying of the poison shows us a Romeo grown out of all knowledge away from the sentimental, phrase-making adorer of Rosaline.

> There is thy gold; worse poison to men's souls,
> Doing more murder in this loathsome world
> Than these poor compounds that thou mayst not sell:
> I sell thee poison, thou hast sold me none.

This ageing of Romeo is marked by more than one touch. To the contemptuous Tybalt he was a boy; now Paris to him, when they meet, is to be ' good gentle youth.'

Then, after one more needed link in the story has been riveted, we reach the play's last scene. Producers are accustomed to eliminate most of this, keeping the slaughtering of Paris as a prelude, concentrating upon Romeo's death and Juliet's, possibly providing a sort of symbolic picture of Montagues and Capulets reconciled at the end. This is all very well, and saves us the sweet kernel of the nut, no doubt; but it happens not to be the scene that

Shakespeare devised. To appreciate that we must once more visualise the stage for which it was devised. The authorities are in dispute upon several points here, but only of detail. Juliet lies entombed in the inner stage; that is clear. The outer stage stands for the churchyard; as elastically as it stood before for the street or the courtyard of Capulet's house in which the Maskers marched about, while the serving-men coming forth with their napkins converted it, as vaguely, into the hall. Now it is as near to the tomb or as far from it as need be, and the action on it (it is the larger part of this that is usually cut) will be prominent and important. The tomb itself is the inner stage, closed in, presumably, by gates which Romeo breaks open, through the bars of which Paris casts his flowers. Juliet herself lies like a recumbent effigy upon a rectangular block of stone, which must be low enough and wide enough for Romeo to lie more or less beside her; and other such monuments, un-effigied, Tybalt's among them, may surround her.[1]

Once more Shakespeare hurries us through a whole night of confusion; from the coming of Paris,

---

[1] We need not comb the text for objections to this arrangement, which is practicable, while no other is. For an explanation of

Why I *descend* into this bed of death . . . .

for instance, we have only to turn to Brooke's poem (lines 2620–2630). The frontispiece to Rowe's edition of the play is (incidentally) worth observing. It does not show a stage-setting, even a Restoration stage setting, but the tomb itself may well be the sort of thing that was used. Paris and Romeo, it can be seen, wear semi-Roman costume. Is this, by any hazardous chance, explicable by the fact that Otway's perversion of the play, *Caius Marius,* was then current in the theatres (*Romeo and Juliet* itself was not, it seems, revived till 1744; and then much altered)? Did du Guernier begin his drawing with the Roman lovers in his mind?

the cheated bridegroom, and Romeo, the robbed
husband, to this ghastly bride-bed, through one
tragic miscarrying after another, to the Prince's
summing up :

> A glooming peace this morning with it brings. . . .

Everything is hurry and confusion. Paris [1] is fearful of disturbance, and Romeo, when he comes, is
strained beyond endurance or control. It is not
till he has fleshed the edge of his desperation upon
poor Paris, till he is sobered by seeing what he
has done, that, armed securely with his poison,
he can take his calm farewell. Once he is dead,
confusion is let loose. The Friar approaches with

> Saint Francis be my speed! How oft to-night
> Have my old feet stumbled at graves! . . .

Balthasar and he whisper and tremble. Then
Juliet wakes; but before he can speak to her, the
Watch are heard coming. He flies; and she has
but time to find the empty phial in Romeo's hand,
bare time to find his dagger and stab herself before
they appear, and the hunt is up :

Paris' page.	This is the place; there, where the torch doth burn.
Captain of the Watch.	The ground is bloody; search about the church-yard:
	Go, some of you, whoe'er you find, attach.
	Pitiful sight! here lies the county slain,
	And Juliet, bleeding, warm and newly dead,
	Who here hath lain this two days buried.[2]
	Go, tell the Prince; run to the Capulets;
	Raise up the Montagues; some others search. ..

---

[1] For no compelling reason; but Shakespeare felt the need
of striking this note at once, since a first note will tend to be
the dominant one.

[2] Another instance of Shakespeare's use of time for momen-
tary effect—or of his carelessness. Or will someone find a
subtle stroke of character in the Watchman's inaccuracy?

Cries, confusion, bustle; Some of the watch bring back Balthasar, some others the Friar; the Prince arrives with his train, the Capulets surge in, the Montagues; the whole front stage is filled with the coming and going, while, in dreadful contrast, plain to our sight within the tomb, the torchlight flickering on them, Romeo and Juliet lie still.[1]

The play is not over, another hundred lines go to its finishing; and, to appease our modern impatience of talk when no more is to be done, here, if nowhere else, the producer will wield the blue pencil doughtily. Why should the Friar recount at length—after saying he'll be brief, moreover!— what we already know, with Balthasar to follow suit, and Paris' page to follow him? There are half a dozen good reasons. Shakespeare neither could nor would, of course, bring a play to a merely catastrophic end; the traditions of his stage no less than its conditions forbade this. Therefore the Prince's authoritative

> Seal up the mouth of outrage for a while,
> Till we can clear these ambiguities,
> And know their spring, their head, their true descent;
> And then I will be general of your woes.
> And lead you even to death: meantime forbear. . . .

with which he stills a tumult that threatens otherwise to end the play, as it began, in bloody rough-and-tumble—this is the obvious first note of a formal full-close. But the Friar's story must be told, because the play's true end is less in the death of the star-crossed lovers than in the burying of their parents' strife; and as it has been primarily a play

---

[1] It is of some interest to note that *Antony and Cleopatra* ends with a similar stage effect.

30

of tangled mischances, the unravelling of these, the bringing home of their meaning to the sufferers by them, is a natural part of its process. How else lead up to the Prince's

> Where be these enemies? Capulet—Montague!
> See what a scourge is laid upon your hate. . . .

and to the solution with Capulet's

> O brother Montague, give me thy hand.

For us also—despite our privileged vision—it has been a play of confused, passion-distorted happenings, and the Friar's plain tale makes the simple pity of them clear, and sends us away with this foremost in our minds. Again, declamation is the norm of the play's method, and it is natural to return to that for a finish. Finally, as it is a tragedy less of character than of circumstance, upon circumstance its last emphasis naturally falls. Yet, all this admitted, one must own that the penultimate stretch of the writing, at least, is poor in quality. Shakespeare has done well by his story and peopled it with passionate life. But, his impulse flagging, his artistry is still found immature. Compare the poverty of this ending with the resourceful breadth of the effect made in the rounding of the story of *Cymbeline* to a close.

THE QUESTION OF ACT DIVISION

Neither Quartos nor Folio mark act division; Rowe first supplies it, and his arrangement has commonly been accepted since. There are several questions involved. Did Shakespeare plan out the play as an indivisible whole? If he did, was it so acted; and, if not, were the pauses made mere formal pauses, or intervals, in which the emotional tension would not only relax, but lapse altogether? And, pauses or intervals, is Rowe's placing of them authentic? With the historical aspect of all this I am incompetent to deal. But Rowe's dividing up of the action is, clearly, neither here nor there; and even if it is not his, but a somehow inherited tradition, that still will not make it Shakespeare's. A play, as we know, soon passed beyond its author's control, and Elizabethan practice may have differed from play to play, and as between the public theatre and the private. How did Shakespeare *plan* his play? That is what we have to divine if we can; and from that we may pass directly to the question of our own convenience in the acting of it.

The one internal piece of evidence of a lost scheme of act division is the second chorus. This, incidentally, does not appear in the first Quarto. Is it capable of any other explanation? It has little dramatic point, as to this Johnson's robust verdict suffices; '. . . it conduces nothing to the progress of the play, but relates what is already known, or what the next scene will show; and relates it without adding the improvement of any moral sentiment.' It has been held very doubtfully Shakespearean. There is one thing to note about it and the scene which precedes it. This requires stools to be set on the outer stage for the use of Capulet and his cousin. They are presumably the joint-stools of the text, and the text makes provision for their setting. But we find none for their taking away, no dialogue to help out the business, and they could not well be moved during the latter half of the scene, when Romeo and Juliet are love-making.

In an act-pause they could presumably have been moved; but if there were none—was the chorus by chance written in to cover this technical clumsiness? It is possible; but the remedy seems as clumsy as the fault.[1]

Later, Shakespeare lands himself in a more serious technical difficulty, from which, though at some sacrifice of dramatic effect, an act-pause would have extricated him. He wants to show us Romeo and Juliet parting on their wedding night, Romeo descending from the very balcony which had seen their wooing and their brief happiness, and to follow this quickly by the bringing of the news to Juliet that she is to marry Paris. The double blow, no respite given, was the important thing to him dramatically, without doubt. But would he not have saved himself, if he well could, from the present ensuing clumsiness that brings Juliet from upper stage to lower in the middle of a scene, her bedroom on her back, as it were? Though an Elizabethan audience might make light of a lapse of this sort, it is none the less clumsy, and from the beginning he was an apt if a daring craftsman.[2]

[1] It looks as if another stool were needed on the outer stage when the Nurse returns to Juliet with her news of Romeo. But in this case no special provision is made either for its placing or removing.

[2] The scene could have been staged in no other way. *Enter Romeo and Juliet at the window*, says Q1; *Enter Romeo and Juliet aloft*, says Q2. Later Q1 tells us, *He goeth downe*; and later still we have

Enter Nurse hastily.

Nurse. Madame, beware, take heed the day is broke,
    Your Mother's comming to your Chamber. Make
      all sure.
        She goeth downe from the window.

ii. 4

Lastly, was the scene between Peter and the musicians written for its own sake, or to please Will Kempe, or (possibly) to make more time than the two scenes which carry on the plot allow for the moving of the bed and the setting of the tomb upon the inner stage? [1] If Rowe's act-pause had intervened there would have been time enough. These are trivial matters, but not wholly negligible.

If five acts there must be, Rowe's five may serve. But one could vary the division as legitimately in half a dozen different ways; and this in itself, argues against any division at all. Nor is there any scene-division in the play, where an act-division might fall, over which some immediate bridge does not seem to be thrown. Either a strong contrast is devised between the end of one scene and the beginning of the next that a pause would nullify, or the quick succession of event to event is an integral part of the dramatic effect Shakespeare is seeking. (But it is, of course, in the very nature of the play, of its precipitate passion, to forge ahead without pause.) What value is

---

Whether Juliet or the Nurse, does not matter. In fact they both must go down; for there follows immediately:

Enter Juliet, Mother, Nurse.

And a second later, after her

" How now, who calls? "

Juliet is on the stage. By Q2 the scene has been much rewritten. The Nurse is given more time for her descent. The later stage directions are less explicit. But that the business was approximately the same is certain, if for no other reason than that the last part of the scene, containing Capulet's outburst, could have been played nowhere but on the lower stage.

[1] 'Or/and,' as the lawyers sometimes have it, with regard to the last possibility.

there in an act pause after Capulet's supper, between Romeo's first meeting with Juliet and the balcony scene? There is no interval of time to account for, nor has the action reached any juncture that asks for the emphasis of a pause. An act-pause after the marriage falls with a certain effect, but it nullifies the far better effect by which Tybalt is shown striding the streets in search of Romeo at the very moment when the Friar is marrying him to Juliet; and that Romeo should seem to come straight from the marriage to face Tybalt's challenge is a vital dramatic point. The whole action surges to a climax with the deaths of Tybalt and Mercutio and Romeo's banishing; and here, one could argue, a pause while we asked 'What next?' might have its value. But Rowe marks no act-pause here; and if he did, the fine effect by which Juliet's ecstatic

> Gallop apace, you fiery-footed steeds. . . .

follows pat upon the Prince's

> . . . let Romeo hence in haste
> Else, when he's found, that hour is his last. . . .

would be destroyed. The break made between Juliet's departure to the Friar's cell for counsel how to escape the marriage with Paris and her arrival there and the encounter with him relates to no pause, nor check, nor turn in the action. Rowe's Act IV, we may say, then begins with the new interest of the giving of the potion, as it ends upon an echo of its taking. And a pause—a breathing space before the great plunge into tragedy—before we find Romeo in Mantua waiting for news (before Rowe's Act V, that is to say) may have dramatic value. But the comic scene with the musicians provides just such a breathing space. And if we remove it (and there may have been, as I suggest, merely incidental reasons for putting it in) a continuity of action is restored which gives us a most dramatic contrast between the mourning over Juliet and Romeo's buoyant hopes. What we should look for, surely, in act division, is some definite advantage to the play's acting. Where, in this play, do we find that? But the gains are patent if we act it without check or pause. Whatever the Elizabethan practice may have been, and whatever concessions are to be made to pure convenience, everything seems to point to Shakespeare having *planned* the play as a thing indivisible. It can be so acted without much outrunning the two hours traffic.[1] If this will overtax the weakness of the flesh—the audience's; actors will profit by the unchecked flow of action and emotion— some sacrifice of effect must be made. The less the better. And, if any pause is an error, a producer must simply weigh one disadvantage against another. A single pause after the banishing of Romeo would be my own solution.

STAGING, COSTUME, MUSIC, TEXT.

The producer wishing to enscene the play must devise such scenery as will not deform, obscure or prejudice its craftsmanship or its art. That is all. But it is not easy to do.

There are no signs in the text that Shakespeare saw Italian touches added to the players' normal costumes. Italian costumes will serve, as long as

[1] A casual phrase, surely, which means nearer two hours than either one or three.

36

rapier and dagger go with them, and may add something to the effect of the play upon us ; but Elizabethan doublet and hose will take next to nothing of it away.

The text tells us pretty plainly what music is needed. It is a consort of recorders that Paris brings with him to the wedding ; and the musicians either enter with him, playing, to be stopped incontinently by the sight of the tragic group round the bed ; or (this is, I think, more likely) they stay playing the bridal music without, a tragically ironical accompaniment to the lamenting over Juliet, till they are stopped and come clustering—scared, incongruous figures—into the doorway.[1]

> Faith, we may put up our pipes and be gone,

says the leader, when the mourners depart (all but the Nurse, who needs a line or two to speak while she draws the inner-stage curtains), leaving them alone.

The recorders could play for the dance at Capulet's too. But a consort of viols is perhaps likelier here, for there is dialogue throughout the music, and one does not speak through wood-wind

---

[1] According to Q1 they were fiddlers, *i.e.* a consort of viols, so they could not enter playing. Also, viols would not be well heard through dialogue except from the musicians' gallery, so their entrance was perhaps delayed by the time it took them to finish there and descend. Q2 has the first reference to ' pipes.' (Had the Globe acquired another quartet in the meantime ?) These could easily be heard playing ' off.' Q2, however, marks no entrance for them. They are there when the mourners depart ; that is all. The entrance with Paris and the Friar belongs to the undated Quarto, which is of doubtful authority.

with impunity. The musicians probably sat in their gallery.

The text itself raises many minor questions that need not be dealt with here. But no one should omit to read the first Quarto. For all its corruptions, it gives us now and then a vivid picture of a performance Shakespeare himself must presumably have supervised. It may not be much to know that Juliet entered *somewhat fast* and embraced Romeo; [1] that when Romeo *offers to stab himself* the Nurse *snatches the dagger away*; that (but this point we have remarked as important) at one juncture *Paris offers to goe in and Capolet calls him againe*; that they cast rosemary on the Juliet they think dead; and that Paris comes with his page to the tomb bringing flowers and *sweete water* with him too. But Shakespeare's stage directions are rareties indeed; and these and other such small touches give life to the rudimentary text, and an actuality to the play that scrupulous editing seems, somehow, to reform altogether.

Not but that the text has needed editing enough; and there are puzzles, such as the notorious ' runaway's eyes ' (twenty-eight pages devoted to it in the Furness Variorum!), yet unsolved. But few, if any, of them are of dramatic moment; and there is amply varied authority to bow to. The producer has his own few problems to face. There is the minor one of indecency. One or two of Mercutio's jokes are too outrageous for modern public usage; they will create discomfort among a mixed audience instead of laughter. But this full-

[1] But this scene was badly muddled, either by the reporter of these performances, or the actors, or by somebody. For further discussion of the point, see p. 63 n.

blooded sensuality is (as we have seen) set very purposefully against Romeo's romantic idealism, and the balance and contrast must not be destroyed. A Mercutio who lets his mouth be stopped by a prim Benvolio each time he launches on a smutty joke will be a cowed, a ' calm, dishonourable, vile ' Mercutio indeed.

But a producer is tempted to far more cutting than this, and most producers fall. The play as commonly presented to us starts fairly true to Shakespeare, a troublesome passage suppressed here and there ; but, as it advances, more and more of the text disappears, till the going becomes hop-skip-and-jump, and 'Selections from the tragedy of Romeo and Juliet ' would be a truer title for it. This will not do. The construction, very naturally, does not show the skill of Shakespeare's maturity, nor does every character stand consistent and four-square ; the writing runs to extravagant rhetoric and often to redundancy. But his chosen method of close consecutive narrative will be lamed by muti-lation ; and rhetoric and redundancy, the violence, the absurdities even, are the medium in which the characters are quite intentionally painted. To omit the final skurry of Montagues and Capulets and citizens of Verona to the tomb and the Friar's redundant story for the sake of finishing upon the more poignant note of Juliet's death is, as we have seen, to falsify Shakespeare's whole intention ; and to omit the sequel to the drinking of the potion is as bad and worse! Restoring the play to its own sort of stage will serve to curb these follies, at least.

The verbiage and its eccentricities—as they sound to our modern incurious ears—seem, at

39

first blush, harder to compass. No producer need be pedantic; it is his business to gain an effect, not to prejudice it. But much that strikes one as strange in print, that may jar under the repetition and cold-blooded analysis of rehearsals, will pass and make its own effect in the rush of performance. The cutting of a speech or two from a scene is like the removal of a few bricks from a wall; it may be a harmless operation and it may not. The structure may stand up as strongly with the hole in it, or it may sag, or come tumbling altogether. The antiphonal mourning over Juliet is crude, doubtless, and one is tempted to get rid of it, or at least to modify it. Do so, and what becomes of the calming effect of Friar Laurence's long speeches? There will be nothing for him to calm. Cut this too, and Capulet will have to turn without rhyme or reason from distracted grief to dignified resignation, while the others, the Friar included, stand like foolish lay figures.

To protest against the omission of the—to us—incongruous pun which bisects Romeo's passionate outburst, his

This may flies do, when I from this must fly . . .

would be pedantry. The play will not be the worse for its loss; the only question is whether it is worth omitting. But to shirk Juliet's delirium of puns upon ' Ay ' and ' I ' and ' eye ' is to lower the scene's temperature and flatten it out when Shakespeare has planned to lift it, by these very means, to a sudden height of intoxicated excitement, giving us a first and memorable taste of the Juliet of quick despair, who later, in a flash of resolution, will sheath Romeo's dagger in her heart.

There is no more dangerous weapon than the blue-pencil.

THE CHARACTERS

This is a tragedy of youth, as youth sees it, and age is not let play a very distinguished part. Friar Laurence is sympathetic, but he is compact of maxims, of pedagogic kindness; he is just such a picture of an old man as a young man draws, all unavailing wisdom. There is no more life in the character than the story asks and gives; but Shakespeare palliates this dramatic weakness by keeping him shadowed in his cell, a ghostly confessor, a refuge for Romeo, Paris and Juliet alike, existing—as in their youthful egoism we may be sure they thought—in their interests alone.

It is noteworthy what an arbitrary line is drawn between youth and age; arbitrary, but at times uncertain. Capulet and Montague are conventionally 'old,' though their children are young enough for them not to have passed forty. Capulet gives some excuse for this by saying of Juliet that

The earth hath swallowed all my hopes but she . . .

So we may surmise, if we will, a cluster of sons killed in the vendetta, or that sad little Elizabethan procession of infant effigies to be carved in time on his tomb. But Lady Capulet passes from saying that she was but fourteen herself at Juliet's birth fourteen years ago to telling us in the end that

. . . This sight of death is as a bell
That warns my old age to a sepulchre.[1]

---

[1] In her speech to Juliet 'a' mother has been read for 'your' mother; but without any warrant.

And the Nurse is old, though not fourteen years ago she had a child of her own and was suckling Juliet. It is futile trying to resolve these anomalies. Shakespeare wants a sharp conflict set between youth and age; he emphasises every aspect of it, and treats time of life much as he treats time of day—for effect.

The Nurse

The Nurse, whatever her age, is a triumphant and complete achievement. She stands four-square, and lives and breathes in her own right from the moment she appears, from that very first

> Now, by my maiden-head at twelve year old,
> I bade her come.

Shakespeare has had her pent up in his imagination; and out she gushes. He will give us nothing completer till he gives us Falstaff. We mark his confident, delighted knowledge of her by the prompt digression into which he lets her launch; the story may wait. It is not a set piece of fire-works such as Mercutio will touch off in honour of Queen Mab. The matter of it flows spontaneously into verse, the phrases are hers and hers alone, character unfolds with each phrase. You may, indeed, take any sentence the Nurse speaks throughout the play, and only she could speak it. Moreover, it will have no trace of the convention to which Shakespeare himself is still tied (into which he forces, to some extent, every other character)—none, unless we find her burlesquing it; and then we might fancy that he himself, in half-conscious mischief, is thus forecasting his freedom. But the good Angelica—which we at last discover to be her perfect name—needs no critical expanding, she expounds herself on all occasions; nor explanation, for she is plain as daylight; nor analysis, lest it lead to excuse, and she stays blissfully unregenerate. No one can fail to act her well that can speak her lines. Yet they are so supercharged with life that they will accommodate the larger acting—which is the revelation of a personality in terms of a part—and to the full; and it may be as rich a personality as can be found. She is in everything inevitable; from her

> My fan, Peter,

when she means to play the discreet lady with those gay young sparks, to that all unexpected

> Faith, here 'tis; Romeo
> Is banished; and all the world to nothing
> That he dares ne'er come back to challenge you;
> Or if he do, it needs must be by stealth.
> Then, since the case so stands as now it doth,
> I think it best you married with the county.

—horrifyingly unexpected to Juliet; but to us, the moment she has said it, the inevitable thing for her to say.

This last turn, that seems so casually made, is the stroke that completes the character. Till now we have taken her—the ' good, sweet Nurse '—just as casually, amused by each comicality as it came; for so we do take the folk that amuse us. But with this everything about her falls into perspective, her funniments, her endearments, her grossness, her good-nature; upon the instant, they all find their places in the finished picture. And for a last

43

enrichment, candidly welling from the lewd soul
of her, comes

> O, he's a lovely gentleman;
> Romeo's a dishclout to him; an eagle, Madam,
> Hath not so green, so quick, so fair an eye
> As Paris hath. Beshrew my very heart,
> I think you are happy in this second match,
> For it excels your first; or if it did not,
> Your first is dead, or 'twere as good he were
> As living hence and you no use of him.

Weigh the effect made upon Juliet, fresh from the
sacrament of love and the bitterness of parting,
by the last fifteen words of that.

> Speak'st thou from thy heart?
> And from my soul too,
> Or else beshrew them both.
> Amen.

It is gathered into the full-fraught Amen. But
best of all, perhaps, is the old bawd's utter uncon-
sciousness of having said anything out of the way.
And when she finds her lamb, her ladybird, returning from shrift with merry look—too merry!—
how should she suppose she has not given her the
wholesomest advice in the world?

We see her obliviously bustling through the
night's preparations for this new wedding. We
hear her—incredibly!—start to stir Juliet from her
sleep with the same coarse wit that had served to
deepen the girl's blushes for Romeo's coming near.
We leave her blubbering grotesquely over the
body she had been happy to deliver to a baser
martyrdom. Shakespeare lets her pass from the
play without comment. Is any needed? [1]

[1] Unless it be for Juliet's youthful, ruthless
    Ancient damnation! O most wicked fiend. . . ;

Capulet

Capulet, again, is a young man's old man. But he is more opulently done than the Friar, if he has not the flesh, blood, bones and all of the good Angelica. He suffers more than any other character in the play by its customary mutilations; for these leave him a mere domestic tyrant, and Shakespeare does not. With his benevolent airs, self-conscious hilarity, childish ill-temper, he is that yet commoner type, the petted and spoiled husband and father and head of the house; and the study of him might be more effective if it were not strung out through the play, and so intermittently touched in. But he is planned consistently—with all his inconsistencies—from the beginning.

The flavour of gratified vanity in

> But Montagu is bound as well as I
> In penalty alike . . .

puts us at once upon easy terms with him. And Shakespeare hardly wrote

> But woo her, gentle Paris, get her heart,
> My will to her consent is but a part. . . .

without having

> An you be mine, I'll give you to my friend;
> An you be not, hang, beg, starve die in the streets . . .

in his mind already. Our next sight of him gives us the breeze with Tybalt, the chop and change of

> Well said, my hearts! You are a princox; go:
> Be quiet, or—More light, more light!—For shame!
> I'll make you quiet—What, cheerly, my hearts. . . .

This is Capulet at home, a familiar figure in many

45

a home; the complete gentleman, the genial host,
the kindliest of men—as long as no one crosses him.

Old as he is, he was ready enough to take part in
the earlier brawl; but we note that he stands
silent before Tybalt's body, and Lady Capulet is
left to cry out for revenge. He did not the less
love Tybalt dearly because he can turn promptly
from the thought of him to Juliet's marriage to
Paris, and change his decorous resolve to

> . . . keep no great ado; a friend or two;
> For, hark you, Tybalt being slain so late,
> It may be thought we held him carelessly,
> Being our kinsman, if we revel much.

into

> Sirrah, go hire me twenty cunning cooks.

He is incorrigibly hospitable, that is one thing.
For another, it is obviously a wise move, Capulets
and Montagues both being now in worse odour
than ever in Verona, to marry Juliet as soon as
may be to this kinsman of the Prince. And except
for the haste of it (nor would even that greatly
astonish them) his

> Sir Paris, I will make a desperate tender
> Of my child's love. I think she will be ruled
> In all respects by me; nay, more, I doubt it not . . .

would not seem to an Elizabethan audience very
unusual. His vituperative raging against the
obstinate girl does bring his wife and the Nurse to
her rescue.

> Out, you green-sickness carrion! out, you baggage!
> You tallow face!

—moves even Lady Capulet to protest. But he is
merely raging; and parents of the day, finding their
fingers itch to chastise young ladies of riper years

46

than Juliet, did not always let them itch in vain.
For a thrashing then and there ample precedent
could be cited. And an hour or two later he is
quite good-tempered again.

How now, my headstrong! where have you been gadding?

he hails her.

He is not insincere, as he is not undignified, in
his heartbroken outcry at her supposed death, if
we may divine Shakespeare's intention through a
crudely written scene. And he stands, dignified
and magnanimous in his sorrow, at the last. It
is a partial picture of a man, no doubt, ill-empha-
sised at times, and at times crippled by convention; but of a most recognisable man, and never
untrue. Note lastly that it is the portrait of a
very English old gentleman. When did the
phlegmatic Englishman—or the legend of him—
come into fashion as the type of his kind?

The minor Characters; and Mercutio

The play has its full share of merely conventional
figures, from the Prince to Peter, Abram and his
fellows, to Balthasar and Paris' page; and they
must be treated for what they are. Lady Capulet
is sketchily uncertain. Benvolio is negative enough,
confidant to Romeo, foil to Mercutio. But there
are such men; and Shakespeare endows him with a
kindly patience, sharpens his wit every now and
again to a mild irony, gives him a steady consistency that rounds him to something more than
a shadow.

Tybalt we must see somewhat through Mercutio's
eyes. Pretty obviously we are meant to; and the

47

actor must take the hint, nor make him a mere
blusterer, but something at least of a

> . . . courageous captain of compliments . . . the very
> butcher of a silk button, a duellist, a duellist; a gentleman
> of the very first house, of the first and second cause.

He need not, however, place him irretrievably
among the

> . . . antic, lisping, affecting fantasticoes, these new tuners
> of accents . . . these fashion-mongers, these *pardonnez-*
> *mois.* . . .

He may reasonably discount a little Mercutio's
John Bull prejudices.

For Mercutio, when Shakespeare finally makes
up his mind about him, is in temperament very
much the young John Bull of his time; and as
different from the stocky, stolid John Bull of our
later picturing as Capulet from the conventional
heavy father. There can be, of course, no epitom-
ising of a race in any one figure. But the dominant
qualities of an age are apt to be set in a pattern,
which will last in literature, though out-moded,
till another replaces it.

We learn little about Mercutio as he goes racket-
ing to Capulet's supper, except that John Bull is
often a poetic sort of fellow, or as he returns,
unless it be that a man may like smut and fairy
tales too. But he is still in the toils of conventional
versifying, and a victim besides, probably, to his
author's uncertainty about him. The authentic
Mercutio only springs into life with

> Where the devil should this Romeo be? Came he not
> home to-night?

when he springs to life indeed. From now on he

abounds in his own sense, and we can put him to
the test the Nurse abides by ; not a thing that he
says could anyone else say. He asks as little
exposition, he is what he is with perfect clarity ;
the more so probably because he is wholly Shakespeare's creation, his namesake in Brooke's poem
giving no hint of him. And (as with the Nurse) we
could transport this authentic Mercutio into the
maturest of the plays and he would fall into place
there, nor would he be out of place on any stage, in
any fiction.

A wholesome self-sufficiency is his cardinal
quality ; so he suitably finds place among neither
Capulets nor Montagues. Shakespeare endows
him, we saw, with a jolly sensuality for a set off to
Romeo's romancings ; and, by a later, significant
touch, adds to the contrast. When their battle
of wits is ending—a breathless bandying of words
that is like a sharp set at tennis—suddenly, it would
seem, he throws an affectionate arm round the
younger man's shoulder.[1]

Why, is not this better now than groaning for love?
Now art thou sociable, now art thou Romeo, now art thou
    what thou art. . . .

Mercutio's creed in a careless sentence! At all
costs be the thing you are. The more his—and
the more John Bullish—that we find it dropped
casually amid a whirl of chaff and never touched
on again! Here is the man. No wistful ideals for
him ; but life as it comes and death when it comes.
A man of soundest common-sense surely ; the com-

---

[1] We are not definitely told so, but certainly Mercutio
seems a little the older of the two; and here again he is
exempt from that other party-division into young and old.

plete realist, the egoist justified. But by the day's
end he has gone to his death in a cause not his own,
upon pure impulse and something very like principle. There is no inconsistency in this; such
vital natures must range between extremes.

> Rightly to be great
> Is not to stir without great argument,
> But greatly to find quarrel in a straw,
> When honour's at the stake.

That is a later voice, troublously questioning.
Mercutio pretends neither to greatness nor philosophy. When the moment comes, it is not even
his own honour that is at stake; but such calm,
dishonourable, vile submission is more than flesh
and blood can bear. That the Mercutios of the
world quarrel on principle they would hate to be
told. Quarrel with a man for cracking nuts
having no other reason but because one has hazel
eyes; quarrel, with your life in your hand, for
quarrelling's sake, since quarrelling and fighting
are a part of life, and the appetite for them human
nature. Mercutio fights Tybalt because he feels
he must, because he cannot stand the fellow's airs
a moment longer. He'll put him in his place, if
no one else will. He fights without malice, not
in anger even, and for no advantage. He fights
because he is what he is, to testify to this simple
unconscious faith, and goes in with good honest
cut and thrust. But *alla stoccata* carries it away;
and he, the perfect realist, the egoist complete,
dies for an ideal. Extremes have met.

No regrets though; nor any hypocrisy of
resignation for him! He has been beaten by the
thing he despised, and is as robustly angry about

it as if he had years to live in which to get his own back.

> Zounds, a dog, a rat, a mouse, a cat, to scratch a man to death! A braggart, a rogue, a villain, that fights by the book of arithmetic.

He is brutally ingenuous with Romeo:

> Why the devil came you between us? I was hurt under your arm.[1]

He says no more to him after that, quite ignores the pitifully futile

> I thought all for the best.

He dies with his teeth set, impenitently himself to the last.

Romeo

We have Romeo and Juliet themselves left to consider; the boy and girl—they are no more—caught with their love as in a vice between the hatreds of their houses, to be crushed to death there.

Romeo has been called an early study for Hamlet. It is true enough to be misleading. The many ideas that go to make up Hamlet will have seeded themselves from time to time in Shakespeare's imagination, sprouting a little, their full fruition delayed till the dominant idea ripened. We can find traits of Hamlet in Romeo, in Richard II, in Jacques, in less likely habitations. But Romeo is not a younger Hamlet in love, though Hamlet in love seem a disillusioned Romeo. The very likeness, moreover, is largely superficial, is a common likeness to many young men, who take life desper-

---

[1] All the technical talk of sword-play must, of course, have been a dozen times livelier to the Elizabethans than it ever can be to us.

ately seriously. The study of him is not plain sailing. If Hamlet's melancholy is of the soul, Romeo's was something of a pose; and there is Shakespeare's own present pose to account for, the convention of word-spinning and thought-spinning in which he cast much of the play, through which he broke more and more while he wrote it; there are, besides, the abundant remains of Brooke's Romeus. Romeo is in the making till the end; and he is made by fits and starts. Significant moments reveal him; but, looking back, one perceives screeds of the inessential, more heat than light in them. The actor's first task will be to distinguish between the significant and the merely effective, and his last, as he plays the part, to adjust and reconcile the two.

Decorative method allowed for, the Romeo of

> Why then, O brawling love! O loving hate!
> O anything of nothing first create!
> O heavy lightness! serious vanity!
> Misshapen chaos of well-seeming forms!
> Feather of lead, bright smoke, cold fire, sick health!
> Still-waking sleep, that is not what it is . . .

pictures an actual Romeo truly enough; and, if it seems to over-colour him, why, this Romeo was busy at the moment over-colouring himself. Yet amid all the phrase-mongering we may detect a phrase or two telling of a deeper misprision than the obduracy of Rosaline accounts for. The inconsequent

> Show me a mistress that is passing fair,
> What doth her beauty serve but as a note
> Where I may read who passed that passing fair? . . .

is very boyish cynicism, but it marks the unhappy nature. And Rosaline herself was a Capulet, it

52

seems ; so, had she smiled on him, his stars would
still have been crossed. He is posing to himself
certainly, more in love with love than with
Rosaline, posing to his family and friends, and not
at all displeased by their concern. But beneath all
this, the mind that, as he passes with the Maskers
and their festive drum to Capulet's feast,

> . . . misgives
> Some consequence yet hanging in the stars . . .

shows the peculiar clarity which gives quality to a
man, marks him off from the happy-go-lucky crowd,
and will at a crisis compel him to face his fate.
By a few touches, then, and in a melody of speech
that is all his own, he is set before us, a tragic figure
from the first.

He sees Juliet. Shakespeare insists on the youth
of the two, and more than once on their innocence,
their purity—his as well as hers. It is not purpose-
lessly that he is given the Dian-like Rosaline for a
first love ; nor that his first words to Juliet, as he
touches her finger tips, are

> If I profane with my unworthiest hand
> This holy shrine. . . .

nor that their first exchange is in the pretty
formality of a sonnet, the kiss with which it ends
half jest, half sacrament.[1] But their fate is sealed
by it, there and then. They cannot speak again,
for Lady Capulet calls Juliet away ; and Benvolio,
ever cautious, urges Romeo out of danger before

[1] Elizabethan kisses were given and taken with greater
freedom and publicity and less significance than Victorian
kisses, at any rate, were. But one supposes that the kiss
of greeting (which Erasmus found so pleasant) was a kiss on
the cheek. Romeo kisses Juliet on the lips.

53

there may be question of unmasking and discovery. Not before he has accepted his fate, though, and she hers—for better, for worse, without doubt, question, or hesitation ! He (if we are to note niceties) accepts it even more unquestioningly than she. But her cry when she first hears his name gives us early promise of the rebellious Juliet, the more reckless and desperate of the two.

They look into the abyss and then give no more heed to it. Virginal passion sweeps them aloft and away, and to its natural goal. What should hinder? Nothing in themselves, none of the misgiving that experience brings ; and for counsellors they have Nurse and Friar, she conscienceless, he as little worldly as they. Juliet is no questioner, and Romeo's self-scrutinies are over. The balcony scene is like the singing of two birds ; and its technical achievement lies in the sustaining at such length—with no story to tell, nor enlivening clash of character—of those simple antiphonies of joy.

Rosaline's adorer, aping disillusioned age, is hardly to be recognised in the boyishly, childishly happy Romeo that rushes to the Friar's cell. From there he goes to encounter Mercutio, still overflowing with spirits, apt for a bout of nonsense, victorious in it, too. From this and the meeting with the Nurse, back to the cell, to Juliet and the joining of their hands !

Note that the marriage and its consummation are quite simply thought of as one, by them and by the Friar. And fate accepts Romeo's challenge betimes.

> Do thou but close our hands with holy words,
> Then love devouring death do what he dare;
> It is enough I may but call her mine.

It is of the essence of the tragedy that, for all their passionate haste, the blow should fall upon their happiness before it is complete, that they must consummate their marriage in sorrow.   And, in a sense, it is Romeo's ecstatic happiness that helps precipitate the blow.   It lets him ignore Tybalt's insult:

> O sweet Juliet,
> Thy beauty hath made me effeminate,
> And in my temper softened valour's steel.

But, for all that, it has fired him to such manliness that he cannot endure the shame put upon him by Mercutio's death.   Nothing is left now of the young Romeo, love-sick for Rosaline, and so disdainful of the family feud.   His sudden hardihood is the complement to his chaffing high spirits of a few hours earlier ; even as the grim

> This day's black fate on more days doth depend,
> This but begins the woe others must end.

makes a counterpart to his confident challenge to fate to give him Juliet and do its worst after.   He must seem of a higher stature as he stands over Tybalt's body, stern, fated, and passive to the next Capulet sword that offers, did not Benvolio force him away.

The hysterics of the next scene with the Friar, when he hears of his banishment, may seem as retrograde in character as they certainly are in dramatic method ; but Shakespeare has taken the episode almost intact—and at one point all but word for word—from Brooke.   And it does attune us, as we noted, to the fortuitous disasters of the story.   Then the tragic parting of the two echoes the happy wooing of the first balcony scene ; and

55

later in Mantua we find Shakespeare's Romeo, come to his full height.

Euphuism has all but vanished from the writing now. We have instead the dynamic phrase that can convey so much more than its plain meaning, can sum up in simplicity a ferment of emotion and thought.

> Is it even so? Then I defy you, stars! . . .

is his stark comment on the news of Juliet's death; but what could be more eloquent of the spirit struck dead by it? He knows in a flash what he means to do. We are not told; Balthasar is to hire horses, that is all. Then, when he is alone:

> Well, Juliet, I will lie with thee to-night.

And what better epitome of the love in death, which is all that is left them! [1]

There follows the scene with the apothecary; its skeleton Brooke's, its clothing Shakespeare's, who employs it, not so much for the story's sake, as to give us, in repose, a picture of the Romeo his imagination has matured.

> How oft, when men are at the point of death
> Have they been merry! which their keepers call
> A lightning before death. . . .

he lets him say later. He does not make him merry; but he gives him here that strange sharp clarity of eye and mind which comes to a doomed man, a regard for little things when his

---

[1] This whole passage is also notable in that it calls for sheer acting, for the expression of emotion without the aid of rhetoric. This demand was a comparatively new thing when the play was written. Its fulfilment will have been one of the factors in the great success won.

56

own end means little to him. He brings him to a
view of life far removed from that first boyish,
selfish petulance, to a scornful contemplation of
what men come to, who will not dare to throw
with fate for happiness, and be content to lose
rather than be denied. As he watches the
apothecary fumble for the forbidden poison:

> Art thou so bare and full of wretchedness
> And fearest to die? . . .

But for him it is:

> Come, cordial and not poison, go with me
> To Juliet's grave, for there must I use thee.

Life has broken him, and he in turn breaks all
compact with life. If Balthasar dares to spy into
the tomb his blood be on his head. He knows that
he sins in killing himself: very well, he will sin.
He implores Paris not to provoke him ; but, provoked, he slaughters him savagely. At last he is
alone with his dead.

At this juncture we lose much by our illegitimate
knowledge of the story's end, and actors, presum-
ing on it, make matters worse. They apostrophise
Paris and Tybalt and Juliet at their leisure. But
the dramatic effect here lies in the chance that at
any minute, as we legitimately know, Juliet may
wake or Friar Laurence come ; and it is Romeo's
haste—of a piece with the rest of his rashness—
which precipitates the final tragedy. Shakespeare
has provided, in the speech to the dead Juliet,
just enough delay to stimulate suspense, but it
must appear only as the last convulsive checking
of a headlong purpose. He has added a last
touch of bitter irony in letting Romeo guess at the

57

truth that would have saved him, and her, and never guess that he guesses it.

> . . . O my love! my wife!
> Death, that hath sucked the honey of thy breath,
> Hath had no power yet upon thy beauty:
> Thou art not conquered; beauty's ensign yet
> Is crimson in thy lips and in thy cheeks,
> And death's pale flag is not advanced there . . .

After his glance at the dead Tybalt he turns to her again, obscurely marvelling:

> . . . Ah, dear Juliet,
> Why art thou yet so fair? . . .

And it is upon a sardonic echo of the eloquence to which his love's first happiness lifted him that he ends. Then it was

> I am no pilot, yet, wert thou as far
> As that far shore washed by the farthest sea
> I would adventure for such merchandise.

Now, the phial in his hand, it is

> Thou desperate pilot, now at once run on
> The dashing rocks thy sea-sick weary bark!
> Here's to my love . . .

With that he drinks and dies.

From the beginning so clearly imagined, passionately realised in the writing, deeply felt at the end; this Romeo, when he had achieved him, must have stood to Shakespeare as an assurance that he could now mould a tragic figure strong enough to carry a whole play whenever he might want to.

Juliet

The first thing to mark about Juliet, for everything else depends on it, is that she is, to our thinking, a child. Whether she is Shakespeare's fourteen or Brooke's sixteen makes little difference; she is meant to be just about as young as she can be; and her actual age is trebly stressed.[1] Her tragedy is a child's tragedy; half its poignancy would be gone otherwise. Her bold innocence is a child's, her simple trust in her Nurse; her passionate rage at the news of Tybalt's death is easily pardonable in a child, her terrors when she takes the potion are doubly dreadful as childish terrors. The cant saying that no actress can play Juliet till she is too old to look her should therefore go the way of all parroted nonsense. A Juliet must have both the look and the spirit of a girl of from fourteen to sixteen, and any further sophistication—or, worse, a mature assumption of innocence—will be the part's ruin. One must not compare her, either, to the modern girl approaching independence, knowing enough to think she knows more, ready to disbelieve half she is told. Life to Juliet, as she glimpsed it around her, was half jungle in its savagery, half fairy tale; and its rarer gifts were fever to the blood. A most precocious young woman from our point of view, no doubt;

[1] It has been held that Shakespeare may have taken her age from a later edition of Brooke's poem in which the XVI had perhaps been transformed by the printer into XIV; also that he may have reduced her age to suit the very youthful appearance of some boy-actress. This is at any rate unlikely; fourteen is not distinguishable from sixteen on the stage. Moreover, he has other almost as youthful heroines: Miranda is fifteen, Perdita sixteen.

59

but the narrower and intenser life of her time ripened emotion early.

Not that there is anything of the budding sensualist in her; for to be sensual is to be sluggish, not fevered. Her passion for Romeo is ruled by imagination. And were this not the true reading of it, Shakespeare would have been all but compelled, one may say, to make it so; doubly compelled. Of what avail else would be his poetry, and through what other medium could a boy-actress realise the part? The beauty of the girl's story, and its agonies too, have imagination for their fount. The height of her joy (anticipated, never realised) is reached in the imaginative ecstasy of

> Gallop apace, you fiery-footed steeds. . . .

And she suffers to the full, even in thinking of them, all the shame of the marriage to Paris and the terrors of the vault.

Her quick florescence into womanhood is the more vivid for its quiet prelude; for the obedient

> Madam, I am here.
> What is your will?

when she first appears, for the listening to the Nurse's chatter, the borrowed dignity with which she caps her mother's snub that ends it, the simple

> It is an honour that I dream not of.

with which she responds to the hint of the great match awaiting her, the listening to her mother's talk of it and the

> I'll look to like, if looking liking move;
> But no more deep will I endart mine eye,
> Than your consent gives strength to make it fly.

60

that seal our first impression of her.   Where could
one find a more biddable young lady?

What could one guess, either, from her first
meeting with Romeo, from the demure game of
équivoque she plays; though something shows,
perhaps, in the little thrust of wit—

> You kiss by the book

—by which she evades the confession of a kiss
returned.[1] One moment later, though, there comes
the first flash of the true Juliet; a revelation to
herself, is it, as to us?

> My only love sprung from my only hate. . . .

And she stands, lost in amazement at this miracle
that has been worked in her (even as Romeo will
stand later lost in the horror of Tybalt's slaying),
till the puzzled Nurse coaxes her away.

We next see her at her window. Yet again
Shakespeare holds her silent a little, but for that
one ' ay me ' to tell us that now the still depths in
her are brimming; when they brim over, again
it is to herself she speaks.[2] The scene is conven-
tionalised to a degree, with its overheard soliloquies, its conceits, its lyric flow. It turns every
exigency of stage and acting to account, and its
very setting, which keeps the lovers apart, stimu-
lates passionate expression and helps sustain it.
It left the boy-actress in imaginative freedom;
nothing asked of him that his skill could not give.
But the conceits come to life and blend insensibly
with the simplicities.   The fanciful

[1] And how admirably suited to the effective resources of
the boy-actress the pretty formality of this passage is!
[2] Not a sigh, this! There is nothing sentimental about
Juliet.

> Thou know'st the mask of night is on my face
> Else would a maiden blush bepaint my cheek. . . .

flows into the frank coquetry of

> O gentle Romeo,
> If thou dost love, pronounce it faithfully;
> Or if thou think'st I am too quickly won,
> I'll frown and be perverse and say thee nay,
> So thou wilt woo; but, else not for the world.

and

> My bounty is as boundless as the sea,
> My love as deep; the more I give to thee
> The more I have, for both are infinite.

comes from her as naturally as the very practical

> Three words, dear Romeo, and good-night indeed.
> If that thy bent of love be honourable,
> Thy purpose marriage, send me word to-morrow. . .

And the scene's finest moment comes with

> *Juliet.* Romeo!
> *Romeo.* My dear?
> *Juliet.* At what o'clock to-morrow
> Shall I send to thee?
> *Romeo.* By the hour of nine.
> *Juliet.* I will not fail. 'Tis twenty years till then.
> I have forgot why I did call thee back.
> *Romeo.* Let me stand here till thou remember it.
> *Juliet.* I shall forget, to have thee still stand there,
> Remembering how I love thy company.
> *Romeo.* And I'll still stay to have thee still forget,
> Forgetting any other home but this.

This is the commonplace made marvellous. What is it, indeed, but the well-worn comic theme of the lovers that cannot say good-bye turned to pure beauty by the alchemy of the poet? Modesty, boldness, shyness, passion, each and all shot through with innocence, chase their way through the girl's speech; and Romeo, himself all surrender, sings

62

to her tune. Together, but still apart, this is their one hour of happiness, and she is enskied in it, even as he sees her there.

We find her next, two scenes later, impatient for the Nurse's return with news of him ; and in reckless delight and quick imagery for its expression she rivals Romeo now—the Juliet that could stand so mute ! Then comes the quiet moment of the marriage. Making her reverence to the Friar, she may seem still to be the self-contained young lady we first saw ; but even in the few lines of formal speech we hear a stronger pulse-beat and a deeper tone. She stands, not timidly at all, but just a little awed upon the threshold of her womanhood.[1]

After the tragic interval that sees Mercutio and Tybalt killed we find her alone again, and again her newly franchised self, expectant of happiness, pending the blow that is to kill it. To the modern Juliet, as we have noted, this scene probably presents more difficulties than any other in the play. Victorian Juliets customarily had theirs drastically eased by the eliminating of

Gallop apace, you fiery-footed steeds. . . .

---

[1] I make no attempt to say how and why this scene as it is in Q1 is so completely changed in Q2. But it is worth while remarking that we have far more than a re-writing of the words.

Enter Juliet somewhat fast and embraceth Romeo.

says Q1 ; and her first word is " Romeo." In Q2, on the contrary, it is

Good even to my ghostly confessor.

and there is no sure sign that she embraces Romeo at all. I think myself that she does not, that the short scene was kept formal and dignified, the lovers standing on either side the Friar as if they were already before the altar.

63

(some of the finest verse in the play) on the ground
—God save the mark!—of its immodesty. One
hopes that the last has been heard of such nonsense. But few performances since Shakespeare's
time can have given the rest, with its elaborately
embroidered rhetoric, intact.[1] It will all of it,
needless to say, be out of place upon a realistic
stage; acted by a mature, ultra-feminine Juliet
it will be intolerable. But we can hardly blame
Shakespeare for that. He took here full advantage of his theatre's convention. The epitha-
lamium has no more realism about it than a
song or a sonnet would have; and the verbal
embroideries which follow, meant to be taken at a
high pitch of emotion and at a surprising pace,
owe their existence in great part to the bravura
skill of the boy-actresses who could compass such
things with credit. The actress of to-day need
not lack the skill, though the audiences may (and
no great harm done) less consciously admire it;
they probably will not break into applause as
audiences at an opera do, as do French audiences
at the declaiming of a fine passage of verse.
She must think of the scene largely in terms
of virtuosity; but there is far more in it, of course.
It brings us the first clash of Montague and
Capulet in other and sharper terms than sword
play, in the heart agonies of this child, as she
is torn, now one way, now the other:

The Nurse. Will you speak well of him that kill'd your
cousin?
Juliet. Shall I speak ill of him that is my husband?

The tragedy is summed up for the first time in that.

[1] For whatever reason, much of this is missing from Q1.

Till now, we have seen Juliet at intervals; but with Romeo's farewell to her and his passing to Mantua she becomes for a space the sole centre of the play, while misfortune batters at her. In her helpless courage is the pathos, in her resolve from the first to kill herself sooner than yield—she is fourteen!—is the high heroism of the struggle. She is a child in the world's ways still. But she faces her mother when the marriage to Paris is broached, dignified and determined—and takes that good lady very much aback. The next moment, though, she has broken into a storm of impotent tears, which puzzle her father, but move him not at all, except to match and outdo her in storming. Her mother repulses her, her Nurse betrays her; the trap is closing on her. She flies to the Friar. There is Paris himself; and for appearance sake she must stop and parley with him while he claims her with calm assurance as his wife, must let him kiss her, even! Back she flies again from the shaken old man, armed with the only aid he can give her, one little less desperate than the dagger that never leaves her. The time is so short; and, in her distraction—playing the hypocrite as she must, and over-playing it—she even contrives to make it shorter. It escapes her quite that she is now—and fatally—not following the Friar's directions.[1] She easily hoodwinks her mother and her nurse; then, left alone, outfacing terror, she drinks the potion.

[1] And us too, probably—which may show we are not meant to remark it. Quite possibly Shakespeare didn't. At any rate he makes no use of the mistake, but brings in Friar John's mishap instead. The immediate effect of the extra haste was all he cared about.

She wakes in the vault, hopefully, happily:

> O comfortable friar, where is my lord?
> I do remember well where I should be
> And there I am. Where is my Romeo?

to have for all answer

> Thy husband in thy bosom there lies dead.

and to see Friar Laurence—even he!—turn and desert her. Should we wonder at the scorn sounded in that

> Go, get thee hence, for I will not away . . .

Romeo's dagger is all she has left.

The simplest reason for Juliet's leave-taking of life being short is that Romeo's has been long. But, theatrical effect apart, the sudden brutal blow by which her childish faith in the ' comfortable Friar ' is shattered, and her unquestioning choice of death, make a fitting end to the desperate confidence of her rush to escape from what is worse than death to her. In the unreflecting haste of it all lies her peculiar tragedy. One day a child, and the next a woman! But she has not grown older as Romeo has, nor risen to an impersonal dignity of sorrow. Shakespeare's women do not, for obvious reasons, so develop. They are vehicles of life, not of philosophy. Here is a life cut short in its brightness ; and it is a cruel business, this slaughter of a child betrayed.

THE MERCHANT OF VENICE

THE MERCHANT OF VENICE is a fairy tale. There is no more reality in Shylock's bond and The Lord of Belmont's will than in Jack and the Beanstalk.

Shakespeare, it is true, did not leave the fables as he found them. This would not have done; things that pass muster on the printed page may become quite incredible when acted by human beings, and the unlikelier the story, the likelier must the mechanism of its acting be made. Besides, when his own creative impulse was quickened, he could not help giving life to a character; he could no more help it than the sun can help shining. So Shylock is real, while his story remains fabulous; and Portia and Bassanio become human, though, truly, they never quite emerge from the enchanted thicket of fancy into the common light of day. Æsthetic logic may demand that a story and its characters should move consistently upon one plane or another, be it fantastic or real. But Shakespeare's practical business, once he had chosen these two stories for his play, was simply so to charge them with humanity that they did not betray belief in the human beings presenting them, yet not so uncompromisingly that the stories themselves became ridiculous.

What the producer of the play must first set

himself to ascertain is the way in which he did
this, the nice course that—by reason or instinct—
he steered. Find it and follow it, and there need
be no running on the rocks. But logic may land
us anywhere. It can turn Bassanio into a heart-
less adventurer. Test the clock of the action by
Greenwich time, it will either be going too fast
or too slow. And as to Portia's disguise and
Bellario's law, would the village policeman be
taken in by either? But the actor will find that
he simply cannot play Bassanio as a humbug, for
Shakespeare does not mean him to. Portias and
Nerissas have been eclipsed by wigs and spectacles.
This is senseless tomfoolery; but how make a
wiseacre producer see that if he does not already
know? And if, while Shylock stands with his
knife ready and Antonio with his bared breast, the
wise young judge lifting a magical finger between
them, we sit questioning Bellario's law—why, no
one concerned, actors or audience, is for this
fairyland, that is clear.

The Merchant of Venice is the simplest of plays,
so long as we do not bedevil it with sophistries.
Further, it is—for what it is!—as smoothly and
completely successful, its means being as well
fitted to its end, as anything Shakespeare wrote.
He was happy in his choice of the Portia story;
his verse, which has lost glitter to gain a mellower
beauty and an easier flow, is now well attuned to
such romance. The story of Shylock's bond is
good contrast and complement both; and he can
now project character upon the stage, uncompromising and complete. Yet this Shylock does
not overwhelm the play, as at a later birth he
might well have done—it is a near thing, though!

Lastly, Shakespeare is now enough of the skilled playwright to be able to adjust and blend the two themes with fruitful economy.

THE CONSTRUCTION OF THE PLAY
The Problem of 'Double Time'

This blending of the themes would, to a modern playwright, have been the main difficulty. The two stories do not naturally march together. The forfeiture of the bond must be a matter of months; with time not only of the essence of the contract, but of the dramatic effect. But the tale of the caskets cannot be enlarged, its substance is too fragile ; and a very moderate charge of emotion would explode its pretty hollowness altogether. Critics have credited Shakespeare with nice calculation and amazing subtlety in his compassing of the time-difficulty. Daniel gives us one analysis, Halpin another, Eccles a third, and Furness finds the play as good a peg for the famous Double Time theory as Wilson, its inventor, found Othello. All very ingenious ; but is the ingenuity Shakespeare's or their own? [1] For him dramatic time

---

[1] If the effect is one and the same, one might think the question unimportant. But Daniel, making out his three months, is generous of ' intervals,' not only between acts, but between scenes; and even Furness, on his subtler scent, can say, " One is always conscious that between the acts of a play a certain space of time elapses. To convey this impression is one of the purposes for which a drama is divided into acts." Therefore an important and a much-disputed question is involved—and begged. And, in practice, the pernicious hanging up of performances by these pauses is encouraged, to which scenery and its shifting is already a sufficient temptation.

was a naturally elastic affair. (It still is, though
less so, for the modern playwright, whose half-hour
act may commonly suggest the passing of an hour
or two; this also is Double Time.) Shakespeare
seems to think of it quite simply in terms of effect,
as he thought of dramatic space, moving his
characters hither and thither without measure-
ment of yards or miles. The one freedom will
imply and enhance the other. The dramatist
working for the 'realistic' stage must settle
definitely where his characters are to be and keep
them there till he chooses to change the scenery.
Shakespeare need not; and, in fact, he never
insists upon place at all, unless it suits him to; and
then only to the extent that suits him.[1] In this
play, for instance, where we find Shylock and
Antonio will be Venice, but whereabouts in
Venice is usually no matter; when it is—at Shylock's door or in Court before the Duke—it will
be made clear enough to us. And where Portia
is, is Belmont. He treats time—and the more
easily—with a like freedom, and a like aim. Three
months suits for the bond; but once he has
pouched the money Bassanio must be off to
Belmont, and his calendar, attuned to his mood,
at once starts to run by hours only. The wind
serves, and he sails that very night, and there is no
delay at Belmont. Portia would detain him some
month or two before he ventures; and what could
be more convenient for a Shakespeare bent on
synchronising the two stories? For that matter,
he could have placed Belmont a few hundred
miles off, and let the coming and going eke out
the time. Did the problem as a whole ever even

[1] See also preface to *Antony and Cleopatra*.

70

occur to him? If it did, he dismissed it as of no consequence. What he does is to set each story going according to its nature ; then he punctuates them, so to speak, for effect. By the clock they are not even consistent in themselves, far less with each other. But we should pay just the sort of attention to these months, days or hours that we do, in another connection, to the commas and semi-colons elucidating a sentence. They give us, and are meant to, simply a *sense* of time and its exactions. It is the more easily done because our own sense of time in daily life is far from consistent. Time flies when we are happy, and drags in anxiety, as poets never tire of reminding us. Shakespeare's own reflections on the phenomenon run to half a column of the concordance, and he turns it quite naturally to dramatic account.

The True Problem

How to blend two such disparate themes into a dramatically organic whole ; that was his real problem. The stories, linked in the first scene, will, of themselves, soon part company. Shakespeare has to run them neck and neck till he is ready to join them again in the scene of the trial. But the difficulty is less that they will not match each other by the clock than that their whole gait so differs, their very nature. How is the flimsy theme of the caskets to be kept in countenance beside its grimly powerful rival? You cannot, as we said, elaborate the story, or charge it with emotion ; that would invite disaster. Imagine a Portia seriously alarmed by the prospect of an Aragon or a Morocco for husband. What sort of a barrier, on the other hand, would the caskets be to a flesh-and-blood hero and heroine fallen in love? Would a Romeo or Rosalind give a snap of the finger for them? As it is, the very sight of Bassanio prompts Portia to rebellion; and Shakespeare can only allow his lovers a few lines of talk together, and that in company, dare only colour the fairy-tale with a rhetorically passionate phrase or so before the choice is made and the caskets can be forgotten—as they are!—altogether. Nor does anything in the play show the artist's supreme tact in knowing what *not* to do better than this?

But you cannot neglect the Portia story either, or our interest in her may cool. Besides, this antiphony of high romance and rasping hate enhances the effect of both. A contrasting of subjects, scene by scene, is a trick (in no depreciatory sense) of Shakespeare's earliest stage-craft, and he never lost his liking for it.[1] Then if the casket-theme cannot be neglected, but cannot be elaborated, it must somehow be drawn out, its peculiar character sustained, its interest husbanded while its consummation is delayed.

Shakespeare goes straightforwardly enough to work. He puts just as little as may be into Portia's first scene; but for the one sounding of Bassanio's name there would be nothing but the inevitable tale of the caskets told in tripping prose and the conventional joking upon the suitors. Portia and Nerissa, however, seen for the first time in the flesh, give it sufficient life, and that ' Bassanio ' one vivid spark more. Later, in due

[1] It is, one may say, a commonplace of stagecraft, Elizabethan or other; but none the less worthy for that.

course, come Morocco's choice of the gold casket and Aragon's of the silver. We remark that Morocco is allotted two scenes instead of one. The reason is, probably, that Shakespeare has now enriched himself with the Lorenzo–Jessica story (not to mention the episode of the Gobbos, father and son), and, with this extra weight in the Venetian scale of the action, is put to it to maintain the balance. He could, of course, finish with both Morocco and Aragon earlier and give Bassanio two scenes instead of one.[1] And if a romantic hero could not well wait till after dinner to make his choice, as Morocco does, Solanio's arrival with the ill news of Antonio could easily have been kept for the later scene. But this will not do either—most characteristically will not do for Shakespeare. He has held his lovers apart, since the air of the Belmont of the caskets is too rarefied for flesh and blood to breathe. And Portia herself has been spellbound ; we have only had jaunty little Nerissa to prophesy that love (by the pious prevision of the late lord) would somehow find out the way.[2] But once he brings them

---

[1] And such interest as there is in Aragon's scene is now lessened, perhaps, by our knowledge that Bassanio is on his way ; even more, by the talk in the scene before of Antonio's misfortune. But Shakespeare, as his wont is, plucks some little advantage from the poverty of the business by capping Aragon's vapidity with the excitement of the news of Bassanio's arrival.

[2] Though there are commentators who maintain that Nerissa—even Portia, perhaps—gives Bassanio the hint to choose lead, or has it sung to him :

Tell me, where is fancy *bred*
In the heart, or in the *head*,
How begot, how nouri*shed*?

73

together Bassanio must break the spell. It is the
story of the sleeping beauty and the prince in
another kind ; a legitimate and traditional outcome. And once Shakespeare himself has broken
free of the fairy-tale and brought these two to life
(for Bassanio as well has been till now a little blood-
less) it is not in him to let them lapse from the
scene unproven, and to the full. The long re-
straint has left him impatient, and he must, here
and now, have his dramatic fling. We need not
credit—or discredit him, if you like—with much
calculation of the problem. It was common
prudence both to keep Belmont as constantly in
our view as Venice, and the emancipating Bassanio
clear of it for as long as possible. And he is now
in the middle of his play, rather past it, ready to
link his two stories together again. He worked
forthright ; that is written plain over most of his
work. Though he might now find that he had
here material for two scenes, he would not return
in his tracks, telescope Aragon and Morocco—and
take, in fact, all the sort of trouble we, who are
his critics, must take to explain what a much more
compact job he could have made of it ! Besides,

And if he'll only listen carefully he will note that they all
rhyme with *lead*.

Shakespeare was surely of a simpler mind than this—his
audiences too. And he had some slight sense of the fitness
of things. Would he—how *could* he ?—wind up this innocent
fairy-tale with such a slim trick ? Besides, how was it to be
worked ; how is an audience to be let into the secret ? Are
they likely to tag extra rhymes to the words of a song as
they listen to it ? Or is Nerissa—not Portia, surely !—at
some point to tip Bassanio the wink while he smiles know-
ingly back to assure her that he has cottoned on ? Where,
oh where indeed, are such dramatic fancies bred ? Not in
any head that will think out the effect of their realisation.

here is his chance to uplift the two as hero and heroine, and he will not dissipate its effectiveness.

For Bassanio, as we said, has been till now only little less bound than Portia in the fetters of a fairy-tale; and later, Shylock and the bond will condemn him to protesting helplessness, and the affair of the rings to be merrily befooled.[1] The wonder indeed is, considering the rather poor figure—painfully poor by the gospel according to Samuel Smiles—the coercion of the story makes him cut, that throughout he measures up so well to the stature of sympathetic hero. Shakespeare contrives it in two ways. He endows him with very noble verse; and, whenever he can, throws into strong relief the Bassanio of his own un-covenanted imagination. He does this here. The fantasy of the caskets brought to its due climax, charged with an emotion which blows it for a finish into thin air, he shows us Bassanio, his heart's desire won, agonised with grief and re-morse at the news of Antonio's danger. Such moments do test a man and show him for what he is; and this one, set in bright light and made the scene's turning point, counts for more in the effect the character makes on us than all the gentlemanly graces of his conventional equipment. Unless the actor is much at fault, we shall hear the keynote to the true Bassanio struck in the quiet

[1] Little to be found in him, upon analysis, to refute the frigid verdict lately passed upon him by that distinguished and enlightened—but in this instance, surely, most mis-takenly whimsical—critic, Sir Arthur Quiller-Couch, of fortune-hunter, hypocrite and worse. Is anything more certain than that Shakespeare did not *mean* to present us with such a hero? If Sir Arthur were producing the play, one pities the actor asked to give effect to his verdict.

75

simplicity—such contrast to his rhetoric over the caskets, even though this was less mere rhetoric than Morocco's and Aragon's—of the speech which begins

> O sweet Portia,
> Here are a few of the unpleasant'st words
> That ever blotted paper. . . .
> Rating myself at nothing, you shall see
> How much I was a braggart. When I told you
> My state was nothing, I should then have told you
> That I was worse than nothing, for indeed
> I have engaged myself to a dear friend,
> Engaged my friend to his mere enemy,
> To feed my means. . . .

Here speaks Shakespeare's Bassanio ; and it is by this, and all that will belong to it, that he is meant to live in our minds.

Producer and actors must look carefully into the means, by which in this scene the method that has served for the casket story is resolved into something better fitted to the theme of the bond (dominant from the beginning of the play, and now to absorb and transform the dedicated Portia and her fortunes). It is a change—though we must not insist on the contrast more than Shakespeare does—from dramatic convention to dramatic life. From the beginning the pulse of the scene beats more strongly ; and Portia's

> I pray you, tarry: pause a day or two
> Before you hazard; for in choosing wrong,
> I lose your company; therefore forbear awhile. . . .

is not only deeper in feeling (there has been little or nothing to rouse her till now ; she has had to be the picture of a Portia, hardly more, with a spice of wit to help her through) but how much simpler in expression! When Bassanio turns to those

76

obsessing caskets she must lapse again for a space into fancies of his swan-like end, her eye the watery death-bed for him, into talk about Hercules and Alcides (borrowed, one fears, from Morocco), about Dardanian wives and the like—even as he will be conventionally sententious over his choice. But note how, within the convention, preparing an escape from it, emotion is roused and sustained. With the rhetoric of Portia's

> Go, Hercules!
> Live thou, I live: with much, much more dismay
> I view the fight, than thou that mak'st the fray.

for a spring-board, the song and its music are to stir us,

> *whilst Bassanio comments on the caskets to himself.*

So (let the actor remember) when he does at last speak, the emotional ascent will have been half climbed for him already. And while he pays his tribute of trope and maxim, Portia, Nerissa and the rest watch him in silence, at full strain of attention, and help to keep us, too, intent. The speech itself sweeps unhindered to its climax, and the pause while the casket is unlocked is filled and enriched by the intensity of Portia's

> How all the other passions fleet to air . . .

most cunningly contrived in meaning and melody, with its emphasis on ' despair ' and ' ecstasy ' and ' excess,' to hold us upwrought. The fairy-tale is finally incarnate in the fantastic word-painting of the portrait and the reading of the scroll. Then, with a most delicate declension to reality, Bassanio comes to face her as in a more actual world, and the curtains can be drawn upon

77

the caskets for the last time. Observe that not for a moment has Shakespeare played his fabulous story false. He takes his theatre too seriously to go spoiling an illusion he has created. He consummates it, and turns the figures of it to fresh purpose, and they seem to suffer no change.

Throughout the scene—throughout the play, and the larger part of all Elizabethan drama for that matter—effects must be valued very much in terms of music. And, with the far adventuring of his playwriting hardly begun, Shakespeare's verse is already fairly flawless, and its manœuvring from mood to mood masterly, if still simple. We have the royal humility of the speech in which Portia yields herself (Bassanio slips back to his metaphors for a moment after this) ; then, for contrast, the little interlude of Gratiano and Nerissa, with the tripping monosyllables of Gratiano's

> I wish you all the joy that you can wish ;
> For I am sure you can wish none from me . . . .

to mark the pace and the tone of it. Then follows the arrival of Antonio's messenger with Lorenzo and Jessica ; done in plain, easy-moving verse that will not discount the distressed silence in which he reads the letter, nor the quiet candour of his confession to Portia. Now comes another crescendo—two voices added to strengthen it—leading up to her generous, wide-eyed

> What sum owes he the Jew?
> *Bassanio.*　For me, three thousand ducats.
> *Portia.*　　　　　　　　　What, no more!
> Pay him six thousand, and deface the bond,
> Double six thousand, and then treble that . . .

which itself drops to the gentleness of

> Since you are dear bought I will love you dear.

78

Then, to strengthen the scene's ending, we have the austere prose of Antonio's letter, chilling us to misgiving. And since—in stage practice, and with the prevailing key of the play's writing to consider—this will not do for an actual finish, there is a last modulation into the brisk coda of

> Since I have your good leave to go away,
> I will make haste: but till I come again,
> No bed shall e'er be guilty of my stay,
> Nor rest be interposer 'twixt us twain.

Lorenzo and Jessica make another link (though their relation to Belmont is pretty arbitrary) between the two stories. This, however, is but the secondary use of them. There must be a sense of time passing in Venice while the bond matures, yet we must have continuous action there too while the ritual at Belmont goes its measured way; so, as there can be little for Shylock and Antonio to do but wait, this third, minor theme is interposed. It brings fresh impetus to the action as well as new matter; and it shows us—very usefully—another and more human side of Shylock. Shakespeare does not scheme it out over carefully. The masking and the elopement and the coming and going they involve are rather inconveniently crowded together (the pleasant episode of the Gobbos may have stolen a little necessary space); and one chapter of the story—for were we perhaps to have seen Shylock at supper with Bassanio, Lorenzo and the rest while the disguised Jessica waited on them?—was possibly crowded out altogether.

Once the fugitives, with some disregard of likelihood, have been brought to Belmont, Gobbo in attendance, Shakespeare turns them to account

79

quite shamelessly. They play a mighty poor scene to give Portia and Nerissa time to disguise themselves as doctor and clerk.[1] They will have to play another while doctor and clerk change to Portia and Nerissa again; but for that, as if in compensation, they are to be dowered with the loveliest lines in the play.[2] With the junction of the themes in the trial scene the constructive problem is, of course, solved. Shylock disappearing, the rest is simple.

SHAKESPEARE'S VENICE

If Lorenzo and Jessica and a little poetry and the consort of music, which no well-regulated great household of his time would be without, are Shakespeare's resources (he had no other; and what better should we ask?) for the painting of the star-lit garden of Belmont at the play's end, for its beginning he must show us Venice. He troubles with no verbal scene-painting here; throughout the first scene the very word is but spoken twice, and quite casually. We might be anywhere in the city, or out of it, even. Thereafter we hear of the Rialto, of a gondola, of the common ferry and such-like incidentals; but of the picturesque environment to which modern staging has accustomed us there is no suggestion at all. Yet he does present a Venice that lived in the Elizabethan mind, and it is the Venice of his

[1] Possible extra time was needed for the shifting of the caskets and their furniture and the setting of the chairs of state for the Duke and the Magnificoes. But in that case these last must have been very elaborate.

[2] For the bearing of this upon the question of act division, see p. 107.

dramatic needs ; a city of royal merchants trading to the gorgeous East, of Jews in their gaberdines (as rare a sight, remember, as to us a Chinese mandarin is, walking the London streets to-day), and of splendid gentlemen rustling in silks. To the lucky young Englishman who could hope to travel there Venice stood for culture and manners and the luxury of civilisation ; and this—without one word of description—is how Shakespeare pictures it.

We are used nowadays to see the play begun by the entry of a depressed, sober-suited, middle-aged man and two skipping youths, who make their way with a sort of desperate merriment through such lines as the producer's blue pencil has left them, vanish shamefacedly, reappear at intervals to speak the remnant of another speech or two, and slip at last unregarded into oblivion. These are Solanio and Salarino, cursed by actors as the two worst bores in the whole Shakespearean canon; not excepting, even, those other twin brethren in nonentity, Rosencrantz and Guildenstern.[1] As characters, Shakespeare has certainly not been at much pains with them ; they could exchange speeches and no one would be the wiser, and they move about at everybody's convenience but their own. But they have their use, and it is an important one ; realise it, and there may be some credit in fulfilling it. They are there to paint Venice for us, the Venice of the magnificent young man. Bassanio embodies it also ; but there are other calls on him, and he will be off to Belmont

[1] But Rosencrantz and Guildenstern, as Shakespeare wrote them, are not the mere puppets that the usual mangling of the text leaves them.

soon. So do Gratiano and Lorenzo; but they
will be gone too. Solanio and Salarino will not
fail us; they hoist this flag at the play's beginning
and keep it bravely flying for as long as need be.
When Salarino, for a beginning, addresses Antonio
with

> There, where your argosies with portly sail,
> Like signiors and rich burghers on the flood,
> Or, as it were, the pageants of the sea,
> Do overpeer the petty traffickers,
> That curt'sy to them, do them reverence
> As they fly by them with their woven wings. . . .

—there should be no skipping merriment in this.

They are argosies themselves, these magnificent
young men, of high-flowing speech; pageants to
overpeer the callow English ruffians, to whom they
are here displayed. The talk passes from spices
and silks into fine classical phrases; and with
what elaborate, dignified dandyism it ends!

Enter Bassanio, Lorenzo and Gratiano.

Solanio. Here comes Bassanio, your most noble kinsman,
Gratiano, and Lorenzo; Fare you well;
We leave you now with better company.

Salarino. I would have staid till I had made you merry,
If worthier friends had not prevented me.

Antonio. Your worth is very dear in my regard,
I take it, your own business calls on you,
And you embrace the occasion to depart.

Salarino. Good-morrow, my good lords.

Bassanio. Good signiors both, when shall we laugh? Say, when?
You grow exceeding strange: Must it be so?

Salarino. We'll make our leisures to attend on yours.

No apologetic gabbling here: but such a polish,
polish as might have satisfied Mr. Turveydrop.
Solanio—if one could distinguish between them—

might cut the finer figure of the two. When the Mask is in question:

> 'Tis vile (he says) unless it may be quaintly ordered,
> And better, in my mind, not undertook.

Salarino has a cultured young gentleman's turn for classical allusion. He ranges happily from two-headed Janus and Nestor to Venus' pigeons.

But it is, as we said, when Bassanio and Gratiano and Lorenzo with his Jessica have departed, that the use these two are to the play becomes plainest. They give us the first news of Antonio's losses, and hearsay, filtering through them, keeps the disaster conveniently vague. If we saw the blow fall on Antonio, the far more dramatic scene in which Shylock is thrown from depth to heights and from heights to depth as ill news and this good news strike upon him would be left at a discount. In this scene they are most useful (if they are not made mere targets for a star actor to shoot at). For here again is Venice, in the contrast between sordid Shylock and Tubal and our magnificent young gentlemen, superfine still of speech and manner, but not above a little Jew-baiting. They sustain that theme—and it must be sustained—till it can be fully and finally orchestrated in the trial scene. It is a simple stagecraft which thus employs them, and their vacuity as characters inclines us to forget this, their very real utility. Forgetting it, Shakespeare's histrionic Venice is too often forgotten also.

THE CHARACTERS, AND THE CLIMAX OF THE ACTION

None of the minor characters does much more than illustrate the story; at best, they illuminate with a little lively detail their own passage through it. Not the Duke, nor Morocco, Aragon, Tubal, Lorenzo, Jessica, nor the Gobbos, nor Nerissa, had much being in Shakespeare's mind, we feel, apart from the scenes they played, and the use they were to him. It is as futile, that is to say, to discuss Jessica's excuses for gilding herself with ducats when she elopes as it is to work out her itinerary via Genoa to Belmont; we might as well start writing the life-story of Mistress Margery Gobbo.

Portia

Shakespeare can do little enough with Portia while she is still the slave of the caskets; incidentally, the actress must resist the temptation to try and do more. She has this picture of an enchanted princess to present, verse and prose to speak perfectly, and she had better be content with that. But we feel, nevertheless (and to this, very discreetly, she may encourage us), that here, pent up and primed for escape, is one of that eminent succession of candid and fearless souls: Rosaline, Helena, Beatrice, Rosalind—they embodied an ideal lodged for long in Shakespeare's imagination; he gave it expression whenever he could. Once he can set his Portia free to be herself, he quickly makes up for lost time. He has need to; for from the moment of that revealing

You see me, Lord Bassanio, where I stand. . . .

84

not half the play's life is left her, and during a good part of this she must pose as the young doctor of Rome whose name is Balthasar. He does not very deliberately develop her character; he seems by now to know too much about her to need to do that. He reveals it to us mainly in little things, and lets us feel its whole happy virtue in the melody of her speech. This it is that casts its spell upon the strict court of Venice. The

> Shed thou no blood. . . .

is an effective trick. But

> The quality of mercy is not strained;
> It droppeth as the gentle rain from heaven
> Upon the place beneath. . . .

with its continuing beauty, gives the true Portia. To the very end she expands in her fine freedom, growing in authority and dignity, fresh touches of humour enlightening her, new traits of graciousness showing. She is a great lady in her perfect simplicity, in her ready tact (see how she keeps her guest Antonio free from the mock quarrel about the rings), and in her quite unconscious self-sufficiency (she jokes without embarrassment about taking the mythical Balthasar to her bed, but she snubs Gratiano the next minute for talking of cuckoldry, even as she snubbed Nerissa for a very mild indelicacy—she is fond of Nerissa, but no forward waiting-women for her!) Yet she is no more than a girl.

Here is an effect that we are always apt to miss in the acting of Shakespeare to-day. It is not the actress's fault that she cannot be what her predecessor, the boy-Portia, was; and she brings us compensation for losses which should leave us—

85

if she will mitigate the losses as far as she can—
gainers on the whole. But the constant play made
in the Comedies upon the contrast between
womanly passion or wisdom and its very virginal
enshrining gives a delicacy and humour to these
figures of romance which the limited resources of
the boy left vivid, which the ampler endowment
of the woman too often obscures. This is no
paradox, but the obvious result of a practical
artistry making the most of its materials. Portia
does not abide in this dichotomy as fully as, for
instance, Rosalind and Viola do; but Shakespeare turns it to account with her in half a
hundred little ways, and to blur the effect of them
is to rob her of much distinction.

The very first line she speaks, the

> By my troth, Nerissa, my little body is aweary of this great
>   world

is likely to come from the mature actress robbed
of half its point. This will not matter so much.
But couple that ' little body ' with her self-
surrender to Bassanio as

> . . . an unlessoned girl, unschooled, unpractised;
> Happy in this, she is not yet so old
> But she may learn . . .

and with the mischief that hides behind the formal
courtesies of the welcome to Aragon and Morocco,
with the innocence of the amazed

> What no more!
> Pay him six thousand and deface the bond . . .

with the pretty sententiousness of her talk of
herself, her

> I never did repent of doing good,
> Nor shall not now. . . .

86

followed by the artless

> This comes too near the praising of myself . . .

and the figure built up for us of the heiress and great lady of Belmont is seen to be a mere child too, who lives remote in her enchanted world. Set beside this the Portia of resource and command, who sends Bassanio post haste to his friend, and beside that the schoolgirl laughing with Nerissa over the trick they are to play their new lords and masters. Know them all for one Portia, a wise and gallant spirit so virginally enshrined ; and we see to what profit Shakespeare turned his dis- abilities. There is, in this play, a twofold artistry in the achievement. Unlikelihood of plot is redeemed by veracity of character ; while the artifice of the medium, the verse and its con- vention, and the stylised acting of boy as woman, re-reconciles us to the fantasy of the plot.

But a boy-Portia's advantage was chiefly mani- fest, of course, in the scene of the trial ; and here in particular the actress of to-day must see that she lessens it no more than she need. The curious process of what we may call the ' double negative,' by which an Elizabethan audience first admitted a boy as a girl and then enjoyed the pretence that the girl was a boy, is obsolete for us ; make- believe being the game, there was probably some pleasure just in this complication of it. This beside, there was the direct dramatic effect, which the boy made supremely well in his own person, of the wise young judge, the Daniel come to judgment. Shylock (and Shakespeare) plucks the allusion from the popular story of Susanna ; but there may be some happy confusion, perhaps, with that other

Daniel who was among '. . . the children of
Israel, of the king's seede and of the Prince's:
Springaldes without any blemish, but well-
favoured, studious in all wisdome, skillful for
knowledge, able to utter knowledge, and such as
have livelinesse in them, that they might stand in
the king's palace. . . .' For this is the very
figure we should see. Here is the strict court of
Venice, like enough to any law court, from East
to West, from Shakespeare's time to now, in that
it will seem to the stranger there very dry and
discouraging, airless, lifeless. Age and incredulity
preside ; and if passion and life do enter, they must
play upon muted strings. The fiercely passionate
Shylock is anomaly enough in such surroundings.
Then comes this youth, as brisk and businesslike
as you please, and stands before the judges' bench,
alert, athletic, modest, confident. He is life incarnate and destined to victory; and such a victory
is the fitting climax to a fairy-tale. So the Portia
that will—as most Portias do—lapse into feminine
softness and pitch the whole scene in the key of
the speech on mercy, and that in a key of sentiment, damns the scene and herself and the speech,
all three. This amazing youth has the ear of the
Court at once ; but he'll only hold it by strict
attention to business. Then, suddenly, out of
this, comes the famous appeal, and catches us and
the Court unaware, catches us by the throat,
enkindles us. In this lies the effect. Prepare for
it, or make the beauty of it over-beautiful (all the
more now, because it is famous and hackneyed)
and it becomes a dose of soothing syrup.

This, be it further remembered, is not the scene's
top note; conflict and climax are to come. They

are brought about simply and directly; the mechanical trick of the ' No jot of blood ' that is to resolve them asks nothing else. Shakespeare keeps the medium of the verse as simple ; it flows on with hardly a broken line. The conflict is between Portia and Shylock. Bassanio's agony, Antonio's stoic resignation cannot be given great play ; the artifice of the story will not even now sustain cross-currents of human passion. But the constraint of the business of a court accounts well enough for their quiescence (the actors need do nothing to mitigate it) and the few notes that are struck from them suffice. The action must sweep ahead and no chance be given us to question its likelihood. Even when all is over the Duke departs with not much more comment upon this amazing case than an invitation to the learned young doctor to come to dinner, and Antonio and his friends are as casual about it and almost as calm. There is tactful skill in this. Shylock has gone, that fairy-tale is done with; the less we look back and the sooner we come to fresh comedy again the better.

Throughout the scene a Portia must, of course, by no smallest sign betray to us—as well betray it to Bassanio—that she is other than she now seems. No difficulty here, as we said, for Shakespeare's Portia, or his audience either. There was no wondering as he faced the judges why they never saw this was a woman (since very obviously he now wasn't) nor why Bassanio did not know his wife a yard off. The liquid sentences of the Mercy speech were no betrayal, nor did the brusque aside of a young lawyer, intent upon his brief—

> Your wife would give you little thanks for that,
> If she were by to hear you make the offer.

—lose its quite casual humour. All this straight-forwardness the modern actress must, as far as she can, restore.

Antonio, Gratiano and others

In these early plays character does not as a rule outrun the requirements of the plot. Shakespeare is content enough with the decorative, the senten-tious, the rhetorical, in his casual Venetians, in Aragon and Morocco; with the conventional in Launcelot, who is the stage clown—the juggler with words, neat, agile, resourceful and occasion-ally familiar with the audience, as a clown and a juggler should be—under a thin disguise of character; with old Gobbo for a minute or two's incidental fun; with the pure utility of Tubal.

Antonio is flesh and blood. He is the passive figure of the story's demand; but Shakespeare refines this in the selflessness that can send Bassanio to Belmont and be happy in a friend's happiness, in the indifference to life that lets him oppose patience to his enemy's fury; and he makes him more convincingly this sort of man by making him just a little self-conscious too.

> In sooth I know not why I am so sad . . .

If he does not, it is not for want of thinking about it. He takes a sad pleasure in saying that he is

> . . . a tainted wether of the flock.
> Meetest for death . . .

But there is a redeeming ironic humour in

> You cannot better be employed, Bassanio,
> Then to live still and write mine epitaph.

90

He is sufficiently set forth, and there is conveyed in him a better dignity than mere words give.[1]

Nerissa is echoing merriment ; not much more.

Shakespeare may have had half a mind to make something a little out of the way of Gratiano. He starts him with a temperament and a witty speech ; but by the play's end we have not had much more from him than the ' infinite deal of nothing ' of Bassanio's gibe, rattling stuff, bouncing the play along, but revealing no latent Gratiano. It all makes a good enough pattern of this sort of man, who will be a useful foil to Bassanio, and can be paired off for symmetry with Portia's foil, Nerissa ; and the play needed no more. But there is enough of him, and enough talk about him, for one to feel that he missed by only a little the touch of magic that would have made something more of him and added him to the list of those that survive the lowering of the lights and the theatre's emptying. There is a moment while he waits to take his share in Jessica's abduction, and sits reflecting :

> All things that are,
> Are with more spirit chased than enjoyed.
> How like a yonker or a prodigal,
> The scarfed bark puts from her native bay,
> Hugg'd and embraced by the strumpet wind!
> How like a prodigal doth she return;
> With over-weather'd ribs, and ragged sails,
> Torn, rent and beggared by the strumpet wind!

Harsh enough similes for such an occasion! Is this another side to the agreeable rattle? Does the man who exclaims

---

[1] It is worth remarking that the word 'sad,' as Shakespeare uses it, may mean rather solemn and serious than definitely miserable.

Let me play the fool!
With mirth and laughter let old wrinkles come . . .

find life in fact rather bitter to his taste? But one must beware of reading subtleties into Shakespeare. If such a Gratiano was ever shadowed in his mind, he made no solid substance of him.

Bassanio we have spoken of; play the part quite straightforwardly and it will come right.

Shylock

There remains Shylock. He steps into the play, actual and individual from his first word on, and well might in his strength (we come to feel) have broken the pinchbeck of his origin to bits, had a later Shakespeare had the handling of him. As it is, his actuality is not weakened by the fantasy of the bond, as is Portia's by her caskets. For one thing, our credulity is not strained till the time comes for its maturing, and by then—if ever—the play and its acting will have captured us. For another, the law and its ways are normally so uncanny to a layman that the strict court of an exotic Venice might give even stranger judgments than this and only confirm us in our belief that once litigation begins almost anything may happen. Despite the borrowed story, this Shylock is essentially Shakespeare's own. But if he is not a puppet, neither is he a stalking horse; he is no more a mere means to exemplifying the Semitic problem than is Othello for the raising of the colour question. 'I am a Jew.' 'Haply, for I am black. . . .' Here we have—and in Shylock's case far more acutely and completely—the *circumstances* of the dramatic conflict; but at the heart of it are

92

men; and we may surmise, indeed, that from a maturer Shakespeare we should have had, as with Othello, much more of the man, and so rather less of the alien and his griefs. However that may be, he steps now into the play, individual and imaginatively full-grown, and the scene of his talk with Bassanio and Antonio is masterly exposition.

The dry taciturnity of his

Three thousand ducats, well?

(the lure of that thrice-echoed ' Well '!) and the cold dissecting of the business in hand are made colder, drier yet by contrast with the happy sound of Portia's laughter dying in our ears as he begins to speak. And for what a helpless innocent Bassanio shows beside him; over-anxious, touchy, over-civil! Shylock takes his time; and suddenly we see him peering, myopic, beneath his brows. Who can the new-comer be? And the quick brain answers beneath the question's cover: They must need the money badly if Antonio himself comes seeking me. Off goes Bassanio to greet his friend; and Shylock in a long aside can discharge his obligations to the plot.[1] These eleven lines are worth comment. In them is all the motive power for drama that the story, as Shakespeare found it, provides; and he throws this, with careless opulence, into a single aside. Then he returns to the upbuilding of *his* Shylock.

[1] This is one of the ever-recurring small strokes of stage-craft that are hardly appreciable apart from an Elizabethan stage. Shylock and Bassanio are to the front of the platform. Antonio, near the door, is by convention any convenient distance off; by impression too, with no realistic scenery to destroy the impression. Shylock is left isolated, so isolated that the long aside has all the importance and the force of a soliloquy.

93

Note the next turn the scene takes. From the snuffling depreciation of his present store, from his own wonted fawning on these Christian clients, Shylock unexpectedly rises to the dignities of

> When Jacob grazed his uncle Laban's sheep. . . .

And with this the larger issue opens out between Gentile and Jew, united and divided by the scripture they revere, and held from their business by this tale from it—of flocks and herds and the ancient East. Here is another Shylock; and Antonio may well stare, and answer back with some respect—though he recovers contempt for the alien creature quickly enough. But with what added force the accusation comes:

> Signior Antonio, many a time and oft
> In the Rialto you have rated me. . . .
> You called me misbeliever, cut-throat dog
> And spit upon my Jewish gaberdine. . . .

The two Venetians see the Ghetto denizen again, and only hear the bondman's whine. But to us there is now all Jewry crouched and threatening there, an ageless force behind it. They may make light of the money bond, but we shall not.

Shakespeare keeps character within the bounds of story with great tact; but such a character as this that has surged in his imagination asks more than such a story to feed on. Hence, partly at least, the new theme of Jessica and her flight, which will give Shylock another and more instant grudge to satisfy. It is developed with strict economy. Twenty-one lines are allowed to Jessica and Launcelot, another twenty or so to her lover and their plans; then, in a scene not sixty long, Shylock and his household are enshrined. As an

94

example of dramatic thrift alone this is worth study. The parting with Launcelot: he has a niggard liking for the fellow, is even hurt a little by his leaving, touched in pride too, and shows it childishly.

> Thou shalt not gormandize
> As thou hast done with me. . . .

But he can at least pretend that he parts with him willingly and makes some profit by it. The parting with Jessica, which we of the audience know to be a parting indeed; that constant calling her by name, which tells us of the lonely man! He has looked to her for everything, has tasked her hard, no doubt; he is her gaoler, yet he trusts her, and loves her in his extortionate way. Uneasy stranger that he is within these Venetian gates; the puritan, who, in a wastrel world, will abide by law and prophets! So full a picture of the man does the short scene give that it seems hardly possible we see no more of him than this between the making of the bond and the climacteric outbreak of passion upon Jessica's loss and the news of Antonio's ruin.[1]

References to him abound; Shylock can never

[1] And so strange has this seemed to many a producer of the play and actor of Shylock, that we have been given scenes of pantomime in which Shylock comes back from Bassanio's supper to find Jessica flown. The solitary figure with a lantern, the unanswered rapping at the door, has become all but traditional. Irving did it, Coghlan had already done something of the sort, and—I fancy—Booth. An ingenious variation upon a theme by Shakespeare, that yet merely enfeebles the theme. The lengthier elaboration of a Shylock seen distracted at the discovery of his loss is, of course, sheer stupidity, since Shakespeare has deliberately avoided the situation.

95

be long out of our minds. But how deliberate is
the thrift of opportunity we may judge by our
being shown the first effect of the loss on him
only through the ever-useful eyes of Salarino and
Solanio. This is politic, however, from other
points of view. Look where the scene in question
falls, between Morocco's choice of his casket and
Aragon's. Here or hereabouts some such scene
must come, for the progress of the Antonio and
Shylock story cannot be neglected. But conceive
the effect of such a tragic outcry as Shylock's own,

So strange, outrageous and so variable. . . .

—of such strong dramatic meat sandwiched
between pleasant conventional rhetoric. How
much of the credibility of the casket story would
survive the association, with how much patience
should we return to it? But Salarino and Solanio
tone down tragedy to a good piece of gossip,
as it becomes young men of the world to do.
We avoid an emotional danger zone; and, for
the moment at least, that other danger of an
inconvenient sympathy with ' the dog Jew.'
When Shylock's outbreak of anguish does come,
the play is nearer to its climax, Bassanio's choice
is about to free Portia's story from its unreality,
and his savage certainty of revenge upon Antonio
will now depress the sympathetic balance against
him.

But, considering the story's bounds, what a
full-statured figure we already have! Compare
the conventional aside, the statement of the
theme, in the earlier scene, the bald

I hate him for he is a Christian. . . .

with the deluge of molten passion which descends

96

upon the devoted Solanio and Salarino, obliterating their tart humour; compare the theme, that is to say, with its development, mere story with character, and measure in the comparison Shakespeare's growing dramatic power.

In tone and temper and method as well this scene breaks away from all that has gone before. The very start in prose, the brisk

> Now, what news on the Rialto?

even, perhaps, Solanio's apology for former

. . . slips of prolixity or crossing the plain highway of talk:

seem to tell us that Shakespeare is now asserting the rights of his own imagination, means, at any rate, to let this chief creature of it, his Shylock, off the leash. For verily he does.

The scene's method repays study. No whirling storm of fury is asked for; this is not the play's climax, but preparation for it still. Shylock is wrapped in resentful sorrow, telling over his wrong for the thousandth time. Note the repetition of thought and phrase. And how much more sinister this sight of him with the wound festering than if we had seen the blow's instant fall! His mind turns to Antonio, and the thrice told

> . . . let him look to his bond.

is a rope of salvation for him; it knots up the speech in a dreadful strength. Then, on a sudden, upon the good young Salarino's reasonable supposition that what a money-lender wants is his money back; who on earth would take flesh instead?—

> What's that good for?

ii. 8

—there flashes out the savagery stripped naked of

> To bait fish withal: if it will feed nothing else, it will feed my revenge.

Now we have it; and one salutes such purity of hatred. There follows the famous speech—no need to quote it—mounting in passionate logic, from its

> He hath disgraced me . . . and what's his reason? I am a Jew.

to the height of

> If a Jew wrong a Christian, what is his humility? Revenge. If a Christian wrong a Jew, what should his sufferance be by Christian example? Why, revenge. The villainy you teach me I will execute, and it shall go hard but I will better the instruction.

This is a Shylock born of the old story, but transformed, and here a theme of high tragedy, of the one seemingly never-ending tragedy of the world. It is the theme for a greater play than Shakespeare was yet to write. But if this one cannot be sustained on such a height, he has at least for the moment raised it there.

Solanio and Salarino are quite oblivious to the great moral issue opened out to them; though they depart a little sobered—this Jew seems a dangerous fellow. There follows the remarkable passage with Tubal; of gruesome comedy, the apocalyptic Shylock shrunk already to the man telling his ill-luck against his enemy's, weighing each in scales (love for his daughter, a memory of his dead wife thrown in!) as he is used to weigh the coin which is all these Christians have left him for his pride. It is technically a notable passage, in that it is without conflict or contrast, things generally necessary to dramatic dialogue; but the breaking of a rule will be an improvement, now and then, upon obedience to it. So Shakespeare, for a finish, lowers the scene from its climax, from that confronting of Christian and Jew, of hate with hate, to this raucous assonance of these two of a kind and mind, standing cheek to cheek in common cause, the excellent Tubal fueling up revenge.

Such a finish, ousting all nobility, both shows us another facet of Shylock himself (solid man enough now to be turned any way his maker will) and is, as we saw, a shadow against which the high romance of Bassanio's wooing will in a moment shine the more brightly. Sharp upon the heels of this, he comes again; but once more apocalyptic, law incarnate now.

Shylock. Gaoler, look to him; tell me not of mercy;
This is the fool that lent out money gratis:
Gaoler, look to him.
Antonio. Hear me yet, good Shylock.
Shylock. I'll have my bond; speak not against my bond:
I have sworn an oath that I will have my bond.

Verse and its dignity are needed for this scene; and note the recurring knell of the phrases:

I'll have my bond; I will not hear thee speak:
I'll have my bond, and therefore speak no more.
I'll not be made a soft and dull-eyed fool,
To shake the head, relent, and sigh, and yield
To Christian intercessors. Follow not;
I'll have no speaking: I will have my bond.

Here is a Shylock primed for the play's great scene; and Shakespeare's Shylock wrought ready for a catastrophe, which is a deeper one by far than that the story yields. For not in the missing

99

of his vengeance on Antonio will be this Shylock's tragedy, but in the betrayal of the faith on which he builds.

> I've sworn an oath that I will have my bond . . .

How many times has the synagogue not heard it sworn?

> An oath, an oath.   I have an oath in Heaven . . .

He has made his covenant with an unshakable God :

> What judgment shall I dread, doing no wrong?

—and he is to find himself betrayed.

It is the apocalyptic Shylock that comes slowly into Court, solitary and silent, to face and to outface the Duke and all the moral power of Venice.[1] When he does speak he answers the Duke as an equal, setting a sterner sanction against easy magnanimity—at other people's expense ! One could complain that this first appeal for mercy discounts Portia's.   To some extent it does ; but the more famous speech escapes comparison by coming when the spell of the young doctor is freshly cast on us, and by its finer content and larger scope. Structurally, the Duke's speech is the more important, for it sets the lists, defines the issue and provokes that

> I have possessed your grace of what I purpose ;
> And by our holy sabbath have I sworn
> To have the due and forfeit of my bond . . .

---

[1] Upon the modern stage he usually has Tubal for a companion ; one has even seen him seconded by a small crowd of sympathetic Jews.   How any producer can bring himself so to discount the poignant sight of that drab, heroic figure, lonely amid the magnificence around, passes understanding !

So confident is he that he is tempted to shift ground a little and let yet another Shylock peep— the least likable of all. He goes on

> You'll ask me, why I rather choose to have
> A weight of carrion flesh, than to receive
> Three thousand ducats: I'll not answer that,
> But say it is my humour . . .

Legality gives license to the hard heart. Mark the progression. While the sufferer cried

The villainy you teach me I will execute; and it shall go hard but I will better the instruction.

with the law on his side it is

> What judgment shall I dread, doing no wrong? . . .

from which he passes, by an easy turn, to the mere moral anarchy of

> The pound of flesh, which I demand of him,
> Is dearly bought; 'tis mine, and I will have it . . .

and in satanic heroism stands defiant:

> If you deny me, fie upon your law!
> There is no force in the decrees of Venice.
> I stand for judgment. Answer: shall I have it?

There is a dreadful silence. For who, dwelling unquestioningly under covenant of law, shall gainsay him?

It says much for the mental hypnosis which the make-believe of the theatre can induce that this scene of the trial holds us so spellbound. Its poetry adds to the enchantment—let anyone try re-writing it in prose—and the exotic atmosphere helps. But how much more is due to the embroidering of character upon story so richly that the quality of the fabric comes to matter little!

Shakespeare, at any rate, has us now upon the elemental heights of drama. He cannot keep us there. Portia must perform her conjuring trick; perhaps this is why he gives Shylock full scope before she arrives. But he brings us down with great skill, manœuvring character to the needs of the story, and turning story to character's account.

The coming of the young judge's clerk does not impress Shylock. How should it? Little Nerissa! He has won, what doubt of it? He can indulge then—why not?—the lodged hate and loathing he bears Antonio. The Duke is busy with Bellario's letter and the eyes of the Court are off him. From avenger he degenerates to butcher; to be caught, lickerish-lipped, by Bassanio, and Gratiano's rough tongue serves him as but another whetstone for savagery. He turns surly at first sight of the wise young judge—what need of such a fine fellow and more fine talk?—and surlier still when it is talk of mercy. He stands there, he tells them yet again, asking no favours, giving none.

> My deeds upon my head! I crave the law,
> The penalty and forfeit of my bond.

Why does Shakespeare now delay the catastrophe by a hundred lines, and let Portia play cat and mouse with her victim? From the story's standpoint, of course, to keep up the excitement a while longer. We guess there is a way out. We wonder what it can be; and yet, with that knife shining, Antonio's doom seems to come nearer and nearer. This is dramatic child's play, and excellent of its sort. But into it much finer stuff is woven. We are to have more than a trick brought off; there must be a better victory; this faith in which Shylock abides must be broken. So first she leads him on. Infatuate, finding her all on his side, he finally and formally refuses the money—walks into the trap. Next she plays upon his fanatical trust in his bond, sets him searching in mean mockery for a charitable comma in it—had one escaped his cold eye—even as the Pharisees searched their code to convict Christ. Fold by fold, the prophetic dignity falls from him. While Antonio takes his selfless farewell of his friend, Shylock must stand clutching his bond and his knife, only contemptible in his triumph. She leads him on to a last slaveringly exultant cry: then the blow falls.

Note that the tables are very precisely turned on him.

> . . . if thou tak'st more,
> Or less, than a just pound, be it so much
> As makes it light or heavy in the substance,
> Or the division of the twentieth part
> Of one poor scruple, nay, if the scale do turn
> But in the estimation of a hair. . . .

is exact retaliation for Shylock's insistence upon the letter of his bond. Gratiano is there to mock him with his own words, and to sound, besides, a harsher note of retribution than Portia can; for the pendulum of sympathy now swings back a little—more than a little, we are apt to feel. But the true catastrophe is clear. Shylock stood for law and the letter of the law; and it seemed, in its kind, a noble thing to stand for, ennobling him. It betrays him, and in the man himself there is no virtue left.

> Is *that* the law?

he gasps helplessly. It is his only thought. The pride and power in which legality had wrapped him, by which he had outfaced them all, and held Venice herself to ransom, are gone. He stands stripped, once more the sordid Jew that they may spit upon, greedy for money, hurriedly keen to profit by his shame.

> I take this offer then; pay the bond thrice,
> And let the Christian go.

Here is Shakespeare's Shylock's fall, and not in the trick the law plays him.

He is given just a chance—would the story let him take it!—to regain tragic dignity. What is passing in his mind that prompts Portia's

> Why doth the Jew pause? Take thy forfeiture.[1]

No, nothing, it would seem, but the thought that he will be well out of the mess with his three thousand ducats safe.

Shakespeare has still to bring his theme full circle. He does it with doubled regard to character and story.

> Why, then the devil give him good of it!
> I'll stay no longer question.

If he were not made to, by every canon of theatrical justice Shylock would be let off too lightly; wherefore we find that the law has another hold on him. It is but a logical extending of retribution, which Gratiano is quick to reduce to its brutal absurdity. Here is Shylock with no more right to a cord with which to hang himself than had Antonio to a bandage for his wound. These quibbling ironies are

[1] See Furness for an elaborate, illuminating and witty comment upon the situation.

for the layman among the few delights of law.
Something of the villainy the Jew taught them the
Christians will now execute ; and Shylock, as helpless as Antonio was, takes on a victim's dignity in
turn. He stays silent while his fate, and the
varieties of official and unofficial mercy to be
shown him, are canvassed.[1] He is allowed no
comment upon his impoverishing for the benefit
of 'his son Lorenzo' or upon his forced apostasy.
But could eloquence serve better than such a
silence ?

> *Portia.* Art thou contented, Jew ? What doest thou say?
> *Shylock.* I am content.

With the three words of submission the swung
pendulum of the drama comes to rest. And for
the last of him we have only

> I pray you give me leave to go from hence;
> I am not well. Send the deed after me,
> And I will sign it.

Here is the unapproachable Shakespeare. 'I
am not well.' It nears banality and achieves perfection in its simplicity. And what a completing
of the picture of Shylock! His deep offence has
been to human kindness; he had scorned com-
passion and prayed God himself in aid of his

[1] It is hard to see why Antonio's taking the money to pass
on to ' the gentleman that lately stole his daughter ' and
providing that, for his half-pardon " he presently become a
Christian," should be so reprobated by some critics. If we
have less confidence to-day than had Antonio in the efficacy
of baptism, have we none left in the rightfulness of reparation ?
Not much in its efficacy, perhaps. Antonio, one must
insist, does not mean to keep any of the money for himself.
One hopes he never lapsed into self-righteousness in recalling
this. Nothing is said, however, about the original three
thousand ducats !

vengeance. So Shakespeare dismisses him upon an all but ridiculous appeal to our pity, such as an ailing child might make that had been naughty ; and we should put the naughtiness aside. He passes out silently, leaving the gibing Gratiano the last word, and the play's action sweeps on without pause. There can be no greater error than to gerrymander Shylock a strenuously ' effective exit '—and most Shylocks commit it. From the character's point of view the significant simplicity of that

I am not well.

is spoilt ; and from the point of view of the play the technical skill with which Shakespeare abstracts from his comedy this tragic and dominating figure and avoids anti-climax after is nullified.

THE RETURN TO COMEDY

The tragic interest is posted to oblivion cavalierly indeed. Seven lines suffice, and the Duke's processional departure. The business of the rings is then briskly despatched, and made the brisker by the business-like matter of the signing of the deed being tacked to it. Thence to Belmont ; and while Lorenzo and Jessica paint its moonlit beauty for us, Balthasar and his clerk have time to change costume and tire their heads again for Portia and Nerissa. They have evidently, as we saw, none too much time ; for Launcelot is allowed a last— and an incongruously superfluous—piece of clowning. But the musicians can play ahead for an extra minute or two if hooks and eyes refuse to fasten, and no one will notice the delay. The last stretch of dialogue is lively; a comic quartet coming after the consort of viols, and it asks for a like virtuosity. The play ends, pleasantly and with formality, as a fairy-tale should. One may wonder that the last speech is left (against tradition) to Gratiano; but one practical reason is plain. Portia and Bassanio, Antonio, Lorenzo and Jessica must pace off the stage in their stately Venetian way, while Gratiano's harmless ribaldry is tossed to the audience as an epilogue. Then he and Nerissa, now with less dignity than ever to lose, skip after.

ACT DIVISION AND STAGING

However well the First Folio's five-act rule may fit other plays, and whatever, in Elizabethan stage practice, division into five acts implied, there is ample evidence that *The Merchant of Venice* was meant to be played without an effective break. The scenes, and the padding in them, that give time for Portia and Nerissa to change clothes are one sign of it. The first of these is padding unalloyed, and very poor padding at that. For the second, Shakespeare finds better and pleasanter excuse; but in part, at least, we owe that charming duet between Lorenzo and Jessica to this practical need.[1]

A case of a sort can be made out for the division in the Folio. Granted five acts, this fourth and fifth are manifest; the beginnings and finishings

[1] The two scenes are, to a line, of the same length. Add to the one the opening of the Trial scene, and to the other, for safety's sake, twenty bars or so of music, and we have the time allotted for the change of costume.

of the first three make useful milestones in the
story, but others every bit as useful could be set up.
It is worth noting that this act division does
nothing to elucidate the complex time-scheme of
our anxious editors ; but the Folio's expert play-
divider would be no more bothered by that
problem than Shakespeare had been. Nor was
he concerned to end his acts memorably ; the
second leaves Aragon in our minds and the third
ends with Jessica and Lorenzo's and the play's
worst scene.[1] There might, however, be good
enough reason in the Elizabethan theatre for
making an act's first scene arresting and for
letting its last tail away; for they had, of course,
no curtain to lower upon a climax, and after an
interval interest would need quick re-kindling.
No producer to-day, one hopes, will want to lower
a picture-stage curtain at such points. Nor, if he
is wise, while his stories are working to their joint
climax will he give us pause to think by what
strange leaps in time and space they travel.

But surely there are many signs that—however,
for convenience sake, it is to be acted, with or
without pause—Shakespeare has conceived and
constructed the play indivisibly. There is the
alternating between Venice and Belmont, and
the spinning out of the Portia story to fit with the
other ; neither device gains by or countenances
act division. There is the unhesitating sweep of
the action up to the Trial scene, and indeed beyond

[1] Furness sees dramatic point in the second act ending
with Bassanio on the doorstep. I suggest that Nerissa's tag
is meant to keep Belmont a little in our minds during the
strenuous scene between Shylock and Tubal which follows;
but that, if anything, it tells against an act pause falling here,
rather than for it.

108

it. One can parcel it up in various ways—the Folio's and half a dozen others—and on various pleas; but will any one of them make the story clearer; will it not, on the contrary, do something to disclose its confusions? Prose and blank verse, rhymed couplets and a quatrain are used indifferently for tags; so these form no consistent punctuation. There is no scene, not even the Trial scene, that ends with a full close, until the play ends. There is, in fact, no inherent, no dramatic pause in the action at all; nor can any be made which will not be rather hindrance than help to a performance.

Well-paced acting will take the play straight through in the traditional, vague two hours. But if, for the weakness of the flesh, there must be pauses, division into three parts will be a little less awkward than into two. If you do not stop before the Trial scene you cannot, of course, stop at all; the play will be virtually over. You may reasonably pause at the end of the Folio's Act III. This alone, though, will make very unequal division. For an earlier pause, the moment of Bassanio's departure from Venice will serve.[1] This splits the first three acts of the Folio all but exactly in two. Delay the pause another scene and we shall have done with Morocco. The second part would then begin with the tale of how Shylock took his loss and our first news of Antonio's losses, and would develop this interest till the eve of the trial. Incidentally it would hold all the inordinate time-telescoping; a helpful quickening, this, to its pulse. But these divisions and the

---

[1] There is, as we have seen, a possible contracting of the action here that gives a summariness to the last few lines and suggests (to the modern ear, truly) a 'curtain.'

choice of them have no other validity than convenience ; the play must be thought of as an integral whole.

Needless to say that the confusion of scene-divisions in most modern editions (a very riot of it when Jessica is eloping) is not Shakespeare's ; nor is the expert of the Folio responsible, nor even Rowe, who contents himself with marking the moves from Venice to Belmont and back.[1] For a century editors disputed as to when 'Venice, a street,' shifted to 'A room in Shylock's House,' or to 'Another Street,' or to 'Before Shylock's House,' and chopped up the action and checked its impetus, when one glance at Shakespeare's stage, its doors and balcony and traverses, shows with what swift unity the play and its playing flow on. And whatever picturing of Venice and Belmont a producer may design, this swift-flowing unity he must on no account obstruct. Let that be clear.

But there is little difficulty in the play's production, once its form is recognised, its temper felt, the tune of its verse and the rhythm of its prose rightly caught. The text is very free from errors, there are no puzzles in the actual stagecraft. The music may come from Elizabethan stock, and the costuming is obvious. Nothing is needed but perception and good taste, and from the actors, acting.

[1] Lord Lansdowne's Jew held the stage in Rowe's time; and for this reason, perhaps, he does not trouble to bring the play into closer relation with his own theatre.

ANTONY AND CLEOPATRA

HERE is the most spacious of the plays. It may lack the spiritual intimacy of *Hamlet*, the mysterious power of *Macbeth*, the nobilities of *Othello*, may reach neither to the heights nor depths of *King Lear ;* but it has a magnificence and a magic all its own, and Shakespeare's eyes swept no wider horizon.

Eight years or so earlier he had written *Julius Cæsar.* There already are these rivals Antony and Octavius, comrades then; and the main clash of fortune and character is between Antony and Brutus, between the man of action and the idealist. Antony comes from it victorious ; the tragedy is the soul's tragedy of Brutus. Thereafter Shakespeare gives us play after play upon this theme of the self-torturing soul. Hamlet (its chief exemplar), Othello, Macbeth, Lear are all concerned with the world within themselves. Now he returns to the world of great affairs, and, almost as if for emphasis, to the very pair that he left standing over the dead body of the idealist in defeat.[1]

We have a play of action, then, not of spiritual insight ; that is the first thing to mark. Of a large field of action too. For if with *Julius Cæsar* the insularity of the earlier Histories was left

[1] And a little later he took Coriolanus, another Roman, another man of action, for tragic hero.

behind, we are shown now not Rome in her might only, but the whole range of the Empire, eastward to Athens, Egypt and the Parthian bounds. Antony, the once-triumphant man of action, is hero; we are to watch his defeat by his subtler sometime pupil. Truly it is his passion for Cleopatra that is his ruin, and the action pulses to this; but the wider issue dictates form, method, and the bulk of the play's content.

A tragedy of disillusion, we might call it. As to the lovers, from the beginning they have little to learn about each other.

> She is cunning past man's thought,

says Antony; and Cleopatra is very soon lashing at him with

> O most false love!
> Where be the sacred vials thou shouldst fill
> With sorrowful water? Now I see, I see,
> In Fulvia's death, how mine received shall be.

(though the event belies her). But the whole picture is shaded to this sere hue. 'My son,' said Oxenstierne, 'you will be amazed to discover with how little wisdom the world is governed.' We may sit through this play and add, 'With how little honour or honesty or decency either!' Shakespeare had not idealised the earlier Antony, nor—though the sketch of him is so slight—underrated Octavius.[1] But the dead Cæsar's champion was at least a gallant fellow, able and alert. In his stead we now see

> . . . the triple pillar of the world transformed
> Into a strumpet's fool.

---

[1] And we may even read into passages of *Julius Cæsar* a foreshadowing of the breach between the two.

And that industrious apprentice Octavius, as he nears his reward, grows under our eyes ever colder of heart, more meanly calculating, more deliberately false. We meet Lepidus again, the ' barren-spirited fellow,' as barren still of everything but efforts to keep the peace somehow, since only so can he hope to keep his own weak head above water; and we see Octavius belatedly following Antony's politic advice to

> . . . turn him off,
> Like to the empty ass, to shake his ears
> And graze in commons.

We meet Pompey, the foolish optimist, the lucky fighter cajoled to an unstable peace, standing on his honour, but as willing to profit by the vilest treachery. Ventidius is the one Roman to be found fighting Rome's enemies instead of his fellow Romans; and he dare not push victory home for fear of Antony's jealousy. We have Enobarbus; a man (the bitter paradox!) corrupted most by fidelity to his friend, then turning traitor—too late! Towards the play's end comes a very procession of generals, soldiers and dutiful servants, their fidelity abused, their valour wasted. Some desert while they can and some are caught in their leader's insensate ruin. While as to the Roman people themselves, the republic for which Brutus and Cassius died, the Friends, Romans, Countrymen who were Antony's ' good friends, sweet friends,' what have their saviours and masters to say of them now? For Antony they are

> . . . our slippery people,
> Whose love is never linked to the deserver
> Till his deserts are past.

and Cæsar, a scene or so later (it cannot be for-
tuitously), is made to speak of

> . . . the ebb'd man, ne'er loved till ne'er worth love.

and, with what contempt, of how

> This common body,
> Like to a vagabond flag upon the stream,
> Goes to and fro, lackeying the varying tide,
> To rot itself with motion.

Not, on the whole then, a hopeful picture of the
Roman world. And it is, in the main, Shakespeare's own picture; if he pillages Plutarch for
facts, even for phrases, their interpretation and
emphasis—all that makes a picture—are his.

Bradley will not place the play with the four
great tragedies, because, he says, Antony and
Cleopatra themselves do not kindle pity and
admiration to the full. He admits, though, that
their passion and its ending is by no means the
whole of the story. Certainly it is not. What are
we shown to begin with? Far less a pair of
tragic lovers in the making than—through the
indignant Roman eyes of Philo and Demetrius—
a doting general, effeminate in Egyptian finery,[1]
ignoring Cæsar's messengers, capable of a

> Let Rome in Tiber melt, and the wide arch
> Of the ranged Empire fall.

(whoever will may hear it!), and a debauched
Eastern queen, mocking at things Roman, batten-
ing on his apostasy. Here at once is the larger
theme emphasised, the discord which is to be
resolved at last to a full close in the elaborate

---

[1] The ' strumpet's fool ' is some, if not absolute, warrant
for this.

114

confusions of their defeat and death. The love-tragedy, we might almost say, is not made the main question till no other question is left, till the ruin wreaked by Triumvir and Queen is accomplished. And the action of the play is schemed throughout for the picturing of this wider ruin. Hence its diffuseness; and hence, if this is not understood, much misunderstanding of its artistry.

'*Feliciter audax*,' says Coleridge of the style, and the label has stuck. Dr. Johnson, however, is stern. 'The events, of which the principal are described according to history, are produced without any art of connection or care of disposition.' It never does to neglect Johnson. His plain-sailing sanity will cut a clear way for us through many a metaphysical fog of nineteenth-century criticism. Even if at last we must disagree with him, he takes answering. But he owns besides that 'this play keeps curiosity always busy and the passions always interested' and that 'the continual hurry of the action, the variety of incidents, and the quick succession of one personage to another call the mind forward without intermission from the first Act to the last.' So in the end—Johnson exhibiting, perhaps, less consistency than usual—he and Coleridge are found not so far apart.

Feliciter audax! Shakespeare does seem to be amazingly at his ease. He brings in characters lavishly, flings Plutarch into dialogue; his verse is at its supplest, we are hardly conscious of the convention, and he shifts it to prose and back again without a jar. The action moves forthright and unchecked. Yet little or nothing in it shows superfluous; and, though endowed with but a line or two, the characters never fail to come to life. And if all this comes about 'without any art of connection or care of disposition,' if it all seems haphazard, is it not just possible Shakespeare may mean it to, may at least be content that it should? There is little luck in these matters, as the inexpert playwright who tries his along these lines will find. Do we perhaps pay a tribute to this art in so condemning it? Critics have found themselves performing this feat before now. But, in fact, the play's scheme is plain and ordered enough once we grasp its purpose, and—the essential thing—once we relate it to the theatre of its nativity.

THE PLAY'S CONSTRUCTION:
The Main Problem and Some Minor Ones

We should never, probably, think of Shakespeare as sitting down to construct a play as an architect must design a house, in the three dimensions of its building. His theatre did not call for this, as the more rigorous economics of modern staging may be said to do. He was liker to a musician, master of an instrument, who takes a theme and, by generally recognised rules, improvises on it; or even to an orator, so accomplished that he can carry a complex subject through a two-hour speech, split it up, run it by divers channels, digress, but never for too long, and at last bring the streams abreast again to blend them in his peroration. Clarity of statement, a sense of proportion, of the value of contrast, justness of emphasis—in these lie the technique involved;

and these, it will be found, are the dominant qualities of Shakespeare's stagecraft—of the craft merely, be it understood.

He is apt to lay the main lines of his story very firmly and simply, and to let us see where we are going from the start, to cut the complexities from borrowed plots, and if any side-issue later promises distraction, to make (literally) short work of it. Here he reduces the actual story to simplicity itself. Antony breaks from Cleopatra to patch up an insincere peace with Cæsar, since Pompey threatens them both; he marries Octavia, and deserts her to return to Cleopatra; war breaks out, Cæsar defeats them and they kill themselves. That is the plot; and every character is concerned with it and hardly a line is spoken that does not relate to it. There is no under-plot, nor any such obvious relief as Falstaff, Nym, Bardolph, Pistol and Fluellen give to the heroics of the Henriad.

But, for a broad picturesque contrast, Roman and Egyptian are set against each other; and this opposition braces the whole body of the play, even as conflict between character and character will sustain each scene. He asserts this contrast at once; for we assemble expectant in a theatre, therefore first impressions cut deep and a first stretch of action will be of prime importance. We have the two indignant, hard-bitten Roman campaigners, who must stand aside while the procession passes—

. . . *Cleopatra, her ladies, the train, with Eunuchs fanning her.*

—and see Antony in the toils. Their bitter comments follow it. Next, we have a taste of the chattering, shiftless, sensual, credulous Court, with

its trulls and wizards and effeminates.[1]   Then we
see Antony, with Rome, the 'garboils' of his wife's
making and the threats of Pompey calling him,
breaking his toils for a time; and the statement
of the theme is complete.

Do events now proceed (we ask Dr. Johnson)
'without any art of connection or care of disposition'? We are shown Cæsar, the passionate
Antony's passionless rival, correct and charmless,
in conference with Lepidus—that third and very
feeble pillar of the world!—upon their poor prospects, while Antony's 'lascivious wassails' hold
him in Egypt. The action then swings back to a
Cleopatra sighing after an Antony, who is already
travelling Romeward; then to Pompey, question-
ably confident in his rising star.

> If the great gods be just, they shall assist
> The deeds of justest men.

Much virtue—and some risk—in such an if!
And we pass at once to the knitting up of the
alliance that is to eclipse him.

Cæsar and Antony (when he is in his senses)
are realists both, and there is neat wary work all
round before their bargain is made, with the
marriage to Octavia for a seal to it. A long
passage, comparatively; but how artfully it is

---

[1] There was possibly more matter in the scene at one
time. Lamprius, Rannius and Lucillius, whose entrance
survives, will hardly have been brought on, this first and
last time, for nothing. Was there chaffing between Romans
and Egyptians? Nothing is left of it, if so, but Enobarbus'

> Mine, and most of our fortunes to-night shall be drunk
> to bed.

Or did Shakespeare, having written the stage directions,
discover he could make enough effect without them?

proportioned and modulated! First comes the straight dispute between the rivals. This must, of course, be given full importance, for here is the play's main clash. But it is salted by the ironies of Enobarbus, lightened by Lepidus and his fussiness, eased by Mæcenas and Agricola and their tact. Now, the dispute over and the alliance made, the worth of it will be shown us. The great men depart to the sound of trumpets; the three pillars of the world, mutual in its support again. And while Antony does his brisk wooing Enobarbus talks to the gloating Agrippa, and the somewhat shocked Mæcenas—of Cleopatra! Note that the famous panegyric comes from a coarse-mouthed cynic; he, too, can feel her witchery.

Mæcenas.	Now Antony must leave her utterly.
Enobarbus.	Never! He will not.

Age cannot wither her, nor custom stale
Her infinite variety. Other women cloy
The appetites they feed: but she makes hungry
Where most she satisfies; for vilest things
Become themselves in her, that the holy priests
Bless her when she is riggish.

With this in our ears,

Enter Antony, Cæsar, Octavia between them.

and we hear Octavia, with her gentle gravity, saying

Before the gods my knee shall bow my prayers
To them for you.

So Shakespeare weaves his pattern—to find yet another simile—as he goes along, setting colour against colour, coarse thread by fine. And certainly the thing is done with such seeming ease and natural subtlety that we hardly note the

artistry involved. We should feel the flat poverty
of its absence soon enough.

Now another thread is woven in. The soothsayer, very symbol of the East, comes shadowing
Antony, weakening and poisoning his will.[1] Then
follows (contrast again) a touch of Roman energy;
Ventidius is despatched to Parthia. Then we are
flung back to Egypt and to Cleopatra; and in
redoubled contrast—for Shakespeare has now
begun to bite upon the ironies of his theme—to a
Cleopatra most unlike the golden vision of Cydnus,
a spitting fury that hales the messenger of Antony's
faithlessness up and down by the hair of his head.

> Age cannot wither her, (truly!) nor custom stale
> Her infinite variety.

We return to Cæsar and his policies, to the
successful manœuvring of Pompey to a peace,
thanks to Antony and his prestige. What the
worth of this also will be we learn as before when
the great men have done and their followers talk
things over (harsh truths are heard in ante-
rooms). Or we might judge it for ourselves by
its crowning in a drinking bout. The wretched
Lepidus cannot last this out; and that first bitter
outbreak at the sight of the ' strumpet's fool ' has
its derisive echo in Enobarbus'

> There's a strong fellow, Menas . . . a bears the third part
> of the world, man: seest not?

---

[1] The Romans had their soothsayers too; but this one, by
costume and association, would recall us to Cleopatra's
Court. What modern playwright would so opulently employ
him—bring him from Egypt too, even by Plutarch's permis-
sion—to such seemingly small purpose? Here we see the
extravagant ease of Elizabethan stagecraft. But the episode
yields the exact effect needed, not an iota more.

And the chivalrous Pompey, we find, would be glad to have his guests' throats cut—by someone less chivalrous than he! Cæsar alone keeps his head; but we hardly like him the better for that. Then, sharp upon the crapulous business, Shakespeare shows us

> . . . *Ventidius, as it were in triumph, the dead body of Pacorus borne before him.*

He has beaten back the Parthians. But now he dare not, for his own safety's sake, do Rome better service still, with such masters—hers and his—jealously watching him.

> Oh Silius, Silius,
> I have done enough; a lower place, note well,
> May make too great an act: for learn this, Silius;
> Better to leave undone, than by our deed
> Acquire too high a fame when him we serve's away.

Here is so notable and typical a piece of stage-craft that it is worth while to try and see the full effect of it. There is, of course, the subtler aspect, which the reader easily discovers : the contrasting of the sòldiers at their duty with the rulers at their drinking bout.[1] But we must keep Shakespeare's stage well in mind if we are to realise the dramatic value to the spectator of the quick shift from singing and dancing and the confusion of tipsy embracings to the strict military march that brings Ventidius ' *as in triumph* ' upon the stage. There was no pause at all; Enobarbus and Menas would hardly have vanished, their drunken halloos would still be echoing when

---

[1] Easily discovered by reading the Folio. But Rowe made an act-division between the scenes, and later editors have copied him (of which more on p. 127), so that even this much of the effect may pass unnoticed.

Ventidius and his procession appeared. This set the contrast at its sharpest; yet, since change of scene did not mean change of scenery, there was no distracting of mind or eye, a unity of effect was kept, and the action flowed on unchecked.

With one more interweaving of the pattern we shall be half-way through the play. Enobarbus' and Agrippa's mockeries give an acrid after-taste to feast, treaty, and marriage, all three; and we are to guess that poor Lepidus—so spendthrift of good nature!—will be made bankrupt soon. Antony and Octavia take their loving farewell of Cæsar and lovingly depart. An instant after we see Cleopatra, recovered from her fury, having Octavia's attractions picked to pieces for her comfort by the much repentant messenger.

> Dull of tongue and dwarfish ! . . .
> Widow ! Charmian, hark ! . . .
> Why, methinks by him
> This creature's no such thing. . . .
> The man hath seen some majesty, and should know. . . .
> All may be well enough.

And, watching her smile, we need have little doubt but that it will be. Very little; for as she leaves the stage (yet again only upon an Elizabethan stage will the effect fully count),

Enter Antony and Octavia.

with the rift that is to part them already showing.

Thus (if Johnson still needs answering, we can turn his own words against him now) curiosity has been kept busy and the passions interested, and the continual hurry of the action, the variety of incidents and the quick succession of one personage to another have called the mind forward without intermission . . . which is what Shakespeare has set out to do. He has told his story, woven his pattern, kept conflict alive and balance true, character prompting action, and action elucidating character, neither made to halt for the other. This really is the be-all and end-all of his stagecraft—and might well be said to be of any stagecraft; it is only the application of the method that will differ from stage to stage.

We may note in passing how he turns one small technical difficulty that he stumbles on to his profit (he has always had the faculty of doing this), and thereafter how he cuts his way out of another. Throughout this first part of the play he has more Roman than Egyptian material to deal with. Somehow he must keep the balance true and Cleopatra pretty constantly in our minds; but all the story asks is that she should be left by Antony and then sit waiting, patiently or impatiently, for his return. A more mechanically minded playwright would have begun, then, with Cæsar and Pompey, and so have accounted for some of the overplus at once; would have made, consequently, a mild beginning, and given a minor interest precedence. With Shakespeare what most matters will have pride of place, nor will he, when he has it, abate a chance; and, as we see, he lets the impulse of his opening carry him to the point of Antony's departure, over a stretch of three hundred and sixty-five lines, abundant in life and colour (it is actually a tenth of the entire play), till he has his story's master motive made fertile in our minds. But now he must eke out the rest of the Egyptian material very carefully. The glimpse of Cleopatra pursuing her Antony before he is well away from her with 'twenty several messengers' could (if the need were rather for compression) be dispensed with; but it is true and significant Cleopatra, so this may fill up a space. What next? When the news of her lover's treachery has been brought her the material will have run out; so this episode is split up and spread over two scenes. And at once Shakespeare sees and seizes the chance to show us, first the savage and suffering Cleopatra; next, on the rebound, the colder, baser-natured woman, feeding on deceit. The story is moulded to the development of character. Each scene of Cleopatra's, throughout this first part of the play, adds a specific something to our knowledge of her, that will inform the tragedy of her end.

But now, though the two themes are abreast (Antony's concord with Cæsar seen on the wane, while Cleopatra, spider-like, sits spinning a new web for him), it is clear, both that the Roman political material still out-measures the Egyptian and that it may lengthen this part of the play into dangerous monotony. The Antony-Octavia theme might be elaborated for a variation. Shakespeare decides against this; it would still leave Cleopatra in the air. There is no more for her to do, that's evident, till Antony returns to her. Roman politics, then, must suffer heroic compression. The wars upon Pompey and his murder, Cæsar's new quarrel with Antony, the extinction of Lepidus, are reported in a scene or so.

But neither are we shown Antony's return to Cleopatra; Cæsar recounts it to Octavia and his friends. There were other reasons against this. Shakespeare is not, as we have argued, writing a

124

mere love-story, he is transplanting history to the
stage; the causes and circumstances of the quarrel
and the war that is to end at Actium are, at this
juncture, the more important matter to him, and
they must be given the widest significance words can
give them, a wider if vaguer significance than concrete action will give. He could have shown us
effectively enough how

> In Alexandria . . .
> I' the market-place, on a Tribunal silvered
> Cleopatra and himself [Antony] in chairs of gold
> Were publicly enthroned . . .

But in Cæsar's

> No, my most wronged sister, Cleopatra
> Hath nodded him to her. He hath given his Empire
> Up to a whore; who now are levying
> The kings o' the earth for war. He hath assembled
> Bocchus, the king of Libya; Archelaus,
> Of Cappadocia; Philadelphos, King
> Of Paphlagonia; the Thracian king, Adallas;
> King Manchus of Arabia; King of Pont;
> Herod of Jewry; Mithridates, King
> Of Comagene; Polemon and Amyntas,
> The Kings of Mede and Lycaonia,
> With a more larger list of sceptres.

a threat to the whole Roman world seems sounded.
Besides, the play's crisis is to come. These
scenes are preparation for it, no more; they must
be kept tense, but low in tone. The rivals are still
only strengthening themselves for the struggle,
with indignation as with arms.

Incidentally, Shakespeare will be glad to avoid
a scene of reconciliation if it is to involve his boy-
actress in any sort of 'amorous transports.' The
play is dominated by sexual passion, no bones are
made about the carnality of it either; yet how

carefully he avoids writing any scene which a boy could not act without unpleasantness or in fear of ridicule! [1] The fatal reunion is far more significantly marked by her spitfire quarrel with Enobarbus.

Cleopatra.	I will be even with thee, doubt it not . . .
	Thou hast forspoke my being in these wars,
	And sayst it is not fit. . . .
Enobarbus.	Well, is it, is it? . . .
	Your presence needs must puzzle Antony,
	Take from his heart, take from his brain, from 's time
	What should not then be spared. He is already
	Traduced for levity, and 'tis said in Rome,
	That Photinus an Eunuch, and your maids
	Manage this war.

For from this springs disaster; this is the beginning of the end.

Yet we are but half-way through the play; and here is another sign that a larger theme than the love story is being worked out. Would Shakespeare otherwise be giving, against all precedent, half his play's length to its catastrophe? Now, it is the craft and the art of this long ending that have been most distorted by editors, its intention most grievously misunderstood by critics. A producer must not only start afresh from the untouched text, he must read it in the light of a clear understanding of the stage of its origin.[2]

[1] For the further, and important, implications of this, see p. 203 *et seq.*

[2] The Folio text itself may have been edited, I know; but not to the measure of another stage than Shakespeare's.

126

THE QUESTION OF ACT DIVISION

To begin with he must free the play from act and scene divisions. The Folio gives none. The first five-act division was Rowe's. Johnson thought the first scene of his second act might better be the last scene of his first, but added '. . . it is of small importance, where these unconnected and desultory scenes are interrupted.' Pope made the first scene of Rowe's fifth act into the last scene of Act IV, and after this all the later editors seem to have fallen unquestioningly into line. A five-act division for any play has, of course, its sanctions. The editors of the Folio indulge in it when they think they will. They (they or their printer for them) start out each time with an *Actus Primus, Scæna Prima*; a school-boy's heading for his copybook. Sometimes they keep this up, once or twice they get half-way through the play and give it up; sometimes, as with *Antony and Cleopatra*, they just leave it at that. Now, whatever other dramatists may have done, whatever Shakespeare may have done in other plays, whatever may have been the custom of the public and private theatres for which he wrote—and it was probably a differing and a changing one—in the matter of making pauses during a performance, and whether those pauses were formal or prolonged, in this play there is no *dramatically* indicated act-division at all. There is, that is to say, (as far as I can discover) no juncture where the play's acting will be made more effective by a pause. On the contrary, each scene has an effective relation to the next, which a pause between them will weaken or destroy. There may

127

have been four pauses in the original performing, or three, two, or one; there may have been none at all, though that is hardly likely. But it would always (again, as far as I can discern) be a question of custom or convenience, not of dramatic effect.

Granted five acts, a case can be made for Rowe's choice of them, or Johnson's, or Pope's, or for half a dozen others, doubtless; and as good a one perhaps for a four-act division or a three. And if, pleading weakness of the flesh in actors or audience, a producer thinks it well to split the play into two, he can call a convenient halt, he'll find, at the turn of the action when Antony's drift back to Cleopatra is plainly to be seen. He may pause with some effect after that

> All may be well enough.

or pass on a little further before he pauses and begins again (perhaps with better) with the news that

> Cæsar and Lepidus have made wars on Pompey.

or with Cæsar's own outburst of indignation and the return of Octavia; or, more forcibly still, with the squabble between Cleopatra and Enobarbus and the launching of the war. But let him plead convenience merely; for any halt hereabouts must mean rather the loss of an effect than the making one. And this will be as true of any other pauses in any other places; and the lengthier they are the worse it will be.

For the fact is that Shakespeare's work never parcels up very well. He was not among those writers who industriously gather material, sort and arrange and re-arrange it before they fit it together. When his mood is operative he creates out of an abundance of vitality, and it is no good service to him to start obstructing the flow of it. He keeps, for all his fervour, a keen sense of form; it is largely in this marriage of impulse and control that his genius as pure playwright lies. When inspiration flags, he must come to contriving. He is business-like at that, quite callously business-like sometimes. But even to the most work-a-day stuff he gives a certain force. And should carelessness—for he can be wickedly careless—land him in a tight place, there is, to the practised observer, a sort of sporting interest in seeing him so nimbly and recklessly get out of it.

He does not (*pace* Dr. Johnson) write haphazard; it is not that. He plans—and more spaciously than those that have need to plan. He is seldom to be found following a formula, even a proved one of his own. Incidental devices he'll use again and again, as we all repeat words and phrases—and the deeper (one notices) the feelings beneath them the simpler these are apt to be. He is the last man we should look to find submitting himself to an arbitrary scheme, whatever its sanction, a five-act scheme or any other. Custom might even be imposing this on a play's performance and impose it no further on him. And by now he has brought much to the theatre, broken much new ground, has the medium very plastic in his hands. With such a task as this before him, and his imagination fired, he will be out to do it as effectively as he can. There will be no other question. He will have to muster all his resources, and he will need full freedom for the use of them.

ii. 10

A DIGRESSION, MAINLY UPON THE
MEANING OF THE WORD 'SCENE'

But it is hard for us to meet him with a mind as free. The medium that he worked in so spontaneously is alien to us. Even the nomenclature under which we discuss it betrays us to error. Setting disputable act-division aside, what do we mean by scene-division and by 'scene'? There are no reliable scene divisions in the Quartos.[1] The editors of the Folio sometimes run to them, and they customarily draw their dividing lines at each clearance of the stage. But this does not commit them to an imagined change of place, nor connote any check to the action.[2] By Rowe's time, however, 'scene' had taken on, though still uncertainly, a new meaning. Painted scenery, of a more or less conventional sort, was in current use. This defined locality; and a change of scene meant a change of place, was a diversion and a check to the action in every sense. The old fluidity of the Elizabethan stage, which really could 'call the mind forward without intermission,' was gone.

If Rowe finds act-division in the Folio he leaves it, and he cuts the plays with none to a similar pattern. His chief editorial task is to give them geography; but as he leaves scene-division too

[1] I slip in 'reliable,' because Q1 of *Romeo and Juliet* does happen to show a spasmodic sort of recognition of scenes.

[2] They make their slips, however (see the Preface to *Cymbeline*, p. 267). They followed classic practice, even as to-day the French, going further, generally begin a fresh scene whenever a fresh character enters or when a character leaves the stage. Scene does not connote place at all, and the 'scene' of the play, in the pictorial sense of the word, stays unchanged throughout.

when he finds it he cannot do this very consistently; his 'scene' being no longer the
'scene' of the Folio editors. In *As You Like It*,
for instance, he must leave some of the old scene-
divisions unexplained; there are far too many for
him. In *Othello* there are too few; the action will
not abide where he places it. In *A Midsummer
Night's Dream* he announces, to begin with, *Athens,
and a wood not far from it*, and troubles no more.
He looks at the plays when he can in the light
of his own theatre, for he is presenting them to
readers accustomed to it. He disregards the many
signs that they do not really belong there; the
matter, for one thing, is of no great importance,
for another, some memory of the old theatre still
survives.

Antony and Cleopatra, however, offers him a
clean sheet, and he takes trouble. At first he does
no more scene dividing than the sense of place in
his own stagecraft compels him to. He is content
with a generalised *Alexandria ; Rome ; Sicily ;
The coast of Italy near Misenum ; Athens*. He par-
ticularises the very obvious *Pompey's Galley*, and
later rises to the enthusiasm of *A Magnificent
Monument*. But the comings and goings of the
four days' battle defeat him. *Cæsar's camp* is a
clear enough locality. *Cleopatra's Palace* and *Before
the walls of Alexandria* will do. But the manœuv-
rings of the armies, and, above all, that tiresome
noise of a sea-fight cannot be given exact place;
and he is still free enough from realism to let
them, with a few more such confusions, take
their chance. Nevertheless he has now turned
the long, unchecked stretch of action which was
Shakespeare's into an Act III and IV of eight

131

localised scenes each.[1]   Later editors are to better
him.   As the theatre of their day moves ever
further from Elizabethan freedom and is the more
committed to integrity of place they, for their
part, dissect and define ever more closely; till
modern editions give us a third act of thirteen
scenes and a fourth of fifteen, with *A Plain near
Actium ; Another part of the Plain ; Another part of
the Plain*, following each other breathlessly.   Only
that tiresome *noise of a seafight* still refuses its pigeon-
hole.

What of Shakespeare's stagecraft is left?   What
dramatic purpose of any kind is conveyed by this?

Act III.   *Scene 8.   A Plain near Actium.*
Enter Cæsar and Taurus with his army, marching.

Cæsar.   Taurus.
Taurus.   My lord.
Cæsar.   Strike not by land; keep whole: provoke not battle
Till we have done at sea.   Do not exceed
The prescript of this scroll: our fortune lies
Upon this jump.

Exeunt.

Scene 9.   Another part of the plain.
Enter Antony and Enobarbus.

Antony.   Set we our squadrons on yond' side o' the hill,
I' the eye of Cæsar's battle; from which place
We may the number of the ships behold,
And so proceed accordingly.

Exeunt.

Scene 10.   Another part of the plain.
*Canidius marcheth with his land army one way on the
stage ; and Taurus, the lieutenant of Cæsar, the
other way.   After their going in is heard the noise
of a seafight.*
Alarum.   Enter Enobarbus.

---

[1] Strictly speaking, Rowe begins his four days' fighting
with Act III. sc. 6, *Actium.*

132

Enobarbus. Naught, naught, all naught! I can behold no
        longer:
        The Antoniad, the Egyptian admiral,
        With all their sixty fly and turn the rudder. . . .

This last so-called 'scene' does run on for thirty-five lines more.

The layman must remember that he is reading a play, and should be imaginatively translating it into performance as he reads. Into what sort of performance do the editors help him to translate this, and the whole stretch of action from the eve of the first battle with Cæsar to the carrying of Antony dying to the Monument? They parcel it into twenty-two scenes, two of four lines each, one of six, one of nine, one of ten, three of sixteen lines and two of twenty-two; the rest are of more normal length. Scenes, as the editors of the Folio understood the word, they may be; as localised scenes they make dramatic nonsense.

Do the modern editors mean us to envisage the play in performance with painted scenery shifting every minute or so, transporting us round Actium, from one camp to another, to Alexandria and back again? Apparently. They know that Shakespeare's theatre provided for nothing of the sort; do they never stop to think what the effect of this cinematographic patchwork of their devising must be?[1] But strike out their place headings, and still think in terms of 'scenes,' and even then where are we? For Sir Edmund Chambers, who carries the Elizabethan stage pretty vividly in his eye, can tell us that in these passages 'Shakespeare is in some danger of outrunning the apprehensions of his auditory.'

[1] Modern producers, never looking back past them, have, of course, solved the problem with a liberal blue-pencil.

Is it so? Sir Edmund will be using the word
'auditory' with intention; but is he thinking
of its members, not as listening merely, and looking
at the actors, but imaginatively staring beyond
them, making efforts to conjure up backgrounds
that are never described, barely indicated, and
being kept on the jump, asking themselves—while
Cæsar and his men leave the stage empty for
Antony and his men to fill it, only to leave it in
a moment to Cæsar again—'Where on earth are
we now?'

If the play's first audiences sat trying to do anything of the sort, Shakespeare certainly did outrun
their apprehensions; and if Sir Edmund supposes
that Shakespeare meant them to, no wonder he is
dubious about its stagecraft; and no wonder that
critics with not a tithe of his knowledge, vaguely
agreeing, will cry it down. But (with respect)
Shakespeare's intentions were utterly different,
and his audiences were not puzzled at all.

Convention in art is hard to discount, and we
accept the deceptively natural conventions of the
theatre more unquestioningly than most. The
visual side of our modern 'realistic' drama is
itself conventional; but it has come, by slow de-
grees, so fully to its own that we are apt to apply
the laws of it, quite unconsciously, to every sort of
theatre and play, as if they were natural laws.[1]
The visual law of drama, to the Elizabethans, was
a very different and a very arbitrary and incon-
stant thing. It had existed, crudely, in the miracle
plays, and it became elaborately, decoratively

[1] This is less true certainly than it would have been
twenty years ago, before so many experiments in new-
fangled (which is really old-fangled) staging had been made.
But the normal stage of to-day is still the realistic stage.

dominant in the Masks. But on the public stages it was, for various reasons, unprofitably hard to develop, and only in the candle-lit 'private' theatres were its claims finally made good. By 'visual law' must be understood, of course, not the sight of the actors and their acting, unescapable in any play, but their environment, the background, against which they show, and which can be as histrionic in its kind as they. We are now so used to seeing this pictured, be it as *A drawing-room in Mayfair*, or as *Piccadilly Circus*, or *The Forest of Arden*, or *A street in Venice*, or *Verona*, or *Rome*, that if it is not set before us we set ourselves to imagine it there; and, without argument, we assume that the Elizabethans did the same—for, after all, the characters in a play must be somewhere. Yes, they must be, if we push the enquiry. But the Elizabethan dramatist seldom encourages us to push it; and his first audiences assuredly, as a rule, did not do so in despite of him. For them the actors were very plainly on the stage, but the characters might, half the time, be nowhere in particular. It was, for the dramatist of that day, a privilege akin to the novelist's, who may, if he chooses, detach characters, through page after page, from fixed surroundings. It was a freedom which the promise of the scenic stage gradually sapped; but Shakespeare, at least, never surrendered it, and we here find him in the maturity of his craftsmanship, enjoying and exploiting it to the full.

He will always have, of course, as the novelist has, the whereabouts of his characters in mind, and casual allusion to it will crop out. There may also be the demands of the action for a

house-door, a balcony, a tree or a cavern to be
satisfied; but these things will have rather the
utility of furniture than the value of scenery.
And—this is the point—he need never give more
attention to his play's background than he feels
will be dramatically profitable. Moreover, he
can give it—yet again as does the novelist—the
exact sort of attention he chooses. Look at
Richard II. Poetry is lavished on the characters
and the theme in general. But it is never put to
use for the verbal painting of a background.

> Believe me, noble lord,
> I am a stranger here in Gloucestershire:
> These high wild hills and rough uneven ways
> Draw out our miles and make them wearisome.

is the extremest instance of it. We are left, as a
rule, to judge by the tenor of the action where
the actors are; and in many cases it would be
impossible for the listener to say. If we need to
know with any precision, the simple label of such
a line as

> Barkloughly Castle call they this at hand?

will suffice to tell us.
Now take two of the Comedies.

> Well, this is the Forest of Arden.

sets us (in *As You Like It*) accurately enough
where Shakespeare wishes us to be.[1]   Scene after
scene, so called, once this impression is given us,
may be taking place anywhere thereabouts; and,

[1] This, however (to be accurate oneself), is not our first
introduction there.   But we only know where the Banished
Duke should be when we meet him by a reference to him
in the scene before.

as it is a comedy of character, not much time is spent upon picturing the forest itself. Such description of it as we do get is fantastic and reflects the artifice of the story. But *A Midsummer Night's Dream* is one long lyrical painting of the wood near Athens, with its English banks of primroses and thyme, the oxlip and the nodding violet; for this is what the play's theme demands.

From such direct simplicity as this turn to *Macbeth*, to such passages as

> This castle hath a pleasant seat; the air
> Nimbly and sweetly recommends itself
> Unto our gentle senses. . . .

as

> The west yet glimmers with some streaks of day;
> Now spurs the lated traveller apace
> To gain the timely inn. . . .

to the recurring chorus of the witches—the play's writing is full of pictorial suggestion. It is suggestion rather than description, an elaborate creating of atmosphere:

> Light thickens; and the crow
> Makes wing to the rooky wood. . . .

Description in this play is, indeed, as nothing compared with suggestion. Whereabouts in the castle at Inverness we are throughout the comings and goings of Duncan's tragic sojourn we should never know if the editors did not tell us, nor what the rooms or courtyards look like. But what scene-painter will create such darkness for us as that in which a magic of words wraps the night of the murder?

But all through, and in every phase of Shakespeare's development, it is a question of dramatic profit and the particular need of the play. In *Antony and Cleopatra* we find, except for the one episode of the sentries on guard listening to the mysterious music, no verbal scene-painting of any sort, direct or subtle; nor, as we have noted, more than the very minimum of reference to the locality of the scenes. The reason is plain. It is a play of action and of multiplied incident. The story is simple, but the tributary threads of it are manifold, and the interweaving conflicts of purpose complex enough. Its theme (once again) is not merely Antony's love for Cleopatra, but his ruin as general and statesman, the final ascension of Octavius, and the true end of

> . . . that work the ides of March begun.

Therefore the dead Fulvia's doings, Pompey's grievances, Cæsar's policy, Lepidus and his time-serving, Ventidius baulked of a bigger victory—these things and their like are of first importance, and we must be kept alive to them. But an audience has only a certain amount of attention to bestow, and it must be economised. It does not matter much where Cæsar and Lepidus, Pompey and Menecrates and Menas have their talks, nor whether the bargaining with Antony takes place indoors or out; so Shakespeare spends hardly a thought or a line upon it. Nor upon the beauties of the prospect—nor the weather! Antony and Cæsar, we feel, would take a prosaic view of such things; and, for our part, we shall know them no better for viewing them against a picturesque background. But that each turn in the battle of their quick, ruthless Roman minds should be made clear to us—this matters a great deal, and to this all else, if need be, is sacrificed. Emotion, and at full pitch, is in store; but it will not be freed till the issues of the action are narrowing to the point of solution. Meanwhile, we have clarity, the clarity of a desert landscape, the theme in its stark integrity. *Antony and Cleopatra* is, among other things, the most business-like of plays.

And if, for a beginning, this has been Shakespeare's aim, how much more, when we come to the confusions of the three days' battle, with its blunders and false hopes, its chances and changes, must not perfect clarity be achieved? Nor in the writing only, and by suppressing picturesque inessentials. Could he do what he sets out to do if he did not now exploit to the full the freedom from circumstance which the convention of his stage allows him? For this in itself gives clarity; it lets the dramatist concentrate upon the single subject. Complicate these twenty-two 'scenes' as they flash past us by thinking of their whereabouts, and our limited power of attention will certainly not suffice.[1] But listen without further conjecture to the mere tale as the dialogue unfolds it, and watch just what we are asked to watch, the characters as they come and go and the symbolic marching of the armies, and there is no confusion whatever—only such, at any rate, as Shakespeare is at positive pains to be painting for us, in the hectic uncertainties through which Antony moves to his end.

An audience need do no more than listen and look at what there is to see and ask no questions.

[1] And if our eyes are distracted by changing scenery it will, of course, be worse still.

And audiences, as a fact, do no more than they
are asked to do. Would that they always did
that! Nothing will be heard of Actium, nor of a
plain near it, nor anything of the sort. There is
talk of the obviously distant Toryne and Pelopon-
essus. But from the beginning of this long stretch
of action to the end, till Antony is carried dying to
the Monument, there is hardly a hint to let us
know where, at any moment, we may imaginatively
be. Shakespeare does not set out to inform us,
and he might sometimes be hard put to it to say
himself.

> Cæsar sits down in Alexandria,

we are told. The next day he is to be beaten to
his camp, and Antony will give the order:

> Through Alexandria make a jolly march.

But that same night, with Cæsar still in occupa-
tion, Antony's sentries are on guard 'about the
streets.' What streets? What does it matter?
Just nothing at all. We not only do not want to
know; it would be worse than useless to trouble
us with the information.

If Shakespeare knows these things himself (perhaps he does) and wants to tell us, there are half
a dozen ways open. He never seems to have
rejected simplicities of the

> Barkloughly Castle call they this at hand?

sort merely because they were simple. He can
range from this to the subtle expounding of
geography and history too, by which Ventidius
lets us know where he is in the first few lines
spoken upon his entrance *as in triumph*. But,
simply done or subtly, this sort of thing would

140

over-lengthen the action here, check its flow and distract our attention—as badly, almost, as our own perverse efforts to imagine a whereabouts for each ' scene ' distract it.

To give anything of the spaciousness of a true scene to the four or five terse lines, by which now Cæsar, now Antony show us the quality of their generalship, they would need to be multiplied by four; and this would weaken the present effect even in magnifying it. The larger episodes could easily be localised; but the others would then lose substance by comparison; what is more, the unity of the whole complex event would be destroyed. And it is in this unity that its dramatic strength lies. It is by the welding of the mixed mass of incident and character into a consistent whole, freed from all irrelevant circumstance, that its value is isolated and made clear. Obliterate scenic locality, we have still the stage itself left, certainly. But make-believe makes short work of those familiar features; and, once we are enthralled and they vanish, there is nothing left to stand between us and the essential drama; we are at one with its realities. Here, surely, is a technical achievement of some account.

Why show us this long panorama of detail? Why not (as a Greek and probably a modern dramatist would) plan a few full-charged organic, significant scenes, and compress the story to fit them? Again (if we could imagine Shakespeare putting himself the question) the answer is plain. Antony's is a great captain's downfall, the end of a man who has ruled half the Roman world, and we are to see both why he ends and how; and to see, as near as may be, the very process of it.

141

The poor strategy, the weak will, the useless
bargaining, set against Cæsar's steady mind; these
are as significant every whit as the passion that
wreaks vengeance on the wretched Thidias [1] and
storms at Cleopatra. And the strung-out sequence
of events, that are tense often and feverish while
they matter little, slackened to triteness though
they matter much, now catching up, now shedding
their actors as they pass, time and place apt to
seem the most fortuitous things about them—does
not this both show us the true process of the
matter, and give us, besides, just the impression that
in life will belong to our share in such a crisis?
Bouts of noisy fighting with heart-rent love-scenes
in between would doubtless make a good show.
But here, if Plutarch tells true, is a picture of the
business of war as these Roman realists waged it,
with luck and cunning, passion and judgment and
interest all at odds in leaders and followers too.
It is history directly dramatised.

Shakespeare neither takes nor uses his material
haphazard. If, with one dramatic aim, he frees
himself from ties of place, with another he
creates for himself ties of time. He telescopes
Plutarch's vague weeks into a strict three days.
They mark the ebb and flow and ebb of Antony's
fortunes. First, there is the night's carouse after
defeat, while the sentries keep their strange watch;
then the next night's after victory, while Cæsar's
sentries mark Enobarbus creeping out to die; then

[1] So the Folio calls him, with a variation to Thidius.
Theobald, apparently, first made him into Plutarch's
Thyreus again, and other editors have followed. But the
change is surely too marked for Shakespeare not to have
made it purposely.

the third day's ebb to disaster. This gives him rhythm and form, and increases tension; it makes the story clearer, and our interest easier to hold. It is deliberate stagecraft.

THE PLAY'S CONSTRUCTION, CONTINUED:
The Three Days' Battle

We are plunged, for a beginning to the business, amid the squabbling distractions of Antony's counsels. Enobarbus, level-headed, caustic of tongue, does what he can to stem the tide of folly. Antony stands, weakly obstinate, under Cleopatra's eye. Against all reason, he will meet the enemy at sea—

> For that he dares us to't.

The news accumulates of Cæsar's swift, unchecked advance. We have the veteran legionary breaking all bounds of discipline in a last desperate protest.

> O noble Emperor, do not fight by sea,
> Trust not to rotten planks. Do you misdoubt
> This sword, and these my wounds . . .?

Then, as they disappear,

> *Enter Cæsar, with his army marching.*

The first day's fighting is compressed into the symbolism (it is little else) of a dozen lines of dialogue and business. This is a sort of variation upon the old dumb-show, to an Elizabethan audience a familiar and pregnant convention. But note the niceties of effect. Cæsar enters ' *with his army, marching* '; a formal processional entrance, capping the news of his approach that has threaded the preceding scene. In two sen-

143

tences he shows us his strategy and his quality in
command. Next, Antony and Enobarbus appear
alone on the emptied stage. Antony speaks four
hurried and half-purposed lines, Enobarbus never
a word, but his glum looks will be eloquent; and
they vanish. Then comes the marching and
counter-marching of the armies that are not to
fight (pure symbolism!), each with its subordinate
general in command. The stage empties again,
and its emptiness holds us expectant. Then, of a
sudden, comes the climax, the significant event;
' *the noise of a sea-fight* ' is heard.[1] Then, actual
drama re-asserting itself, Enobarbus, with alarums
to reinforce his fury, bursts upon us, tongue-tied
no more, to interpret disaster with

> Naught, naught, all naught! I can behold no longer;
> Th' Antoniad, the Egyptian Admiral
> With all their sixty fly, and turn the rudder. . . .

He is reinforced by Scarus, younger and fierier
still :[2]

> Gods and goddesses, all the whole synod of them! . . .
> The greater cantle of the world is lost
> With very ignorance; we have kissed away
> Kingdoms and provinces.

---

[1] I cannot pretend to say how ' the noise of a sea-fight '
was made. Professor Stuart-Jones (who speaks with authority
upon one aspect of the matter) suggests that what one
heard was the breaking of the sweeps of the galleys. But is
that—would it have been to Shakespeare's audience—a
recognisable sound? I fancy that a hurly-burly flavoured
with Avasts, Belays and other such sea-phrases from the
landsman's vocabulary would be a likelier refuge in a difficulty for the prompter and his staff. But there may have
been some recognised symbolism of a sea-fight.

[2] There is no authority (that I know of) for Scarus' age.
But the dramatic value of the contrast between his keen
youth and Antony's waning powers is indubitable.

This symbolism of war is not in itself dramatic, one sees. Shakespeare could hardly make it so, but he hardly needs it to be. He gives us, however, very little of it. His drama lies in the consequences of the fighting, as these are reflected in the conduct of his characters. We are shown, it is to be remarked, no actual fighting at all, come no nearer to it than the sight of young Scarus and his fresh wounds. He is marked out for us as the gallant warrior, and Antony gives him generous praise. Antony's own valour we may take for granted. But his challenge to Cæsar to fight him single-handed is stressed, and as a ridiculous thing. Says Enobarbus:

> Cæsar, thou hast subdued
> His judgment too.

This is stressed because in it and all it implies lie his failure and his tragedy.

The sequel to the first battle is shown us at length. Scarus' boyish wrath spends itself; Enobarbus, shame rankling deeper in him, relapses to his gibing; Canidius coolly plans to make his peace with Cæsar, and departs, no man hindering him; Antony appears. The gradation from the convention of the battle to the actuality of the scene to come between the broken Antony and Cleopatra, all repentance, is nicely adjusted. First we have had the angry agony of defeat, which needs human expression; next, the few lines Canidius speaks give us an abstract of many happenings; then Antony, in the exhaustion of despair, sums up against himself and tells to the end the chapter of disaster. Here is Plutarch's '. . . and so Antonius . . . went and sat down

alone in the prowe of his ship, and said never a
word, clapping his head between both his hands . . .
and so lived three days alone without speaking to
any man. But when he arrived at the head of
Tænarus there Cleopatra's women first brought
Antonius and Cleopatra to speak together, and
afterwards to sup and lie together. . . . Now for
himself he determined to crosse over into Africk
and toke one of his carects or hulks loden with
gold and silver and other rich cariage, and gave
it unto his friends, commanding them to depart,
and to seeke to save themselves. They answered
him weeping, that they would nether doe it nor
yet forsake him. Then Antonius very curteously
and lovingly did comfort them. . . .' And it is
interesting to see how Shakespeare, contracting the
circumstances, can yet keep the sense and temper
of the events, can even, by the tune and rhythm
of a dozen lines of verse, and by a suggestive
phrase or so, give us the slack sense of days of
breathing-space following on the blow.

The encounter with Cleopatra brings us back
to matter more his own, and of more immediacy,
closer therefore in tension. It is to be the first
of three in which Antony will face perforce the
truth of what is between them, mounting the scale
of suffering to madness at the last. This one, then,
must be in a low key (Shakespeare even skirts the
edge of the comic at its start, with the leading of
Cleopatra, spectacularly pitiful, up to the weeping
hero), and it holds no contest; he is but too ready
with his

> Fall not a tear, I say; one of them rates
> All that is won and lost . . .

We pass to Cæsar's diplomatic exploiting of his

victory, his curt rejection of Antony's overtures, the sending of Thidias to wean Cleopatra from him. Antony rises to nobility again, with his 'Let her know't' for sole comment upon the offer of peace to Cleopatra if she will yield him up. But with his next breath he falls to the fatuity of the challenge to Cæsar.

There follows Cleopatra's ignoble reception of Thidias. Enobarbus can have at least one taste of revenge upon her, and Antony is fetched to see her smiling on Cæsar's messenger.

> 'Tis better playing with a lion's whelp
> Than with an old one dying.

The savage outburst, which sends the glib fellow back, dumb and bleeding from his stripes, is as futile—and is meant to seem so—as were the heroics of the challenge; so is the moral stripping and lashing of Cleopatra. For, his rage glutted and appeased by the sight of the wretch half-slaughtered at his feet, he can turn back to her, open-eyed to the truth about her, and, listening to the easy lies, can end them with an easier—and such a hopeless

> I am satisfied.

After this we may be sure that he is doomed. Enobarbus is sure of it, and Cæsar's comment is contemptuous and brief. Shakespeare adds, for the ending of the day, the strange little hysterical passage in which, by

> . . . one of those odd tricks which sorrow shoots
> Out of the mind.

we find him melting his followers to tears as he pathetically paints the prospects of his defeat and

147

death—to show us yet again, one supposes, how helplessly off the rails the man has run.[1]

Now comes, to mark the passing of the night, the episode of the sentries on their watch. It is, as we have noted, the one piece of scene-painting in the play; a developing of atmosphere, rather— for the single line,

> Heard you of nothing strange about the streets?

is the only hint of locality—of the ominous atmosphere of a night of reprieve between battles. The means to it are merely a few whispering voices and the

> *Music of the hoboyes . . . under the stage.*

It is after the couples have met, gossipped a moment and parted with ' good-night,' that they hear this.

4th Soldier.	Peace! what noise?
1st Soldier.	List, list!
2nd Soldier.	Hark!
1st Soldier.	Music i' the air!
3rd Soldier.	Under the earth.
4th Soldier.	It signs well, does it not?
3rd Soldier.	No.
1st Soldier.	Peace, I say.
	What should this mean?
2nd Soldier.	'Tis the god Hercules, whom Antony loved, Now leaves him.

They feel their way towards each other and whisper confusedly in the darkness, their nerves a little ragged.

[1] Shakespeare elaborates this from a couple of sentences in Plutarch; and the suggestion (from Enobarbus) that Antony almost deliberately ' makes a scene,' is all his own.

148

2nd Soldier.	How now, masters!
All together.	How now? how now? do you hear this?
1st Soldier.	Ay: is't not strange?
3rd Soldier.	Do you hear, masters? do you hear?
1st Soldier.	Follow the noise so far as we have quarter.
	Let's see how it will give off.
All.	Content! 'Tis strange.

And, holding all together as the music dies into distance, they vanish. The entire effect, simple in itself, is made with masterly economy. The scene has two uses: it preserves the continuity of the action, and is gloom before the bright beginning of the second day.

Antony has not slept. He comes jovial and confident from night-long revelry, calling for his squire. Cleopatra, seeming a lissom girl again, beneath the spell of this still magnificent spend-thrift of fortune, plays at buckling on his armour; and with shouts and the flourish of trumpets and the clangour of the gathering of armed men Shakespeare rings up the dawn. Trumpets sound again; it is as if they set out to sure victory. Two notes of doubt are struck: by a shrewder Cleopatra with her

> That he and Cæsar might
> Determine this great war in single fight!
> Then, Antony—! But now—?

—before she retires to her chamber to recover what she may of her lost night's rest; and by the news, greeting Antony as he marches forth, that Eno-barbus—Enobarbus!—has deserted. He puts the treason behind him with a gentle magnanimity which comes strangely—does it?—from a man who could have his enemy's ambassador half flayed alive. But this is Antony.

149

Next we see Cæsar, an over-confident Cæsar, by
no means the cautious general of the earlier battle.
And between the brilliant opening and the brilliant
end of Antony's day we have, for contrast, Enobarbus repentant. There is, of course, no strict
measuring out of time; and we return to some
degree of symbolism when, after alarum, drums
and trumpets, Agrippa enters with

> Retire, we have engaged ourselves too far:
> Cæsar himself has work, and our oppression
> Exceeds what we expected.[1]

He and his staff pass, unflurried, across the stage.
Antony and Scarus pursue them, the youthful
elation of Scarus a foil to Antony's self-possession.
He is the potent general still, one might believe—
set him free from Cleopatra! Drums and alarums
subsiding in the distance give us the battle's
ending. The emptied stage here is the equivalent
of a line of asterisks on a printed page. Then
with

Enter Antony again in a march.

comes the brilliant consummation of this last day
of good fortune that he is to see. It ends as it
began, with trumpets sounding; and it has shown
us Antony at his best, generous, gallant, a born
leader of men.

Cæsar's sentries on their watch mark the second
night's passing; and our sight of Enobarbus, sick

[1] The Folio's stage direction brings Agrippa on alone, but
this, his speech pretty clearly shows, must be an error. He
may have Dolabella or Mæcenas with him. It will hardly,
however, be a symbolic army in retreat. All the disorder of
battle Shakespeare is giving us by sound, its thrills through
individuals; and his massed entries are processional. The
stage directions hereabouts are all rather cursory.

of his ague, broken in spirit, crawling out into the
misty moonlight to die, gives it a dreary colouring.
The dawn breaks dully.

Drums afar off.

> Hark, the drums
> Demurely wake the sleepers. . . .

The armies parade again.   First Antony leads his
across.   He is smiling grimly, yet there is a
desperate edge to his

> I would they'd fight i' the fire, or i' the air,
> We'd fight there too . . .

Then we see Cæsar, sober caution itself this time.
He passes, heading his men, and the stage stays
empty a moment.

Antony and Scarus appear alone.   No tokens
of fighting so far, and Antony is in suspense.
With

> Yet they are not joined : where yond pine does stand
> I shall discover all : I'll bring thee word
> Straight, how 'tis like to go.

he vanishes, leaving Scarus to turn suspense to
misgiving with

> Swallows have built
> In Cleopatra's sails their nests : the augurers
> Say they know not, they cannot tell ; look grimly,
> And dare not speak their knowledge.   Antony
> Is valiant and dejected, and by starts
> His fretted fortunes give him hope and fear
> Of what he has and has not.

Through this comes sounding an

> *Alarum afar off, as at a sea-fight.*

—to our remembrance, a most ominous sound.
And hard upon it, transformed, wrought to a grand
climacteric of fury, Antony reappears.

151

> All is lost!
> This foul Egyptian hath betrayed me:
> My fleet hath yielded to the foe; and yonder
> They cast their caps up and carouse together
> Like friends long lost.   Triple-turned whore! 'tis thou
> Hast sold me to this novice; and my heart
> Makes only wars on thee.[1]

From now till he is carried exhausted and dying to the Monument Antony's passion dominates the action. Eros, Mardian, the Guard, Dercetas, Diomedes are caught distractedly in the wind of it; we see nothing of Cæsar; panic quickly obliterates Cleopatra. It is a long passage and highly charged; but Shakespeare can find all the change and variety he needs in its own turbulent ebb and flow.   Nor, when the medium is rhetoric

---

[1] The Folio gives the stage direction

Alarum farre off, as at a sea fight.

in the interval between Cæsar's exit with his army and Antony's entrance with Scarus. This is almost certainly wrong. Antony would not enter upon an alarum with a 'Yet they are not joined.' But it does not as certainly follow that the editors (from 1778 onwards, according to Furness) are right in transferring it to the instant before his re-entrance with 'All is lost.' They may be. But it is an 'alarum afar off,' and might come more effectively before, or even during, Scarus' speech. The point is not a very important one. It is hard to tell what sheer dramatic value there was for the Elizabethans in these symbolic alarums and the like, and what variety of effect could be given them. Some without doubt; they speak a language, if a simple one. The effect of that first *noise of a sea-fight* which precipitated Enobarbus' outburst of 'Naught, naught, all naught' is evidently not precisely the same— nor meant to be—as this *alarum afar off* which brings Antony on to the greater crisis of 'All is lost.' We may note that, besides the 'symbolism,' Shakespeare gives about a dozen illustrative lines of dialogue to each of the first two battles, to the third about twenty.

raised to such a pitch and given such colouring,
could any competition be admitted; the audience
must be caught and rapt in the mood.   The shock
of the first outburst should capture us.   Then, the
brilliant Scarus, Enobarbus' successor, Antony's
new right hand, having been sent packing like a
lackey (and as ready to go: or do we wrong him?)
we are held by the simple magnificence of

> Oh, sun, thy uprise shall I see no more:
> Fortune and Antony part here; even here
> Do we shake hands. All come to this?   The hearts
> That spanieled me at heels, to whom I gave
> Their wishes, do discandy, melt their sweets
> On blossoming Cæsar; and this pine is barked
> That over-topped them all.

His fury soon begins to work again; it is like yeast
in him; and when he turns, expectant of Eros
coming to his call, to find Cleopatra herself, he
chokes for a moment, long enough for her smooth
incongruity,

> Why is my lord enraged against his love?

to give a fresh twist to his torture.   In this babyish
line, and in her flabbergasted, tongue-tied, sudden,
very un-queen-like bolting, in his frenzied pursuit
of her, Shakespeare again skirts the ridiculous;
and closely enough this time to provoke in us a
sort of half-hysteria which will attune us to his
next shift of key—into the delirium which brings
Antony, exhausted, to a pause. We must picture
the actor, transfigured to the terms of

> The shirt of Nessus is upon me: teach me,
> Alcides, thou mine ancestor, thy rage:
> Let me lodge Lichas on the horns o' th' moon. . .

and storming from the stage.   While we still hear

him we see Cleopatra with her scared women and her sapless eunuch scurrying across like rabbits. And as they vanish he follows, vertiginous, insensate! It is a wild, roundabout chase, hazardously raised to poetic power.

If we were not first thrown off our emotional balance we might find the fantasy that follows—for all its beauty—too much an intellectual conceit, and too long-drawn-out.

Ant.   Eros, thou yet behold'st me?
Eros.   Ay, noble lord.
Ant.   Sometime we see a cloud that's dragonish,
          A vapour sometime, like a bear or lion,
          A tower'd citadel, a pendant rock,
          A forked mountain, or blue promontory
          With trees upon't, that nod unto the world
          And mock our eyes with air: thou hast seen such
              signs;
          They are black vesper's pageants.
Eros.   Ay, my lord.
Ant.   That which is now a horse, even with a thought
          The rack dislimns and makes it indistinct,
          As water is in water.
Eros.   It does, my lord.
Ant.   My good knave Eros, now thy captain is
          Even such a body. . . .

But now we should feel with Antony the relief this strange sense of dissolution brings from the antics of passion, and how, as he does, one would prolong the respite, playing with these fancies that the half-freed spirit conceives!

From this he sinks to quiet grief. The sight of the 'saucy eunuch,' on tiptoe with his glib tale, sets fury glowing for a moment again. Then comes the news, worded as piteously as ever Cleopatra, safe now in her Monument, could desire—the news that she is dead. He greets

them as Antony must.[1]   The fact that they are
false is of a piece with the other futilities of these
three days that have gone to his undoing.   Yet
another is to follow when he stands waiting for the
merciful sword-stroke which Eros turns on himself;
yet another when he bungles his own, and has to
lie there, begging the guard to dispatch him—and
off they go and let him lie![2]

With his carrying to the Monument this long
phase of particularly 'unlocalised' action, germane
to the three days of fighting, ends.   We have been
ideal spectators, we know what happened, and
why; and just such an impression has been made
on us as the reality would leave behind.   It is a
great technical achievement, and one of great
artistry too.

CLEOPATRA AGAINST CÆSAR

Antony dead, the domination of the play passes
at once to Cleopatra.   She asserts it in the lament
over him; a contrast to his stoic greeting of the
news of her death.   And from now to the end, the
action (but for one short scene) is definitely localised
in the Monument.   As fitting, this, to the intensity
and cunning of Cleopatra's battle with Cæsar as

[1] If we remember his

On:
Things that are past are done with me.

[2] Eros is despatched from the stage for a moment or so by
an apparently motiveless 'From me awhile.'   The practical
need is probably to dispose of Antony's armour; for soon
there will be both Antony and the body of Eros himself to be
carried off by 'four or five of the guard,' Diomed and (more
doubtfully) Dercetas.   But Shakespeare, by merely leaving
it unexplained, lets it seem part of the general slack
confusion.

diversity was to the chances and changes of the other; and by contrast made more telling.

But Antony's death leaves Shakespeare to face one obvious problem: how to prevent Cleopatra's coming as an anti-climax. Though Plutarch is still lavish of material, it will need some choosing and moulding.

Cæsar is surprised by the news—here is one risk of slackening tension avoided—and shocked into more feeling than we expect of him. Then at once the last round of the play's contest is opened, and we see what the struggle is to be. A humble anonymous messenger comes from Cleopatra, his message as humble. Cæsar sends him back with fair words; and promptly thereafter—

> Come hither, Proculeius; go and say
> We purpose her no shame: give her what comforts
> The quality of her passion shall require,
> Lest in her greatness by some mortal stroke
> She do defeat us; for her life in Rome
> Would be eternal in our triumph. . . .

It is to be Cæsar's wits against Cleopatra's pride and despair. He fought Antony to the death; it may take more generalship to save Cleopatra alive. Proculeius, we notice, is sent; the one man about Cæsar, said Antony, that Cleopatra was to trust. Is it in some distrust of him that Cæsar sends Gallus too; and, on second thoughts, Dolabella to watch them both, lest Cleopatra wheedle her way round them? It turns out to be Dolabella that needs watching. But here, unfortunately, the text, as we have it, plays us false. There has been cutting and botching, and the niceties of the business we can now only guess at.[1] The main

[1] This is discussed in more detail on p. 163.

trend of it is clear, though. In their Roman
fashion, Gallus and Proculeius add force to
diplomacy and manage to capture Cleopatra in
her Monument. Proculeius finds a few moments
with this tiger in a trap quite enough for him,
and gladly gives place to Dolabella.

The passage that follows is a notable one. He
fancies himself, does Dolabella; he is a ladies'
man, and quite the gaoler, surely, for this most
wonderful of wantons.

> Most noble Empress, you have heard of me?

is his ingratiating beginning. From a Roman there
is flattery in the very title; it owns her Antony's
widow and ignores Octavia. She is far from
responsive. She sulks and snarls, gives him half
a glance, and forthwith breaks into invidious
praise of her dead hero. But she knows she can
twist the conceited fellow round her finger. She
has only to turn to him with a smile, with an
'I thank you, sir,' and a 'Nay, pray you, sir,'
and he promptly betrays his master to her, blurts
out that, for all these comforting messages, Cæsar
does mean to lead her chained in his Triumph.
At which point Cæsar himself appears.

He comes in full state and circumstance, his
staff surrounding him, guards clearing the way.
And if Cleopatra thinks to impress him in turn, his
opening sally might well damp her somewhat.
For he faces this marvel among women as she
stands there with her mere maids beside her, and
coolly asks which of them is the Queen of Egypt.
Which? And once it was

> Remember
> If e'er thou look'st on majesty.

The duel of lies that follows—a pretty piece of fighting!—epitomises this second and subtler struggle. We have Egyptian against Roman now, neither with much simplicity left to shed; but Cleopatra, passionate and unstable, shows a very child beside Cæsar. She kneels, and he raises her. He repeats his smooth promises, and she smiles her gratitude, alive to the worth of them— had she ever doubted it!—thanks to coxcomb Dolabella. (But, surely, for a man so indifferent to her, he is a little anxious to be gone. Had she any hope of winning him? It is second nature in her to be wily with men—and to lie.) Seleucus and the false inventory of ' money, plate and jewels' make illuminating matter of dispute. These barbarians can be bribed, surely, and tricked as easily. Cæsar is not to be tricked— nor shocked by the attempt on him. And as for her raging and her nobly pathetic attitudes, he counters them, her lies and her flatteries too, with the same cold smile. She is beaten. She cannot even terrify Seleucus now; it is he, contemptuously considerate, who orders the man off. She is helpless in his clutches, but for the one sure escape. And he thinks, does he, to lure her from that with his lies? She fawns on him as he leaves her; let him think he has!

> He words me, girls, he words me;
> That I should not be noble to myself . . .

If any doubt were left, any chance of yet another noble conquest, Dolabella—the paltry proof that she still can conquer—comes back to disperse it.

158

CLEOPATRA AGAINST CÆSAR

Dolabella. Madam, as thereto sworn by your command,
Which my love makes religion to obey,
I tell you this: Cæsar through Syria
Intends his journey, and within three days
You with your children will he send before:
Make your best use of this: I have performed
Your pleasure and my promise.
                                          Dolabella,

Cleopatra. I shall remain your debtor.[1]

She again makes his name sound beautiful in his
ears (it is a name that can be lingered on),
perhaps gives him her hand to kiss (he does not
pay Thidias' price for the honour) and he goes.
Her way is clear now to death.

But she has still to be lifted to that nobility,
with which the sight of the dead Antony inspired
her.

   . . . and then, what's brave, what's noble,
Let's do it after the high Roman fashion,
And make death proud to take us . . .

She climbs there by no straight path. The longing
to die never leaves her; but we all long to die at
times, and there is much protesting, a stealthy
look or so for chances of escape, some backsliding
into the old twisted passions; and she must at
last lash herself—with, for company, poor frail Iras
—through agony and beyond it before she can
repose upon

My resolution's placed, and I have nothing
Of woman in me: now from head to foot
I am marble-constant. . . .

---

[1] He made no promise. Here is an interesting instance
either of the way in which Shakespeare intensifies an effect
by an over-statement, which he knows will pass muster, or
of a subtlety in character-drawing by which Dolabella, in
thrall to Cleopatra, feels he did promise. The critic may
take his choice.

Then, for one more mitigation before the play's last tragic height is reached, Shakespeare gives us the countryman and his figs. By now (here is the art of it) Cleopatra is past bitterness or fear, and can smile and take the simple pleasure in his simplicity that we do. She jokes with him. This must have been, if one comes to think of it, not the least of her charms. When she would royally

> Hop forty paces through the public street . . .

how the people—the common people, so despised by Cæsar and the politicians—how evidently they would adore her! It is very right that one of them should bring her the comfort of death in a basket slung on his arm, and that she should trust him, and joke with him, a great lady at her ease.

From this she turns to a queenliness unapproached before.

> Give me my robe, put on my crown; I have
> Immortal longings in me . . .

Long ago, we learn, a dead king's servants would be slaughtered around him. This is a still more royal death; for Iras' heart breaks silently at the sight of it, and Charmian only lags behind to set a crooked crown straight once again, and to send triumphant mockery echoing to Cæsar's ears.

He accepts his defeat like a gentleman, let us own. The ceremony of his coming matches the ceremony of her dying; and the end of the play, we should note, is sensibly delayed while they stand gazing—tough soldiers that they are—at a queen so strangely throned:

> . . . . she looks like sleep,
> As she would catch another Antony
> In her strong toil of grace.

THE STAGING

The action makes no extraordinary calls upon an Elizabethan stage as we now think we know it to have been. Two things are noticeable, however. There are, for five-sixths of the play, few definite indications of the use of the inner stage. This keys with the scant localisation of the scenes; the inner and upper stages are always likelier to be 'places' than the main stage will be. But the full stage, *i.e.* the main stage with the inner stage curtains open and the inner stage itself accessible, would probably be used from the general entrance of Charmian, Iras, Mardian, Alexas, the soothsayer and the rest to Antony's departure for Rome; for all Cleopatra's scenes while she sits waiting news of him—and receiving it; for the long scene of reconciliation between Antony and Cæsar; and for the scene in Pompey's galley.[1] The intermediate scenes will be played on the main stage, with the inner stage curtains closed. When the battles begin it looks as if Cleopatra's scenes again employed the inner stage (as hinterland at least to the outer); she and Antony retiring to it or through it at such points as

> Some wine
> Within there, and our viands. . . .
> Let's to supper, come,
> And drown consideration.

—the curtains then closing on them. She may come

[1] This, it may be said, was the normal way of employing the inner stage, the action would seldom be wholly confined there. But furniture, and the localisation this implies would tend to focus the action within its bounds. See also the preface to *Cymbeline*, p. 251 *et seq.*

from the inner stage when she welcomes him from his victory; and

Through Alexandria make a jolly march . . .

may imply that they all pass back, as if into the city in triumph. Cæsar's scenes, the marching and counter-marching and the swifter coming and going, take place on the main stage, that is clear.[1] Now comes disputable matter.

Enter Cleopatra and her Maides aloft, with Charmian and Iras.

They are in the Monument, to which, in a moment, the dying Antony has to be hoisted. There are two slight difficulties. The hoisting of a full-grown man ten or twelve feet in the air asks some strength. However, this could be provided ostensibly by the 'and her maides,' actually by stage hands helping from behind the curtains; and Shakespeare makes dramatic capital out of the apparent difficulty. But the upper stage of the public theatre must have had a balustrade at least three feet high. Swinging a dying man over it and lowering him again asks some care. Granted this done with skill and grace, what of the effect of the rest of the scene, of Antony's death and Cleopatra's lament over him, played behind the balustrade as behind bars? Clearly it would be a poor one. The balustrade must, one presumes, have been

---

[1] But the stage direction

> *Canidius marcheth with his land army one*
> *way over the stage and Taurus, the lieutenant of Cæsar*
> *the other way : After their going in* . . . .

could be more slickly obeyed if there were an inner as well as an outer stage to march over. With two doors only available, it will be a long-drawn-out affair.

removed for the occasion or made to swing open, if the ordinary upper stage was used.[1]

When we next see Cleopatra she is obviously still in the Monument; as obviously she is not still upon such an upper stage as we believe the Globe's to have been. Nor is there any sign that—as with Romeo's farewell to Juliet and her encounter with her mother—the acting of the scene began above and finished below. The stage directions, however, are incomplete, and the text may have been altered. In the previous scene Proculeius and Gallus have been sent to parley with Cleopatra and keep her, if they can, from doing herself a mischief. By the Folio's stage direction only Proculeius arrives. A simple supposition is that he finds her on the inner stage behind a barred gate and speaks to her through it.[2] This at any rate reproduces Plutarch's 'For Proculeius came to the gates that were very thick and strong, and surely barred; but yet there were some craneries through the which her voyce might be heard. . . .' When she has protested her submission he evidently makes as if to go, with

> This I'll report, dear lady.
> Have comfort, for I know your plight is pitied
> Of him that caused it.

But now, with no other speech nor stage direction intervening, the Folio has

Pro. You see how easily she may be surpriz'd;
Guard her till Cæsar come.

---

[1] There seems commonly to have been a trap in the floor of the upper stage. But the use of this and the need to place Antony directly under it would rob the dialogue—would rob the all-important 'I am dying, Egypt dying'—of much of its effect.

[2] Just such a barred gate as shuts in Juliet's tomb.

163

Modern editors (following Theobald in the main)
give the speech to Gallus, whom they have brought
on with Proculeius, and add:

> *Here Proculeius and two of the Guard ascend*
> *the monument by a ladder placed against a window,*
> *and, having descended, come behind Cleopatra.*
> *Some of the Guard unbar and open the gates.*[1]

A minor objection to this is that Gallus in the
Folio is *persona muta*; the full speaking strength
of the company is, we may well suppose, already
employed, and here is a super. A more serious
one must be that so much climbing up and climbing
down again would take time. There is no con-
current dialogue, and a long pause at such a
moment is dramatically unthinkable.[2]

No great difficulty arises if we see Gallus and the
guard left at the door while Proculeius advances to
the gate that bars the inner stage. Cleopatra
would not see them. Let him give them the order
quietly as he returns to the door, and, with no
climbing involved, they can be upon the inner
stage by the back way in a couple of seconds,
seize Cleopatra and unbar the gates; and Gallus
may well go off to report to Cæsar; his exit as his
entrance, if he stays *persona muta*, being a likely
omission from stage directions, which would need

[1] Thus, at least, the Arden edition. But it also presumes
(in a footnote) and the Oxford edition definitely states that
Cleopatra has so far been upon the upper stage. How and
when she gets down is left a mystery.

[2] Johnson proposed to insert part of the speech earlier
so that the guards could come quietly behind and seize
Cleopatra at the cue. But the three previous speeches
allow of no such interruption. If Cleopatra had to be
brought down to the lower stage, it would be ten times worse.

to be unwontedly elaborate if all this were to be made clear.[1]

The discussion is fairly barren from a modern producer's point of view; he can provide for all these exigencies without violating the text or distorting the action.

But if for this and all the rest of the action the recognised Elizabethan stage does not content him, then he must devise one which will not violate its fundamental liberties and laws—its liberties, above all. He will probably find in the end that he has devised something not so very different. If he is for painted scenes of Cleopatra's Palace, Cæsar's House, Antony's camp, the plain near Actium and a variety of ' other parts of the same '—well, the reading of this preface will only have wasted his time. He must somehow provide a staging free from actuality of place; that is his problem. He may decorate it; but if the decoration distracts us from the hearing of Shakespeare's lines—and they ask, as we have noted, pretty close attention—it will be a positive nuisance. It is a hard problem to solve; for one thing, because self-effacement is the rarest of artistic virtues. And let the decorator set out, however discreetly, to interpret the play in his own terms, if he find himself—and it is an ever-present danger—competing with the actors, the sole interpreters Shakespeare has licensed, then it is he

[1] There remains the unnatural hiatus between Proculeius' two speeches, if they are both his. Suppose that the upper stage to which Antony is hoisted were not the usual balcony, but something a little more accessible, to which the guards might climb without delay, and from which Cleopatra might be as easily brought down. The hiatus *may* point to some change in staging, or in the stage itself, or to the shifting of the play from one theatre to another of different resources.

that is the intruder, and he must retire. Even if his picturesque effects are but an anodyne to our vigilance—and much modern stage decoration is of this sort—they will do the play negative harm. We need to have our minds kept clear and alert. Still, if we cannot take the Elizabethan stage for granted as the Elizabethans did, producer and decorator must certainly face the problem of providing something that we can.

COSTUME

Once we are freed from pictures of Rome and Alexandria, brought (so to speak) archæologically up to date, the difficulty of costume is not acute.

Cut my lace, Charmian.

summarises it, and, upon a narrow view, may be said almost to exhaust it. Shakespeare's Cleopatra wore a stomacher of some sort, that is evident. But it is an error to suppose that Shakespeare dressed all his plays in the ordinary costume of his time. It is also an error, for that matter, to suppose that nowadays we all carry accurate pictures of the past in our minds. Dress Cleopatra as a Queen of the Tenth Dynasty instead of as an Alexandrian Greek, and how many of us would be the wiser? Careful research might find us an Alexandrian fashion plate of the right period with laces to cut (Sir Arthur Evans has brought us corsets from Knossos), but our conscientiously Egyptian Cleopatra's have so far been left laceless and waistless, and the line without meaning.

In all this, as in everything else of the sort, the
166

Elizabethans thought first and last—whether by choice or necessity—of dramatic profit. It is not likely that Shakespeare troubled to give a French touch to *Love's Labour's Lost* and an Italian to *Much Ado About Nothing*; nor, had his knowledge run to it, would he probably have seen much gain in dressing Romeo and Juliet by ' the paintings of Giotto and his pupils.'[1] But when some dramatic end was to be served it is clear that he did not lack means of a kind, and he used them. In *Macbeth* the Scots and the English can be told apart, British and Romans in *Cymbeline*; and in this play, quite evidently, Roman and Egyptian stood in picturesque contrast. There would be little archæology about the business and less consistency. We can guess at the sort of figures they made by turning to extant designs for the Court Masks. The theatres could not run, perhaps, to such splendour as that; but they were prosperous, finery was popular, and they probably did pretty well. Rome meant the romantic past, Egypt the exotic East; and Shakespeare would do what he could to capitalise both. The dialogue of the play is coloured with every sort of allusion to the wonders of that far world, from the description of Cleopatra at Cydnus, to the talk of Syria and the Parthians, from the story of Antony in the Alps, from his call to Alcides his ancestor, to tales of ' pyramises ' and crocodiles.

[1] This is how Charles Knight tells us they should be dressed (I quote from the quotation in Furness). ' But,' he adds, ' for the younger and lighter characters . . . some very different habit would be expected by the million, and indeed, desired by the artist.' He is writing in the mid-nineteenth century. The quest for accuracy in these matters is a new thing.

We know better about all these things than did Shakespeare; but it is too late now to put him right. We have to interpret, not to correct him; we are committed even to his errors. Our concern is with the Egypt and Rome of his imagination, not of our own. The difference is manifest less in this detail or the other than in the whole texture of the play. Cut the knot of the 'Cut my lace, Charmian' difficulty, and there is still the larger problem. In the National Gallery hangs Paolo Veronese's 'Alexander and the wife and daughter of Darius.' This will be very much how Shakespeare saw his Roman figures habited. Antony would wear Alexander's mixture of doublet, breastplate, sandals and hose. Here too is something very like Octavia's costume; and though Cleopatra might be given some Egyptian stigmata, there would still be laces to cut. It is all grievously incorrect; but we do not like the picture less for that, nor are students set to copy it and told to redraw the costume in the light of the latest information available. Its good painting apart, we even gain by its being a Renaissance view of a Classic subject, for the spirit of the picture is in that. Now, no one will contend that by clothing Antony and Cleopatra and Cæsar and ordering their Court and their armies according to our modern imagination we shall crush the dramatic life out of them, for this is rooted far deeper. But we shall at every moment, both on the main issue and in countless little ways, be falsifying Shakespeare's, and doing him far more damage than the simple logic of the case implies. We do him, of all dramatists, great damage. For he has an extraordinary faculty of making the great things vivid to us by

168

means of the little things, by just such strokes, in fact, as that

> Cut my lace, Charmian.

This play is particularly full of them, very homely things; and it is bare chance that one of the finest, Charmian's

> Your crown's awry:
> I'll mend it, and then play.

does not get us into more sartorial trouble. He has absorbed Rome and Egypt into his own consciousness; but it is a consciousness opening upon his own world, not the historical Antony's, and naturally not upon our vision of that.

Shakespeare in modern dress is as inappropriate as archæological Shakespeare, and for the same good reason. And the very argument that great drama is not dependent upon its trimmings should surely help us to accept the trimmings that we find. Cleopatra in a farthingale! The orthodox play-goer may turn pale at the thought. But surrender to the idea that this is Shakespeare's Cleopatra we are looking at, not the product of our school books (is that more difficult than to look up from our programme and admit that the well-known Miss Blank, lately seen as Nora in *A Doll's House*, is the real thing?), and by the end of the first scene the oddity will be forgotten; and thenceforward we shall be anachronism-proof. There will be one further gain. An historical play of any sort has a double victory to win; the play's own and a victory over our pre-conceptions of its history. The less familiar its figures the better the chance of the play with us—as a play.

THE MUSIC

Trumpets and cornets and drums are needed; and the flourishes, the sounding of a sennet, the beating of the drums have each their import. Enobarbus is borne away dying to the sound of *Drummes afarre offe*. A consort of wood-wind is also used. The 'hoboyes' play under the stage, and their pungent vibrations should make excellent assault on the nerves.

The music for the revels on Pompey's galley is given to wood-wind (the accompaniment of the song included), trumpets and drums reinforcing it occasionally . The clamour is insisted on.

> Make battery to our ears with the loud music. . . .
> These drums! these trumpets, flutes, what!
> Let Neptune hear we bid a loud farewell
> To these great fellows: sound and be hanged, sound out.

It is a soldiers' revel. But it never slips from the distinction of poetry; and the song itself—the boy's voice singing it—is like light beside the darkness of Menas' whisper to Pompey:

> These three world-sharers, these competitors,
> Are in thy vessel: let me cut the cable;
> And, when we are put off, fall to their throats. . . .

The scene falls midway through the play. It is a rest point in the action. Shakespeare has taken care to give it solidity, variety and colour.

Cleopatra calls once for music, but countermands it with her next breath. She would have needed a consort of viols; and it is possible that strings and wood-wind both were more than be could always reasonably demanded at one performance.

THE VERSE AND ITS SPEAKING

Rome and its Empire are ever a clarion call to Shakespeare's imagination; and the strength of his answer to it lies in his power to make the alien characters his own. For he leaves them in no classic immunity, casting his care upon their impressive reputations. They must be sifted through his dramatist's conscience; he brings them to terms on the ground of common humanity. What is Cleopatra's passport to tragic heights?

> No more but e'en a woman, and commanded
> By such poor passion as the maid that milks
> And does the meanest chares. . . .

With this, of course, they risk the loss of their conventionally heroic stature. But it is preserved for them by the magic of poetry.

This is literally a sort of magic, by which the vibrations of emotion that the sound of the poetry sets up seem to enlarge its sense, and break the bounds of the stage to carry us into the lost world of romantic history. Conceive such a story and such characters so familiarly, and then tie their expression to plain prose—Dido will be in danger of becoming a dowdy indeed, and Cleopatra a gipsy; unless some other magic can be found.[1] Shakespeare, however, has travelled far since Mercutio could thus mock Romeo's poetic prowess, and is now himself by no means 'for the numbers that Petrarch flowed in.' He has another choice. He has come to the writing of a verse which combines

[1] Such as Ibsen tried and—surely it will be admitted— failed, on the whole, to find in *Emperor and Galilean*; succeeded in finding, though he had not then the same need of it, in the later prose plays.

actuality and power, and is malleable to every diversity of character and mood. He is at the apogee of his art in this kind; possibly a shade past it already.

Readers of this book have before them the lyricist of *Romeo and Juliet*, still in his dramatic apprenticeship (masterly enough though the work might be for another man), the rather facile achievement of the *Merchant of Venice*, the extreme ease, the technical sophistication, the partiality for what he best likes doing that shows in the later *Cymbeline*, as well as the opulent extravagant strength we find now. Strength still sufficient for every call on it; the passions of an *Antony and Cleopatra* will not defeat him when the transcendent *Lear* did not. Nevertheless, here and there we may feel a strain; sometimes emotion will not quite vivify thought, which stays constricted or confused; or a too constant repetition of effect or an over-simplifying of simplicity may show fatigue. But Shakespeare has always had the tact to seize on the subject that will best fit his artist's mood, or to adapt mood and method to subject—which, it is not our business to inquire. In its qualities and defects alike his present method, resourceful, audacious yet still spontaneous, ripe if to over-ripeness, fits this subject most consummately well.

Big as it is, he feels no need at all to economise strength. He begins at what a pitch!

Nay, but this dotage of our general's
O'erflows the measure; those his goodly eyes,
That o'er the files and musters of the war
Have glow'd like plated Mars, now bend, now turn,
The office and devotion of their view

> Upon a tawny front: his captain's heart,
> Which in the scuffles of great fights hath burst
> The buckles on his breast, reneges all temper,
> And is become the bellows and the fan
> To cool a gipsy's lust.

This is as ample and virile in substance, as luminous and as consonant in its music as anything well could be. One tremendous sentence, the ends of the lines not answering to pauses either; these, such as they are, fall midway (but a bare four of them in nine lines and more, though), so that fresh impulse may overleap the formal division, and the force be the force of the whole. Note, too, the placing of the dominant ' o'erflows the measure' and its complement 'reneges all temper' with the doubled parenthesis between them, and how the 'now bend, now turn' saves this from slackness; how 'files and musters' and 'office and devotion' strengthen the beat of the verse, with ' plated Mars ' coming like the sudden blare of a trumpet, and ' burst the buckles on his breast ' to sound the exploding indignation which culminates in the deadly

> And is become the bellows and the fan
> To cool a gipsy's lust.

A fairly opulent dramatic allowance for this Philo, of whom we know nothing, are never to see again. But throughout the play we shall find the least considered characters, and on no special occasion, with as meaty stuff—is there a better term for it? —in their mouths. Mæcenas greets Octavia, upon her disillusioned return, with

> Welcome, dear Madam.
> Each heart in Rome does love and pity you:
> Only the adulterous Antony, most large

> In his abominations, turns you off;
> And gives his potent regiment to a trull,
> That noises it against us.

The anonymous legionary, even, has no less vivid and stirring a moment to his share than

> O noble emperor, do not fight by sea;
> Trust not to rotten planks: do you misdoubt
> This sword and these my wounds? Let the Egyptians
> And the Phœnicians go a-ducking: we
> Have used to conquer, standing on the earth,
> And fighting foot to foot.

And from Pompey in his first scene (Shakespeare himself well into his stride by this!) comes the full enrichment of

> . . . But all the charms of love,
> Salt Cleopatra, soften thy waned lip!
> Let witchcraft join with beauty, lust with both!
> Tie up the libertine in a field of feasts,
> Keep his brain fuming; Epicurean cooks
> Sharpen with cloyless sauce his appetite;
> That sleep and feeding may prorogue his honour
> Even till a Lethe'd dullness.

Too much rich writing of this sort would be like Cleopatra's feasts, and clog the march of the action. But when mere argument is in hand we fall back to nothing less pedestrian than Antony's

>   Sir,
> He fell upon me ere admitted: then
> Three kings I had newly feasted, and did want
> Of what I was i' the morning: but, next day,
> I told him of myself; which was as much
> As to have asked him pardon. Let this fellow
> Be nothing of our strife: if we contend
> Out of our question wipe him.

This, and such a passage as Cæsar's somewhat smug

> Let's grant it is not
> Amiss to tumble in the bed of Ptolemy;
> To give a kingdom for a mirth; to sit
> And keep the turn of tippling with a slave;
> To reel the streets at noon, and stand the buffet
> With knaves that smell of sweat; say this becomes him—
> As his composure must be rare indeed
> Whom these things cannot blemish—yet must Antony
> No way excuse his foils, when we do bear
> So great weight in his lightness.

or as Pompey's

> To you all three,
> The senators alone of this great world,
> Chief factors for the gods,—I do not know
> Wherefore my father should revengers want,
> Having a son and friends, since Julius Cæsar,
> Who at Philippi the good Brutus ghosted,
> There saw you labouring for him.

may be taken as the norm of the play's poetic method, upon which its potencies are built up. And it is upon this norm, of course, that the actors must model their own style.

The elemental oratory of this verse needs for its speaking a sense of rhythm that asks no help of strict rule. Shakespeare is so secure by now in the spirit of its laws that the letter may go. He does not commonly stray far. A cæsura may fall oddly or there may be none distinguishable, a syllable or so may splash over at the end. Dramatic emphasis is the thing, first and last; to get that right he will sacrifice strict metre—yet never music—grammar now and then, and at a pinch, if need be, sheer sense too.

These freedoms gain in effect as the play's temper heightens. Cæsar's calculated indignation is sounded in the two swelling catalogues:

175

I'the common show place where they exercise,
His sons he there proclaimed the kings of kings.
Great Media, Parthia and Armenia
He gave to Alexander; to Ptolemy he assign'd
Syria, Cilicia and Phœnicia. . . .
                    . . . he hath assembled
Bocchus the king of Libya; Archelaus
Of Cappadocia. . . .

The passage has been quoted already; the scansion is highly individual.

But no Cleopatra, with an ear, can miss the shrill arrogance of

                    Sink Rome, and their tongues rot
That speak against us! A charge we bear i' the war,
And, as the president of my kindgom, will
Appear there for a man. Speak not against it;
I will not stay behind.

The upward run of semi-quavers in 'A charge we bear i' the war' is as plain as any musical stave could make it; and the pauses seem to mark so many snaps of the jaw. The lines are not, of course, here or elsewhere to be reckoned by syllables, but by beat.

Listen, on the other hand, to the weary descent to depression's depths in Antony's

Fall not a tear, I say; one of them rates
All that is won and lost: give me a kiss;
Even this repays me. We sent our schoolmaster;
Is 'a come back? Love, I am full of lead.

—given us by a regular cæsura, followed by an irregular one, followed by a mid-line full stop; the line then finished with an effort by the banal ' We sent our schoolmaster ' (who could get anything but exhaustion out of that ' schoolmaster '?); the next line with its dead monosyllables dragging after, the pause in the middle made the longer because of them. Then comes a sudden rally in the rhymed couplet :

Some wine, within there, and our viands! Fortune knows
We scorn her most when most she offers blows.

—its irregular first line just saving it from sounding mechanical.

The violence of Antony's anger when he finds Thidias kissing Cleopatra's hand has its own notation and tune.

Approach there! Ah, you kite! Now, gods and devils!
Authority melts from me. Of late, when I cried ' Ho! ',
Like boys unto a muss, kings would start forth
And cry ' Your will? ' Have you no ears?
I am Antony yet. Take hence this jack and whip him.

Long lines, giving a sense of great strength. Exclamatory phrases, prefacing and setting off the powerful centre-phrase, with its ringing ' kings ' for a top note. The cæsura-pause of two beats that the short line allows is followed by the repeated crack of two more short phrases, the first with its upward lift, the second with its nasal snarl and the sharp click of its ending; the last line lengthens out, and the business finishes with the bitten *staccato* of

Take hence this jack and whip him.

Note the deadly flick of the last two words!

The sense apart, what an almost wilful pathos we feel in the smoothly sustained, one- and two-syllable worded, predominantly thin-vowelled speech of Antony's to the weeping servants!

Tend me to-night;
Maybe it is the period of your duty:
Haply you shall not see me more; or if,
A mangled shadow: perchance to-morrow

ii. 13

You'll serve another master. I look on you
As one that takes his leave. Mine honest friends,
I turn you not away; but like a master
Married to your good service, stay till death.
Tend me to-night two hours. I ask no more;
And the gods yield you for 't.

Note in particular the importance given to 'A
mangled shadow' by the sustaining tripled consonant, and the two-beat pause that follows
(' to-morrow,' with its weak ending, ranking for a
dissyllable), and how the repeated, 'Tend me to-
night' rounds in the speech a trifle artificially.

Throughout these scenes, throughout the play
indeed, one can so analyse the verse, find its
rhythm and music, often transcending rule, but
always close fitted to mood and meaning. The
best moments need no analysis, and seem to defy
it.   One must not appear to be praising

I am dying, Egypt, dying; only
I here importune death awhile, until
Of many thousand kisses the poor last
I lay upon thy lips.
                    I dare not, dear—,
Dear, my lord, pardon,—I dare not,
Lest I be taken:

merely for the way in which a short first line allows
for the two silent breaths that will show Antony's
flagging strength, nor for the infallible accenting
of Cleopatra's fear, first upon the ' dare,' and then,
with repetition, upon the ' not.' But actors have
to concern themselves with such impertinences.

The passionate hysteria of her

Where art thou, death?
Come hither, come, come, come, and take a queen
Worth many babes and beggars.

178

Proculeius.   O, temperance, lady!
Cleopatra.   Sir, I will eat no meat, I'll not drink, sir—
               If idle talk will once be necessary—
               I'll not sleep neither: this mortal house I'll
                  ruin . . .

asks neither comment nor analysis. Why waste
time trying to scan the last line? It is right, and not
the extremest perversity could speak it wrongly,
one would suppose. Nor will much more be gained
by trying to extract meaning from the last line but
one. If it has any in particular (which seems
doubtful) no audience could be made to grasp it.
But as a setting of hysterical gibbering to verbal
music, it is perfect.

But one technical excellence among many it is
hard to pass by. As Shakespeare nears the last
great moment, that of Cleopatra's death, he wants
to give his verse solid strength and dignity; and
the pulse of it now throbs with a steady intensity,
goes processionally forward, as it were.

> Give me my robe, put on my crown, I have
> Immortal longings in me: now no more
> The juice of Egypt's grape shall moist this lip.
> Yare, yare, good Iras: quick. Methinks I hear
> Antony call; I see him rouse himself
> To praise my noble act; I hear him mock
> The luck of Cæsar, which the gods give men
> To excuse their after wrath. . . .

Regular metre, saved from formality by the subtle
variety of the mid-line stopping; the whole welded
into unity by the constant carrying on of the
sentences from line to line. But, lest the effect grow
all too set, Charmian is let interpose, a little later,
not a single line but one and a half. Then, lest
life die out of it, we have—after the added
emphasis of an irregular line, in which Cleopatra

lays hands on the asp with a heavily accentuated
'Come . . .'—the words clipped, the pace
quickened. Twice more Charmian interrupts,
but now with phrases that sustain rather than
break the rhythm.

Cleopatra.   . . . Come, thou mortal wretch,
            With thy sharp teeth this knot intrinsicate
            Of life at once untie; poor venomous fool,
            Be angry, and despatch. O, could'st thou speak,
            That I might hear thee call great Cæsar ass
            Unpolicied!
Charmian.   O Eastern star!
Cleopatra.   Peace, peace!
            Dost thou not see my baby at my breast,
            That sucks the nurse asleep?
Charmian.   O break! O break!
Cleopatra. As sweet as balm, as soft as air, as gentle!
            O, Antony! Nay, I will take thee too:
            What should I stay—?

Not one beat has been missed till her dying breaks
the last line; yet we have been no more conscious
of the form than when the verse was at its loosest,
only of the added power.

Shakespeare no longer divides his characters
into speakers of verse and speakers of prose, nor
makes this distinction regularly between scenes.
The freedom and variety of his verse writing allow
him to pass almost imperceptibly from poetry to
prose and back again. Thus he ranges an un-
broken scale, from a pedestrian exactitude in stating
plain fact at one end of it to the conventional
flourish of the rhymed couplet at the other. But
he can still make the sharp contrast of a change
effective between scene and scene; or in the
midst of a scene he can bring passion or pretentious-
ness down to earth—and prose, or as suddenly

restore force and dignity with rhythm and tone. And he can go to work more subtly than that. As in stagecraft, so in his play's actual writing, exploiting freedom to the full, he has forged a weapon of extraordinary suppleness and resource.

For instance, in the ostensibly prose scene that follows the play's more formal opening, we have the Soothsayer countering Charmian's impudent chatter with single lines of verse. Their recurrence lends him peculiarity and a slight portentousness; but the surrounding prose is so subtly adjusted that the device itself passes unnoticed.[1] Later, upon Cleopatra's entrance, the scene is suddenly braced to forcefulness by half a dozen consecutive lines of (not too regular, lest the effect be too noticeable) verse. Later still, with a strong dose of prose, Enobarbus turns Antony's philosophic realism very much the seamy side out.

Enobarbus (he in particular) speaks now verse, now prose, either as the scene requires it of him for harmony or contrast, or as his humours dictate; his character being just such a compound of contrasts. Antony only occasionally relapses to prose, and his verse is regular on the whole. Cleopatra hardly touches prose at all; her verse is apt to be a little freer. Cæsar speaks only verse; it is fairly formal, and expressive of his calculated dignity.

But the supreme virtue of the writing lies in its peculiar combination of delicacy and strength, of richness with simplicity. For simple strength take the quick passage in which Menas tempts Pompey

[1] We also find Enobarbus entering with a blank verse line. The scene, it is true (see p. 118), shows some signs of re-writing.

to put to sea and then cut the throats of his guests.

Menas. Wilt thou be lord of all the world?
Pompey. What say'st thou?
Menas. Wilt thou be lord of the whole world? That's twice.
Pompey. How should that be?
Menas. But entertain it,
And though thou think me poor, I am the man
Will give thee all the world.

For simplicity, Cleopatra's

O well-divided disposition! Note him,
Note him, good Charmian, 'tis the man; but note him.
He was not sad, for he would shine on those
That make their looks by his; he was not merry;
Which seemed to tell them his remembrance lay
In Egypt with his joy; but between both:
O heavenly mingle!

For delicacy, her

But bid farewell and go: when you sued staying,
Then was the time for words: no going then;
Eternity was in our lips and eyes,
Bliss in our brows' bent; none our parts so poor,
But was a race of heaven. . . .

or Antony's

Come, let's all take hands;
Till that the conquering wine hath steeped our sense
In soft and delicate Lethe.

or his picture of Octavia:

Her tongue will not obey her heart, nor can
Her heart inform her tongue—the swan's down-feather,
That stands upon the swell at the full of tide,
And neither way inclines.

For strength, his malediction of Cleopatra:

You were half-blasted ere I knew you; ha!
Have I my pillow left unpressed in Rome,

> Forborne the getting of a lawful race,
> And by a gem of women, to be abused
> By one that looks on feeders?

or his dismissal of the half-flayed Thidias.

> Get thee back to Cæsar;
> Tell him thy entertainment: look thou say
> He makes me angry with him; for he seems
> Proud and disdainful, harping on what I am,
> Not what he knew I was.   He makes me angry;
> And at this time most easy 'tis to do't,
> When my good stars, that were my former guides,
> Have empty left their orbs, and shot their fires
> Into the abysm of hell.

We constantly have that favourite device, the enrichment of a simple effect by an echoing phrase; as when Cleopatra turns to Antony in pathetic dignity with

> Sir, you and I must part, but that's not it:
> Sir, you and I have loved, but there's not it. . . .

—as in the soothsayer's response to Antony's command to him to speak no more:

> To none but thee; no more, but when to thee.

The thought besides is echoed in Cleopatra's

> That time—O, times!—
> I laughed him out of patience; and that night
> I laughed him into patience: and next morn
> Ere the ninth hour, I drunk him to his bed. . . .

and in Enobarbus' remorseful

> This blows my heart:
> If swift thought break it not, a swifter mean
> Shall outstrike thought: but thought will do't, I feel.

Such devices easily degenerate into trick; as this comes near to doing with Cleopatra's

> These hands do lack nobility, that they strike
> A meaner than myself; since I myself
> Have given myself the cause.

—even as the power of concentration which can pack three clear thoughts into those seven words of hers:

> Therefore be deaf to my unpitied folly . . .

has overreached itself a moment earlier in

> O, my oblivion is a very Antony,
> And I am all forgotten.

The most delicate and precise accenting of the 'oblivion' and the 'all' may fail to make the meaning of this last clear upon the instant.

But we have concentration, clarity, strength, simplicity all combined in the swift exchange between Alexas and Cleopatra when he brings her the first news of the absent Antony with

> His speech sticks in my heart.
> Mine ear must pluck it thence.

she answers; and in her dark misgiving as the unlucky second messenger faces her:

> But, sirrah, mark, we use
> To say the dead are well: bring it to that,
> The gold I give thee I will melt and pour
> Down thy ill-uttering throat.

and in the primitive

> Call the slave again:
> Though I am mad I will not bite him: call !

Such things seem easy only when they are done—and well done.

Again, there is artistry of the subtlest in the free-

dom and apparent ease of this (the same wretched
messenger is now atoning for his fault by disparaging
Octavia, Charmian abetting him):

Messenger.   She creeps:
    Her motion and her station are as one;
    She shows a body rather than a life,
    A statue than a breather.
Cleopatra.   Is this certain?
Messenger. Or I have no observance.
Charmian.   Three in Egypt
    Cannot make better note.
Cleopatra.   He's very knowing;
    I do perceive 't: there's nothing in her yet;
    The fellow has good judgment.
Charmian.   Excellent.
Cleopatra. Guess at her years, I prithee.
Messenger.   Madam,
    She was a widow.—
Cleopatra.   Widow, Charmian; hark!

—in the way the continuing swing of the verse
keeps the dialogue swift while the dividing of the
lines gives spontaneity.

Note how actual incoherence—kept within
bounds by the strict rhythm of the verse—leads
up to, and trebles the nobility of a culminating
phrase. (She and her women surround the dead
Antony.)

           How do you, women?
What, what, good cheer? Why, how now, Charmian!
My noble girls! Ah women, women, look!
Our lamp is spent, it's out. Good sirs, take heart:
We'll bury him; and then, what's brave, what's noble,
Let's do it after the high Roman fashion,
And make death proud to take us. . . .

The compelled swiftness of the beginning, the
change without check when she turns to the
soldiers, the accordant discipline of the line which

follows, so that the last two lines can come out clarion-clear; here, again, is dramatic music exactly scored. In like fashion Antony's mixed metaphors (when he has been told she is dead), which include something very like a pun, lead up to and enhance a luminous close.

> I will o'ertake thee, Cleopatra, and
> Weep for my pardon. So it must be, for now
> All length is torture: since the torch is out,
> Lie down and stray no further: now all labour
> Mars what it does: yea, very force entangles
> Itself with strength: seal then, and all is done.
> Eros.—I come, my queen: Eros!—Stay for me
> Where souls do couch on flowers, we'll hand in hand,
> And with our sprightly port make the ghosts gaze:
> Dido and her Æneas shall want troops,
> And all the haunt be ours.

While, for a glorious and famous passage that is music itself—but what more?—take:

> O see, my women,
> The crown o' the earth doth melt. My Lord!
> O, withered is the garland of the war,
> The soldier's pole is fall'n: young boys and girls
> Are level now with men; the odds is gone,
> And there is nothing left remarkable
> Beneath the visiting moon.

This, in analysis, is little better than ecstatic nonsense; and it is meant to sound so. It has just enough meaning in it for us to feel as we hear it that it may possibly have a little more. Art must by so much at least improve on nature; in nature it would probably have none. But it gives us to perfection the reeling agony of Cleopatra's mind; therefore, in its dramatic setting, it ranks as supreme poetry.

Utterly sure of himself, Shakespeare has, in fine,

reached in the writing as in the shaping of this play
limits of freedom and daring that he will not, but
for the worse, overpass.

THE CHARACTERS

Antony

In the two early episodes of his breaking from
Egypt and of his welcome to Rome Antony is
painted for us in breadth and detail; they give us
the man complete, and thereafter the drama of
his actions needs no alloy of analysis or explanation.

Shakespeare's first strokes seldom fail to be significant. The four words to the messenger, who
crosses Antony's unchartered path as he and
Cleopatra saunter by, with

> News, my good lord, from Rome.
>   Grates me! The sum?

(the harsh, impatient, yet slightly conscience-
stricken sound of it!); the next three to Cleopatra:

> How, my love?

(the softened vowels!), then the full diapason of
the heroic, yet fustian-flavoured

> Let Rome in Tiber melt, and the wide arch
> Of the ranged empire fall. . . .

—here, in a few phrases, we have the gallant grown
old and the confident conqueror in decline. He
passes on; the keynote has been struck. But
Philo's sad, scrupulous

> Sir, sometimes when he is not Antony
> He comes too short of that great property,
> Which still should go with Antony.

187

promises, and Cleopatra's descent upon her giggling maids preludes another tune in him with

Cleopatra. Saw you my lord?
Enobarbus.   No, lady.
Cleopatra.   Was he not here?
Charmian. No, madam.
Cleopatra. He was disposed to mirth; but on the sudden
A Roman thought hath struck him. . . .

She sees him coming and will have him see her go, her offended nose in the air. But if he does he ignores her.[1]

The so-lately snubbed messenger is with him, talking, and encouraged to, as man to man. (These messengers, by the bye, are not errand boys, but men of responsibility.) This is the Antony—or little less than he—that could coolly out-face and out-scheme the mob of Cæsar's murderers, out-general the ideologue Brutus and Cassius the fanatic; it is Antony the realist, and never a starker one than when he needs to see himself coldly and clearly as he is. And he is enough a master of men to dare to let them see him so!

Who tells me true, though in his tale lie death,
I hear him as he flattered.

This encounter with the messengers sets him very relentlessly before us. Shakespeare has never

[1] The Folio gives us Antony's entrance before Cleopatra's line
We will not look upon him: go with us.

Modern editions are too apt to place it after, and after her departure, quite obliterating the intended effect. There is even the shadow of a further one. If Enobarbus has already gone to look for Antony, it is with a little train of Egyptians that Cleopatra sails off, leaving the barbarian Romans to their business.

had more illusions about Antony than he about himself. In *Julius Cæsar* how swiftly the heroics of the Capitol and the flattering eloquence of the Forum were followed by the calm proposal to Lepidus and Octavius to cheat the citizens, whose hearts he had just won, of part of their legacies; and, Lepidus being sent on this errand, to jockey *him* next out of his share of the spoils. But, whatever he was at, there was a sportsman-like gaiety about him then. He has grown colder with the years, cynically philosophical. It is a quality of greatness in a man, no doubt, that seeks the truth and sees it even in himself, boldly lets others see it. But such truth, seen and shown with such indifference! Colder; and callous, one adds.

The second messenger's appearance is heralded by ominous hesitations. (The play abounds in these delicacies of craftsmanship.) And, when he does appear, Antony, by that unusual

> What are you?

reads trouble in the sight of him. The answer comes straight:

> Fulvia thy wife is dead.

The response, the curt question,

> Where died she?

makes no sentimental pretences; and, the messenger dismissed, he is as honest with himself.

> There's a great spirit gone. Thus did I desire it.
> What our contempts doth often hurl from us,
> We wish it ours again: the present pleasure
> By revolution lowering, does become
> The opposite of itself.—She's good, being gone . . .

189

And Enobarbus, summoned to make ready for departure, is in talk with him a minute or more before, casually abrupt, he says

> Fulvia is dead.
> Sir?
> Fulvia is dead.
> Fulvia!
> Dead.

We recall Brutus and Cassius and Portia's death.[1] This also, then, would seem to be in " the high Roman fashion." But how truly English, too, the avoidance of the subject, the curt exchange to hide emotion—which, it may be, is not there to hide!

Enobarbus' frank brutalities lend by contrast dignity to his chief, as, lost now in ' Roman thoughts,' he passes on to take his leave of Cleopatra. He knows her,

> . . . cunning past man's thought.

He is free of her for ever if he would be; and it is hardly, one would say, a very fatal passion that shows in his farewell. He looks for tantrums.

> I am sorry to give breathing to my purpose . . .

An uncomfortably polite opening; it is an awkward business.

She plays her every pretty trick on him; but she can tell that the Roman thought has, for the

---

[1] *Brutus.* No man bears sorrow better. Portia is dead.
Cassius. Ha! Portia!
Brutus. Dead.

moment, conquered.[1]   His protests come easily;
she makes short work of them.   She stirs him to
candour by twitting him with 'Liar'; but she
unmasks more reality than she bargained for.

> Hear me, queen.
> The strong necessity of time commands
> Our services awhile. . . .

—and when Antony bites thus on his words, it is
as well to be silent and listen.   We are at the pivot
of the scene, its revealing moment.   He unfolds
for her, with all the force of his mind, his tangled
task ahead.   She listens indifferently: what are
politics and Sextus Pompeius to her?   Then he
adds—as if it were an item forgotten in the sum—

> My more particular,
> And that which most with you should safe my going,
> Is Fulvia's death.

Spoiled wanton of a woman she may be, but she
has a sensitiveness he lacks and a humanity he has
lost.   On the instant there possesses her such a
sense of the pitiful transient littleness of life:

> Though age from folly could not give me freedom
> It does from childishness.   Can Fulvia ' die '?

—of her own life too, and of their love :

> . . . Now I see, I see,
> In Fulvia's death, how mine received shall be.

Yet the next instant she is trifling it away and
at her tricks again.

[1] Note a technicality.   Cleopatra has not to be told that
he is going; she guesses or has already heard; she saw him,
indeed, confabulating with that fatal messenger.   This starts
the scene at the needed pitch; no time is wasted working
up to it.

The duel goes on, he obstinately asserting that it is all to her queenly advantage he should go, she pricking and stinging him with her woman's grievances. She cannot change his purpose, but she knows how to conquer in retreat.

> But, sir, forgive me,
> Since my becomings kill me when they do not
> Eye well to you! Your honour calls you hence:
> Therefore be deaf to my unpitied folly,
> And all the gods go with you. Upon your sword
> Sit laurel victory! and smooth success
> Be strewed before your feet!

That, she sees to it, shall be his remembrance of her.

He is found next in Rome, confronting Cæsar and out-topping him; and by how much more the lesser men around, Lepidus, Agrippa, Mæcenas and the rest. In this scene and those deriving from it we have Antony at his ablest, the seasoned states-man. That prefatory hint at his soldiership, peaceably though he now comes,

> 'Tis spoken well,
> Were we before our armies and to fight,
> I should do thus.

the quick opening of the argument, when cour-tesies with Cæsar have been exchanged,

> I learn, you take things ill that are not so,
> Or, being, concern you not.

give him vantage of position. He has, it would appear, a poor enough case to plead. He makes neither useless defence nor impulsive apology, but with clever dialectic shapes the issue, as far as may be, to his liking. Cæsar is pettish, but Antony—diplomatist that he is—remains proof against pin-

pricks. He jokes about Fulvia and her 'garboils.'

> As for my wife,
> I would you had her spirit in such another.
> The third o' the world is yours, which with a snaffle
> You may pace easy, but not such a wife.

He makes shrugging confession of his own fail-
ings; and in all so takes the wind out of Cæsar's
sails that self-conscious respectability is stung at
last into taxing this elderly scapegrace point blank
with perjury—very much to Lepidus' alarm.
Antony still stays unruffled. But, with his adver-
sary trapped into such rashness, we can feel his
wrist harden and see the steely eye above the easy
smile.

> No, Lepidus,
> Let him speak:
> The honour is sacred which he talks on now,
> Supposing that I lacked it. But, on, Cæsar;
> The article of my oath.

Cæsar does not shirk; but he speaks now by the
card. Antony (in his own phrase) paces them all
with a snaffle. Let them take no liberties, though.
He may jest about Egypt; they had better not.

Then Mæcenas and Agrippa take up their allotted
part in the peacemaking. The marriage with
Octavia is broached.

> . . . great Mark Antony
> Is now a widower.

The outmatched Cæsar cannot resist a malicious
gibe.

> Say not so, Agrippa:
> If Cleopatra heard you, your reproof
> Were well deserved of rashness.

ii. 14

He earns the snub direct.

> I am not married, Cæsar: let me hear
> Agrippa further speak.

But business is business, and a peace is patched up between the two, ' according to plan.'

From now to the consummating of the treaty with Pompey, and thereafter to the brotherly parting with Cæsar, Antony stands in the sun. These men know his worth to them and he knows it. Secure in reputation, he can be generous to Pompey, who girds at him too; he is even civil to Lepidus. And he brings to Octavia such a boyish penitence—

> My Octavia,
> Read not my blemishes in the world's report:
> I have not kept my square; but that to come
> Shall all be done by the rule.

—that how should we not, with the good Mæcenas, trust to her beauty, wisdom and modesty to settle his chastened heart? But Enobarbus has warned us betimes; and we see him, on the instant, turn from her to the soothsayer, that sinister shadow of his bewitchment; and the very next we hear is

> I will to Egypt:
> And though I make this marriage for my peace,
> I' the East my pleasure lies.

He is lost. And the significant thing is that he sinks without an effort from sanity to folly. He has won back his lost ground. We have seen him, with easy authority, outmatching Cæsar, and Cæsar, for all his jealousy, shrewdly content to be outmatched. Yet here he is flinging everything away. This is not the Antony of Philippi,

194

of the Capitol and the Forum. His spirit all
afraid to govern him near Cæsar! Is it, indeed!?
Cæsar has all the luck at dicing and cock-fighting.
No doubt! But the naked truth is that the sensual
man in him must find excuse for the

> I will to Egypt. . . .
> I' the East my pleasure lies.

and any is better than none.

This is the nemesis of the sensual man. Till
now Antony's appetites have not fatally played
him false. Such gifts and vitality as his can for
long enough make the best of both worlds, the
sensual and the world of judgment too; for life is
bred in passion, and has continuing need of it.
But the time comes when Nature finds no more
profit in a man, and her saving graces fail him.
Antony has never learnt to bargain with life; his
abundant strength could take politics and love-
affairs, interest and inclination in its stride. And
now that judgment does pull one way and appetite
another there is neither struggle nor dispute, no
overt choice made, even. Appetite wins, while
judgment winks and ignores defeat. He knows
what going back to Cleopatra means.

> These strong Egyptian fetters I must break,
> Or lose myself in dotage.

Yet in the very knitting up of the new ties that are
to save him from her he can say, ' I'll go,' nor
seem to count the cost. He speaks his own doom
in a careless phrase—and forgets it. He will
have his chance to make a brave show still and a
nobler end; but shameful, secret moments such as
this are the true counterpart to that earlier con-

195

scienceless success. No agony, nor darkening of the spirit before defeat, nor a Promethean defiance of the partial gods. This hero's fate is sealed quite casually, in a talk with a soothsayer about dice and fighting cocks.

Shakespeare adds yet one more touch to his disintegrating. Antony, we shall remember, came with Ventidius to the conference, saying

> If we compose well here, to Parthia.

—to avenge his Egypt-bred defeats there. But now it is

> O, come, Ventidius,
> *You* must to Parthia.

while he will wait the chance to step back to his sty.

This phase of the study of him, in sober business-like relation to Cæsar and his fellow-Romans, gives great ballast to the play. Cleopatra's hectic scenes stand in current contrast to it, and it is steadying preparation for the violence of the end. It is prose in its temper, but the pitch and swing of the actual verse lend it a more heroic life. There come no exciting clashes; but these close-woven contrasts of character that are its substance are the very stuff of drama.

Shakespeare is never the vindictive moralist, scourging a man with his sins, blind to all else about him. Antony's ending, when we reach it, is of a piece with his life. It is the garment of his good fortune turned inside out; and if some virtues have more lustre, some vices are more tolerable in failure than success. Once again, here is no spiritual tragedy of ideals betrayed. The man has had what he wanted from the world; with luck,

196

daring and judgment to bring it him. A debauched judgment, no luck left to draw upon, mere daring become folly, and he loses it; that is the whole story. But he loses like a man, and there is some spiritual tragedy in it too; for if no ideals betray him, yet at every turn he is conscious that he betrays himself. He knows—who better?—that he should not fight Cæsar by sea. He has no reasons to give but

> For that he dares us to't.

All his answer to argument, as he stands supine under Cleopatra's eye, is a weakly obstinate

> By sea, by sea!

though he adds, for excuse, a futile

> But if we fail,
> We then can do't at land.

His mind seems a blank. He has no plan of battle; and with one defeat his nerve and self-respect are gone.

This is his lowest fall, and there in helpless ignominy we might have to leave him

> . . . unqualited with very shame.

to humble himself before his conqueror, to

> . . . dodge
> And palter in the shifts of lowness . . .

—but for Cæsar! Thanks to his enemy, the old courage and a new nobility are made to stir in him. There is a cold unloveliness about Cæsar. With Antony at his mercy—well, he might accord it or refuse it; but surely he need not so promptly send an envoy to win Cleopatra from

him who has lost everything for her sake, to tempt
her at any price to drive from Egypt

> . . . her all-disgraced friend
> Or take his life there.

Conquerors, it would seem, cannot even learn the
common sense of magnanimity. The clever trick
comes near, though, to costing Cæsar all he has
won and more.

Antony has been no great precisian in such
matters himself; but he is thinking now, we may
suppose, less of his own shortcomings than of old
days of comradeship with Cæsar when the diffi-
dent schoolmaster-ambassador returns.

> Is *that* his answer?
> Ay, my lord.
> The queen shall then have courtesy, so she
> Will yield us up.
> > He says so.
> > > Let her know't.

He recovers his stature as hero with that.

But if this is not spiritual tragedy, still less is it
a moral tale, with the scales of vice and virtue
neatly tipped for our edifying; Shakespeare has
left all that behind with artifice of plot and
characters cut to suit it. The light is shining for
us here upon things as they were and men as they
are. So the heroic gesture can be followed by the
folly of the challenge to Cæsar and the savagery
of the whipping of Thidias; by the bitter purging
of the illusion that was Cleopatra, and at her beck,
the prompt re-embracing of it with a narcotic

> I am satisfied.

Yet if Cleopatra is all that in his fury he says she
is, and even readier, it may be, to betray him than

he thinks, she is not cold-hearted toward him, strange though that may seem.[1] And while (by every rule of ready-made morality) his open-eyed return to bondage and debauch should bring him swiftly to defeat,—and Enobarbus the moralist makes sure it will—on the contrary, it preludes victory, and it is the over-confident Cæsar that must learn a lesson.

But Cæsar is apt to learn, and Enobarbus will prove right in the end (though remorse and malaria end him before he finds it out), and Shakespeare forthwith shows us very plainly the rifts in the prospect.   There is the omen of the strange music that the soldiers hear, the sign that

> . . . the god Hercules, whom Antony loved,
> Now leaves him.[2]

and the strange mood in Antony himself that sets him, on the eve of battle, to making his followers weep his likely death.

> The gods make this a happy day to Antony!

is the old legionary's greeting to him as he marches out in the morning; and the response is generous enough.

> Would thou and those thy scars had once prevailed
> To make me fight at land!

The gods do grant him one more happy day, and we see him at his best in it.   Shakespeare shows it as the briefest of the three; as a ray shooting through sunset clouds.

[1] Enobarbus believes the very worst of her. But, of course, *he* would!

[2] Shakespeare finds this in Plutarch, of course; but there it occurs before the last defeat. He adds an ironic value to it by setting it before the intermediate day of victory.

He begins it with what may be called the single touch of sentiment in the play. Antony and Cleopatra come out in the early dawn—come from a night of revel, moreover!—like a young bride and bridegroom, laughing together at her pretty fumblings as she helps him put his armour on. A spoiled child's useless fingers; Octavia would have made a neater job of it, one fears! He flatters and pets her:

> Well, well:
> We shall thrive now!

Her glee when she has slipped a strap into place!

> Is not this buckled well?
> Rarely, rarely! . . .
> Thou fumblest, Eros, and my queen's a squire
> More tight at this than thou.

Seen among his soldiers he is still the Antony of her worship:

> The demi-Atlas of this earth, the arm
> And burgonet of men.

But there are qualities in him that a little pass her understanding, perhaps. For, even as he sets forth, he learns that Enobarbus has deserted; and, very quietly, with no touch of anger, and but one most human shade of bitterness, comes

> What say'st thou?
> *Soldier.* Sir,
> He is with Cæsar.
> *Eros.* Sir, his chests and treasure
> He has not with him.
> *Antony.* Is he gone?
> *Soldier.* Most certain.
> *Antony.* Go, Eros, send his treasure after; do it;
> Detain no jot, I charge thee: write to him—
> I will subscribe—gentle adieus and greetings;

> Say that I wish he never find more cause
> To change a master. O, my fortunes have
> Corrupted honest men! Despatch. Enobarbus!

He goes to fight, not confident of the issue (not stained with such over-confidence as Cæsar's, certainly), nor braggart of his cause. And when he beats his enemy and returns in triumph, his first thought is to thank his soldiers and to praise before them all the young and wounded Scarus, the hero of the day, who, for his reward, shall kiss Cleopatra's hand. Does she remember Thidias at this juncture, and *his* wounds?

Not much is made of the third day's fighting; nor does Shakespeare trouble with the question which Plutarch leaves unanswered, whether Cleopatra did " pack cards " with Cæsar or no. It is enough that fortune crashes upon Antony in final ruin. There is little noble about him now, in his beast-like rage and thirst for her blood; much though that is pitiful in the wreck of such a man.

> The soul and body rive not more in parting
> Than greatness going off.

For, if but in his folly, he has been great. He has held nothing back, has flung away for her honour and power, never weighing their worth against her worthlessness; there is a sort of selfless greatness in that. The lust to kill her before he kills himself is the due backwash of such spendthrift love. He sees her and cannot; folly is folly and weakness is weakness still, he can only damn her to a shamefuller end. Fury racks him again; and then the merciful riving of spirit from body begins. Shakespeare turns, as we have seen, to pure poetry to express it:

Antony.　Eros, thou yet beholdst me?
Eros.　　　　　　　　　　　　Ay, noble lord,
Antony.　Sometimes we see a cloud that's dragonish . . .

He is coming to the end of his strength—even his!
—and the body's passions begin to seem unreal,
and he to be slipping free of them.　Yet another
wrench or so of anger, suffering and shame; and
the news comes that, in despite of him, she it is
that has slipped free.

It is a lie; and he will be a laughing-stock in
death.　What more fitly tragic end for the brilliant
general and statesman, the great realist and
paragon of worldly wisdom, than to be tricked into
emulating the heroism of a Cleopatra, who is, we
know, even now safe in her Monument; than to
be outdone in quiet courage by his servant; than
to bungle his own death-stroke and have to lie
begging, in vain, to be put out of his misery?　And,
as he lies there, he learns the ridiculous truth.

Shakespeare spares him no ignominy; yet out
of it rises, not, to be sure, an Antony turned angel,
but a man set free of debt to fate, still abiding in his
faith, justified of it, then, at the last.　When the
news of Cleopatra's death comes, he reproaches
her no more, says not a word of any loss but this,
has no thought but to follow her.　What purpose
is left him?

> Unarm, Eros; the long day's task is done,
> And we must sleep.

He is nothing without her; the world is empty and
time has no meaning.

> Since Cleopatra died,
> I have lived in such dishonour, that the gods
> Detest my baseness . . .

Since she died, the single minute's passing has been to him as years. And when, dying, he learns that she lives he makes no comment upon that; what do Fate's pettinesses matter now? He asks only to be carried to her that he may die in her arms. Even of this he comes near to be cheated. She will not risk her safety for his sake. But she has them draw him up to her; and his thoughts are for her safety and peace of mind.

> The miserable change now at my end
> Lament nor sorrow at; but please your thoughts
> In feeding them with those my former fortunes,
> Wherein I lived the greatest prince o' the world,
> The noblest; and do now not basely die,
> Not cowardly put off my helmet to
> My countryman—a Roman by a Roman
> Valiantly vanquished. Now my spirit is going;
> I can no more.

He has loved her, the worst and the best of her; and given her the best and the worst of him. He won much from the world, so he had much to lose. Losers ought not to whine. Antony stays a soldier and a sportsman—and a gentleman, by his lights —to the end.

Cleopatra

Shakespeare's Cleopatra had to be acted by a boy, and this did everything to determine, not his view of the character, but his presenting of it. Think how a modern dramatist, a practical man of the theatre, with an actress for his Cleopatra, would set about the business. He might give us the tragedy of the play's end much as Shakespeare does, no doubt—if he could; but can we conceive him leaving Cleopatra without one single scene in which to show the sensual charm which drew Antony to her, and back to her, which is the tragedy's very fount? Yet this is what Shakespeare does, and with excellent reason: a boy could not show it, except objectionably or ridiculously. He does not shirk her sensuality, he stresses it time and again; but he has to find other ways than the one impracticable way of bringing it home to us. What is the best evidence we have (so to speak) of Cleopatra's physical charms? A description of them by Enobarbus—by the misogynist Enobarbus—given us, moreover, when she has been out of our sight for a quarter of an hour or so. Near her or away from her, Antony himself never speaks of them. He may make such a casual joke as

> The beds i' the East are soft.

or reflect in a fateful phrase,

> I will to Egypt . . . :
> I' the East my pleasure lies.

but Shakespeare will not run even so much risk of having a lover's ecstasies discounted. Enobarbus may grumble out gross remarks about her; but Antony's response, as he plans his escape, is

> She is cunning past men's thought.

The lovers are never once alone together; and the only approach to a 'love-scene' comes with our first sight of them, walking in formal procession and reciting antiphonally:

Cleopatra. If it be love indeed, tell me how much.
Antony. There's beggary in the love that can be reckoned.
Cleopatra. I'll set a bourn how far to be beloved.
Antony. Then must thou needs find out new heaven, new earth.

204

This is convention itself. Antony's

> Here is my space.
> Kingdoms are clay: our dungy earth alike
> Feeds beast as man: the nobleness of life
> Is to do thus; when such a mutual pair
> And such a twain can do't. . . .

is pure rhetoric.[1] And the poetry of

> Now, for the love of love and her soft hours,
> Let's not confound the time with conference harsh.
> There's not a minute of our lives should stretch
> Without some pleasure now.   What sport to-night?
>
> *Cleopatra.* Hear the ambassadors.
> *Antony.*   Fie, wrangling queen!
> Whom everything becomes, to chide, to laugh,
> To weep, whose every passion fully strives
> To make itself in thee, fair and admired. . . .

is sensuality sublimated indeed.

Not till their passion deepens as tragedy nears does Shakespeare give it physical expression. Antony leaves her for battle with "a soldier's kiss" (it is the first the action shows) and, returning triumphant, hails her with

> O thou day o' the world,
> Chain my armed neck: leap thou attire and all
> Through proof of harness to my heart, and there
> Ride on the pants triumphing.

A very open and above-board embrace.   And not till death is parting them do we reach

> I am dying, Egypt, dying; only
> I here importune death awhile, until
> Of many thousand kisses the poor last
> I lay upon thy lips.

---

[1] The '*embracing*' which Pope and editors after him tagged on to 'thus,' is not Shakespeare. This was *not* what he meant by suiting the action to the word and the word to the action.

with, for its matching and outdoing, her

> . . . welcome, welcome ! die where thou hast lived :
> Quicken with kissing : had my lips that power,
> Thus would I wear them out.

By which time, if dramatist and actors between them have not freed the imaginations of their audience from the theatre's bonds, all three will have been wasting it. Throughout the play Cleopatra herself gives us glimpses enough of her sensual side.

> Thou, eunuch Mardian !
>   What's your highness' pleasure?
> Not now to hear thee sing.   I take no pleasure
> In aught an eunuch has : 'tis well for thee
> That, being unseminared, thy freer thoughts
> May not fly forth of Egypt.

But Shakespeare never has her turn it towards a flesh-and-blood Antony, inviting response.

His only choice, then, is to endow her with other charms for conquest : wit, coquetry, perception, subtlety, imagination, inconsequence—and this he does to the full.   But had he a veritable Cleopatra to play the part, what other and what better could be do?   How does a Cleopatra differ from the common run of wantons but in just such gifts as these?   It would take a commonplace dramatist to insist upon the obvious, upon all that age does wither, while custom even sooner stales its infinite monotony !

It is, of course, with his magic of words that Shakespeare weaves Cleopatra's charm.   To begin with, we may find ourselves somewhat conscious of the process.   Though that first duet between the lovers is with good reason conventional, they seem slightly self-conscious besides ; less themselves, at the moment, than advocates for themselves. Not till Cleopatra re-appears has this cloud about her vanished; but nothing of the sort ever masks her again.

Cleopatra.	Saw you my lord?
Enobarbus.	No, lady.
Cleopatra.	Was he not here?
Charmian.	No, madam.
Cleopatra.	He was disposed to mirth; but on the sudden A Roman thought hath struck him. Enobarbus.
Enobarbus.	Madam.
Cleopatra.	Seek him and bring him hither. Where's Alexas?
Alexas.	Here, at your service. My lord approaches.
Cleopatra.	We will not look upon him; go with us.

And when she returns:

> See where he is, who's with him, what he does:
> I did not send you: if you find him sad,
> Say I am dancing: if in mirth, report
> That I am sudden sick: quick, and return.

Here is actuality; and forged in words of one syllable, mainly. This is the woman herself, quick, jealous, imperious, mischievous, malicious, flagrant, subtle; but a delicate creature, too, and the light, glib verse seems to set her on tiptoe.

For the scene with Antony, Shakespeare rallies his resources. We have the pouting

> I am sick and sullen.

the plaintive

> Help me away, dear Charmian; I shall fall:
> It cannot be thus long, the sides of nature
> Will not sustain it.

the darting ironic malice of

> I know, by that same eye, there's some good news.
> What says the married woman? You may go. . . .

and pretty pettishness suddenly throbbing into

207

> Why should I think you can be mine and true,
> Though you in swearing shake the throned gods,
> Who have been false to Fulvia? . . .

Then the vivid simplicities melt into a sheer magic
of the music of words.

> But bid farewell and go: when you sued staying
> Then was the time for words: no going then:
> Eternity was in our lips and eyes,
> Bliss in our brows' bent; none our parts so poor
> But was a race of heaven. . . .

And so, up the scale and down, she enchants the
scene to its end.

For a moment in the middle of it we see another
Cleopatra, and hear a note struck from nearer the
heart of her. She is shocked by his callously calculated gloss upon Fulvia's death. Vagaries of
passion she can understand, and tricks and lies to
favour them. But this hard-set indifference! She
takes it to herself, of course, and is not too shocked
to make capital of it for her quarrel. But here,
amid the lively wrangling, which is stimulus to
their passion, shows a dead spot of incomprehen-
sion, the true division between them. They stare
for an instant; then cover it, as lovers will. Fulvia's
wrongs make the best of capital; there are poisoned
pin-pricks in them, and the second round of the
fight leaves him helpless—but to turn and throttle
her. The rules of the ring are not for Cleopatra.
She takes woman's leave to play the child, and the
great lady's to outdo any wench in skittishness; she
matches vulgar gibing with dignity and pathos,
now loses herself in inarticulate imaginings, now is
simple and humble and nobly forgiving. He must
leave her; she lets him go. But to the unguessed
riddle that she is, he will return.

208

Let the actress of to-day note carefully how the brilliant effect of this first parade of Cleopatra is gained. There is no more action in it than the dignity of a procession provides, and the swifter coming and going and returning which ends in this duel of words danced at arm's length with her lover. There is no plot to be worked out; Antony is departing, and he departs, that is all. What we have is the transposing of a temperament into words; and it is in the changing rhythm and dissolving colour of them, quite as much as in the sense, that the woman is to be found. Neither place nor time is left for the embroidery of "business," nor for the over-painting of the picture by such emotional suggestion as the author of to-day legitimately asks of an actress. Anything of that sort will cloud the scene quite fatally. If the shortcomings of a boy Cleopatra were plain, we can imagine his peculiar virtuosity. To the adopted graces of the great lady he would bring a delicate aloofness, which would hover, sometimes very happily, upon the edge of the absurd. With the art of acting still dominantly the art of speech—to be able to listen undistracted an audience's chief need—he would not make his mere presence disturbingly felt; above all, he could afford to lose himself unreservedly—since his native personality must be lost—in the music of the verse, and to let that speak. So in this scene must the Cleopatra of to-day, if *we* are not to lose far more than we gain by her. There will be the larger demands on her later, those that Shakespeare's indwelling demon made on him; he had to risk their fulfilment then, as now.

But her presenting continues for awhile to be

ii. 15

very much of a parade. She is never, we notice, now or later, left to a soliloquy.[1] Parade fits her character (or if Shakespeare fits her character to parade the effect is the same). She is childishly extravagant, ingenuously shameless; nothing exists for her but her desires. She makes slaves of her servants, but she jokes and sports with them too, and opens her heart to them in anger or in joy; so they adore her. It is not perhaps an exemplary Court, in which the Queen encourages chaff about her paramours, and turns on her lady-in-waiting with

> By Isis, I will give thee bloody teeth,
> If thou with Cæsar paragon again
> My man of men.

but it is at least a lively one, and its expansiveness would be a boon to any dramatist.

She is indeed no sluggardly sensualist; double doses of mandragora would not keep her quiet. What she cannot herself she must do by proxy; she cannot follow Antony, but her messengers gallop after him every post. Her senses stir her to potent imagery:

> O happy horse, to bear the weight of Antony!
> Do bravely, horse! for wot'st thou whom thou movest. . . .

—if perverted a little:

>   . . . now I feed myself
> With most delicious poison.

---

[1] Nor is anyone else in the play for more than a few lines; another token of it as drama of action rather than of spiritual conflict. We see in this too how far Shakespeare's stagecraft had outgrown the older, conventional, plot-forwarding use of soliloquies. In his earlier plays of action they abound.

And in that

> Think on me,
> That am with Phœbus' amorous pinches black,
> And wrinkled deep in time.

there is elemental power. And if her praise of Antony for his ' well-divided disposition ' seems incongruous; why, a nature so sure of itself can admire the qualities it lacks.

Shakespeare shirks nothing about her. What will be left for us of her womanly charm when we have seen her haling the bringer of the news of Antony's treachery up and down by the hair of his head, and running after him, knife in hand, screaming like a fish-fag? But this also is Cleopatra. He allows her here no moment of dignity, nor of fortitude in grief; only the pathos of

Cleopatra. In praising Antony, I have dispraised Cæsar?
Charmian. Many times, madam.
Cleopatra.   I am paid for't now.

—which is the pathos of the whipped child, rancorous against its gods, resigned to evil. There is the moment's thought, as she calls the scared messenger back again:

> These hands do lack nobility, that they strike
> A meaner than myself; since I myself
> Have given myself the cause.

And this is a notable touch. It forecasts the Cleopatra of the play's end, who will seek her death after the ' high Roman fashion '; it reveals, not inconsistency, but that antithesis in disposition which must be the making of every human equation. It is the second touch of its sort that Shakespeare gives to his picturing of her; and both, in the acting, must be stamped on our memories.[1]

The end of the scene sees her, with her maids fluttering round her, lapsed into pitifulness, into childish ineptitude. But again, something of spiritual continence sounds in its last note of all, in the

> Pity me, Charmian;
> But do not speak to me.

The complementary scene, in which the unlucky messenger is re-examined, would be more telling if it followed a little closer; but, as we have seen, Shakespeare has hereabouts an overplus of Roman material to deal with. It is pure comedy, and of the best. She is calm again, very collected, making light of her fury; but an echo of it can be heard in that sudden nasty little snarl which ends in a sigh. Charmian and Iras and Alexas have evidently had a trying time with her. They conspire to flatter her back to confidence—and she lets them. The messenger has been well coached too. But the best of the comedy is in Cleopatra's cryptic simplicity. She likes flattery for its own sake. There is a sensuality of the mind that flattery feeds. What does it matter if they lie to her; of what use is the truth? Anger is crippling; but in the glow of their adulation she uncurls and feels her lithe strength return, and this is her only need.

> All may be well enough.

Yet the words savour faintly of weariness, too.

Now comes the war and her undoing. Her dis-

---

[1] The first, her stinging reproach to him for his callousness at Fulvia's death.

illusion first; for Antony, won back, is no longer
the all-conquering captain, from whom she may
command Herod of Jewry's head—or Cæsar's!
—nor does her own reckless generalship prove
much help. We do not, as we have noted, see
the re-uniting of the lovers; we find her at a
nagging match with Enobarbus, and turned, with
her Antony, to something very like a shrew. And
if to the very end she stays for him an unguessed
riddle, 'cunning past man's thought,' there is
much in which Shakespeare is content to leave her
so for us—thereby to manifest her the more consummately. By what twists of impulse or of calculation is she moved through the three fateful days
of swaying fortune? How ready was she to 'pack
cards' with Cæsar? What the final betrayal
amounted to, that sent Antony raging after her,
Shakespeare, it may be said, could not tell us,
because he did not know; and her inarticulate
terror at this point may therefore show us his stagecraft at its canniest. But in retrospect all this
matters dramatically very little; what does matter
is that as we watch her she should defy calculation.

It is futile, we know, to apply the usual moral
tests to her, of loyalty, candour, courage. Yet
because she shamelessly overacts her repentance
for her share in that first defeat it by no means
follows that she feels none. She lends an ear to
Thidias, and the message to Cæsar sounds flat
treason; this is the blackest count against her.
But soft speech costs nothing, and perhaps it was
Cæsar who was to be tricked. Can we detect,
though, a new contempt for Antony as she watches
him, his fury glutted by the torment of the
wretched envoy? She might respect him more had

213

he flogged her instead! Is there in the sadly smiling

> Not know me yet?

with which she counters his spent reproach, and in her wealth of protest, something of the glib falsity of sated passion? Next morning she buckles on his armour and bids him good-bye like a happy child; but, his back turned:

> He goes forth gallantly. That he and Cæsar might
> Determine this great war in single fight!
> Then, Antony—! But now—?

It is a chilling postscript.

She is like Antony in this at least—and it erects them both to figures of heroic size—that she has never learnt to compromise with life, nor had to reconcile her own nature's extremes. To call her false to this or to that is to set up a standard that could have no value for her. She is true enough to the self of the moment; and, in the end, tragically true to a self left sublimated by great loss. The passionate woman has a child's ardours and a child's obliterating fears, an animal's wary distrust; balance of judgment none, one would say. But often, as at this moment, she shows the shrewd scepticism of a child.

From now till we see her in the Monument and Antony is brought to die in her arms, Shakespeare sinks the figure into the main fabric of the play. He makes a moment's clear picture of the welcome to Antony returned from victory. The

> *Enter Cleopatra, attended.*

might be radiance enough; but, for surplus, we have her ecstatic

214

> Lord of lords!
> O infinite virtue, comest thou smiling from
> The world's great snare uncaught!

When defeat follows quickly, her collapse to terror is left, as we saw, the anatomy of a collapse and no more. Then, from being but a part of the general swift distraction, she emerges in fresh strength to positive significance again; and—this is important—as a tragic figure for the first time.

From wantonness, trickery and folly, Shakespeare means to lift her to a noble end. But, even in doing it, he shirks no jot of the truth about her. She loses none of her pristine quality. If she victimises the complacent Dolabella with a glance or two, who shall blame her? But how far she would go in wheedling Cæsar—were there a joint to be found in that armour of cold false courtesy—who shall say? She cheats and lies to him as a matter of course, and Seleucus would fare worse with her than did that once unlucky messenger. Misfortune hardly lends her dignity, the correct Cæsar may well think as he leaves her there. He will think otherwise when he sees her again. But it is not till the supreme moment approaches that she can pretend to any calm of courage. She must sting herself to ever fresh desperation by conjured visions of the shame from which only death will set her free; we hear that 'Be noble to myself,' 'my noble act,' repeated like a charm. Yet she is herself to the end. It is the old wilful childishness, tuned to a tragic key, that sounds for us in

> O Charmian, I will never go from hence.
> *Charmian.* Be comforted, dear madam.
> *Cleopatra.*   No, I will not:
> All strange and terrible events are welcome,
> But comforts we despise. . . .

and in the extravagant magnificence of her grief
she is the Eastern queen, who could stir even an
Enobarbus to rhapsody, and beggar all description.
She has no tears for Antony.[1]   The shock of his
death strikes her senseless, but her spirit is un-
quelled.   Defiant over his body:

> It were for me
> To throw my sceptre at the injurious gods,
> To tell them that this world did equal theirs
> Till they had stolen our jewel. . . .

The rest may find relief in grieving; not she!
   Shakespeare allows her one touch of his favourite
philosophy.   She reappears, confirmed in her loss.

> My desolation does begin to make
> A better life.   'Tis paltry to be Cæsar;
> Not being Fortune, he's but Fortune's knave,
> A minister of her will. . . .

This is the note, once struck by Brutus, sustained
by Hamlet, of failure's contempt for success.   We
hear it in life, more commonly, from quite successful
men, who also seem to find some needed comfort
in the thought.   It is a recurring note in all Shakespearean tragedy, this exalting of the solitary
dignity of the soul; and he will not end even this
most unspiritual of plays without sounding it.
He passes soon to a somewhat truer Cleopatra—
here is the same thought pursued, though—when
she counters Dolabella's bland assurance with

> You laugh when boys or women tell their dreams.
> Is't not your trick? . . .
> I dreamt there was an Emperor Antony.
> O, such another sleep, that I might see
> But such another man!

---

[1] Throughout the play Cleopatra never weeps.   Antony
does.

and utterly bewilders him with the hyperbole that
follows, strange contrast to Cæsar's recent decorous
regret. But it is on such ridiculous heights that
genius—even for wantonness—will lodge its happiness. And the next instant he appears, the
manikin Cæsar, who has triumphed over her
'man of men'! She stares, as if incredulous, till
Dolabella has to say

> It is the emperor, madam.

Then she mocks their conqueror with her humilities. But the scene is, besides, a ghastly mockery
of the Cleopatra that was. Compare it with the
one in which she laughed and pouted and turned
Antony round her finger. She is a trapped animal
now, cringing and whining and cajoling lest the
one chink of escape be stopped. There is no
cajoling Cæsar. He betters her at that with his

> Feed and sleep:
> Our care and pity is so much upon you,
> That we remain your friend.

Even so might a cannibal ensure the tenderness of
his coming meal. She knows; and when he is
gone:

> He words me, girls, he words me, that I should not
> Be noble to myself!

One last lashing of her courage; then a flash of
glorious, of transcendent vanity—

> Show me, my women, like a queen: go fetch
> My best attires: I am again for Cydnus,
> To meet Mark Antony.

—a last touch of the old frolicsomeness as she jokes
with the clown, peeping the while between the
fig-leaves in which the aspics lie; and she is ready.

217

Give me my robe, put on my crown: I have
Immortal longings in me: now no more
The juice of Egypt's grape shall moist this lip:
Yare, yare, good Iras: quick! Methinks I hear
Antony call; I see him rouse himself
To praise my noble act; I hear him mock
The luck of Cæsar, which the gods give men
To excuse their after wrath. Husband, I come:
Now to that name my courage prove my title! . . .

The dull Octavia, with her still conclusions, defeated and divorced!

I am fire and air; my other elements
I give to baser life. So; have you done?
Come then, and take the last warmth of my lips.
Farewell, kind Charmian, Iras, long farewell. . . .

Iras so worships her that she dies of the very grief of the leave-taking.

Have I the aspic in my lips? Dost fall?
If thou and nature can so gently part,
The stroke of death is as a lover's pinch,
Which hurts and is desired. Dost thou lie still?
If thus thou vanishest, thou tell'st the world
It is not worth leave-taking.

Sensuous still, still jealous; her mischievous, magnificent mockery surpassing death itself.

This proves me base.
If she first meet the curled Antony
He'll make demand of her, and spend that kiss
Which is my heaven to have. Come, thou mortal wretch,
With thy sharp teeth this knot intrinsicate
Of life at once untie. Poor venomous fool,
Be angry and despatch. O, couldst thou speak,
That I might hear thee call great Cæsar ass
Unpolicied!

Charmian sees her uplifted, shining:

O eastern star!

Then follows the consummate

> Peace, peace!
> Dost thou not see my baby at my breast,
> That sucks the nurse asleep?

and in another moment she is dead.

Very well, then, it is not high spiritual tragedy; but is there not something still more fundamental in the pity and terror of it? Round up a beast of prey, and see him die with a natural majesty which shames our civilised contriving. So Cleopatra dies; defiant, noble in her kind, shaming convenient righteousness, a miracle of nature that —here is the tragedy—will not be reconciled to any gospel but its own. She is herself to the very end. Her last breath fails upon the impatient

> What should I stay . . .?

Her last sensation is the luxury of

> As sweet as balm, as soft as air, as gentle!

And what more luminous summary could there be of such sensual womanhood than the dignity and perverse humour blended in this picture of her yielded to her death—suckling an asp? It defies praise. So, for that matter, does Charmian's

> Now boast thee, death, in thy possession lies
> A lass unparalleled.

—the one word 'lass' restoring to her, even as death restores, some share of innocence and youth.

This scene shows us Shakespeare's artistry in perfection, and all gloss upon it will doubtless seem tiresome. But though the reader be teased a little, it cannot hurt him to realise that this close analysis of every turn in the showing of a character and composing of a scene—and much besides—must go to giving a play the simple due of its acting. As reader he cannot lose by knowing what demands the play's art makes on the actor's. The greater the play, the more manifold the demands! When he sees them fulfilled in the theatre his enjoyment will be doubled. If they are not, he will a little know why, and so much the worse for the actor; but, at long last, so much the better.

Octavia

Octavia speaks a bare thirty lines, and they are distributed, at that, through four scenes. She is meant to be a negative character, set in contrast to Cleopatra; but if only as an instance of what Shakespeare can do by significant 'placing,' by help of a descriptive phrase or so, and above all by individualising her in the music of her verse, she ranks among the play's achievements. She first appears hard upon the famous picturing of Cleopatra in her barge on Cydnus, with this for preface:

> If beauty, wisdom, modesty can settle
> The heart of Antony, Octavia is
> A blessed lottery to him.

—turned, though, to irony by the comment of Enobarbus' grimmest smile and shrug. We then have but a passing sight of her, and only hear her innocently answer Antony's most ambiguous

> The world and my great office will sometimes
> Divide me from your bosom.

with

>   All which time
> Before the gods my knee shall bow my prayers
> To them for you.

she departs with her brother; but before the scene
ends the ambiguity is resolved. Antony, we learn,
will take his first chance to go back to Cleopatra,
and Octavia is already befooled. An unpromising
beginning for her.

Next we see her parting from her brother, setting out with an already faithless husband, pledge
of an amity between the two as hollow to the
sound as mocking comment and bland protest can
show it; she helpless to make the false thing true.
She weeps at the parting. Antony is kindly in
deceit—

> The April's in her eyes: it is love's spring.
> And these the showers to bring it on. Be cheerful.

—and, as she turns back to whisper some woman's
misgiving to Cæsar, he sums up their usage of her,
and paints her quite inimitably in the sense and
very music of

> Her tongue will not obey her heart, nor can
> Her heart inform her tongue—the swan's down-feather
> That stands upon the swell at the full of tide,
> And neither way inclines.

A gentler victim of great policies one could not
find. Another scene shows her shaken off by
Antony with the same kindly deceit, grown colder
now; another, her return to Cæsar, to a welcome
humiliating in its sympathy; and so, impotent in
goodness, she vanishes from the play. But we
should remember her, if only by such melodies as

> A more unhappy lady
> If this division chance, ne'er stood between,
> Praying for both parts.

as

> The Jove of power make me most weak, most weak,
> Your reconciler! . . .

The gentle and sustained purity of the cadence is all her own. To Cleopatra, of course, she is ' dull Octavia,' and Antony, in the fury of defeat, can credit her with revengefully ' prepared nails '; their obvious tribute to a woman they have wronged.

Octavius Cæsar

Cæsar is the predestinate successful man. Beside his passionate rival, he is passionless; no puritan though. If, as he says, Antony merely

> filled
> His vacancy with his voluptuousness. . . .

it would be his own affair. But how not lose patience with a partner, and such a man as Antony, when he behaves even as boys will,

> . . . who being mature in knowledge,
> Pawn their experience to their present pleasure,
> And so rebel to judgment.

Still, it is his business as politician, to see things as they are, and he knows well enough that his prosaic virtues will never fire the enthusiasms of the Roman mob. He must have the gallant Antony to counter the danger that the gallant Pompey has now become. Not that he under-values himself— far from it! Much as he needs Antony, he makes no concessions to him; insists rather on his own correct conduct:

> You have broken
> The article of your oath; which you shall never
> Have tongue to charge me with.

He must not only be in the right, but keep proving that he is. This alone labels him second-rate.

But is not this the sort of man that Rome now needs to bring the pendulum of conflict to a stand? Such genius as Julius Cæsar's was not to be endured. There was small profit in the zealotries of a Cassius and a Brutus; and to what Antony will bring the Empire we see. Octavius Cæsar may seem no great general. Doubtless at Philippi he "dealt in lieutenantry"; but at least he does not now send a Ventidius to Parthia to do his work for him, while he is yet so jealous that the work stays half done. And is not the best general the one who does deal in lieutenantry—when he has chosen his lieutenants well? Here is, at any rate, the industrious, un-flagging, cautious man, who wins through in the end, and can say and mean, most luckily for Rome,

> The time of universal peace is near.
> Prove this a prosperous day, the three-nook'd world
> Shall bear the olive freely.

—though, as we saw, the moment's over-confidence in which he says it is followed by a day's defeat. Not even the best-regulated characters can wholly discipline fortune!

Personally he is in many ways, no doubt, an estimable man. If he sells his sister to Antony—and we should not, of course, take a sentimental view of such a marriage—he still holds her dear, and is jealous of her honour. His grief for Antony's death, for his one-time

> . . . mate in empire,
> Friend and companion in the front of war. . . .

is not hypocrisy, even though he has, in his own interest, just passed from trying to bribe Cleopatra to have " the old ruffian's " throat cut to orders that he be ' took alive,' to be brought to Rome after (as Antony well knows) chained in his conqueror's Triumph. And if he lies to Cleopatra he does but pay her in her own coin. Nor when she outwits him is he angry; he respects her rather.

> Bravest at the last;
> She levelled at our purposes, and, being royal,
> Took her own way. . . .

Not a lovable man, but a very able one; and we see him growing in ability—such ungenerous natures do—as opportunity matures. If he were 'not rather humourless, we might suspect him of irony in giving as his excuse for getting rid of Lepidus—having had his use of him—that this meekest of incompetent parasites ' was grown too cruel.' And there is a savour of cant, perhaps, in the assurance to poor wronged Octavia that

> . . . the high gods
> To do you justice, make their ministers
> Of us and those that love you.

But one may poke fun at a Lepidus with safety; and righteousness—even self-righteousness—is an asset in public life. In sum, he knows the purblind world for what it is, and that it will be safer in his hands than in a greater man's. And while this is so, does it become us, who compose that world, to criticise him very harshly?

Enobarbus [1]

When at last this good friend turns traitor Antony says remorsefully:

[1] Enobarbus, it is worth remarking, is wholly Shakespeare's own, with nothing owed to Plutarch but the incident of the restored treasure and the (altered) name.

224

> O, my fortunes have
> Corrupted honest men! . . .

And Enobarbus himself very early shows a sense of some small part of the corruption:

> Mine and most of our fortunes to-night shall be—drunk to bed.

His is the tragedy of cynic mind coupled with soft heart, a tragedy of loyalty to something other than the best one knows.

He is a misogynist confessed, and his talk about women is brutal. Misogyny is recognised armour for a soft-hearted man. But he is as plain-spoken about men, and to their faces besides; nor sparing of himself. Nor is this mere bombast. He sees these chaffering traders in the event as they truly are, and further into consequences than do any of them. Antony is his master, and when things go ill he does his best to save him; but good sense and plain speaking will not serve. So far he is a simple variant of the outspoken, honest, disillusioned fellow, a type very useful to the dramatist lacking a chorus; Shakespeare has found it so often enough.

But Enobarbus is not all prose and fault-finding. The rhapsody upon Cleopatra stands out significantly; and when, later, the disintegrating rays of his mind turn inward, they discover him to himself a part and a victim of this time-serving world that he so scorns. It is in the process of his lapse from loyalty, in his sudden collapse from cynicism to pitifulness, that we find Shakespeare's maturer mind and art.[1] We see the moral self-destruction

---

[1] This minor tragedy is worked out in a few asides. It is done, as it seems, very casually, but it shows what can be

of the man upon whom no man's weakness has imposed, and the completing of a figure of far subtler purport than the conventional, plain blunt image which, at a too careless glance, he may seem to be.

The competent soldier rages against Antony's blundering. But when, with the rest, he could save himself from its consequences, he will not. He chooses the losing side, though his reason ' sits in the wind ' against him.

> The loyalty well held to fools does make
> Our faith mere folly.   Yet he that can endure
> To follow with allegiance a fall'n lord,
> Does conquer him that did his master conquer,
> And earns a place i' the story.

This is strange doctrine for an admitted cynic. Then he argues back and forth as things go from bad to worse; at last cold reason conquers, and he rats. It is too late now; and he is but half-hearted in treason. We next see him standing silent, aloof, ignored by the sufficient Cæsar—and not sorry to be. Then Antony, by one simple, generous gesture of forgiveness, breaks his heart.

There is excellent irony in his end. That the rough-tongued, thick-skinned Enobarbus, of all men, should expire sentimentally, by moonlight, of a broken heart! But the superficial effect is not

---

done with thrifty skill in the freedom of the Elizabethan stage; divorced from this, it will be ineffective, probably. It is worth remarking that the asides might well, most of them, be joined up into a long soliloquy; and by Shakespeare's earlier method they probably would be. But by parcelling the matter out he preserves the unity and prominence of the main action, and keeps it flowing on. And the whole episode, in its detached quietness, helps to throw Antony's vociferation into high relief.

226

all. Thus ends another unbalanced man; and whether the inequity lies between passion and judgment as with Antony, or, more covertly, as with Enobarbus, between the armoured and the secret self, there was tragedy prepared. And we have seen the waste of a man. For this it is to bring sound sense and loyalty into the service of the Antonys of the world. With blind folly to serve, loyalty and good sense must come to odds; then one will oust the other, and master and man and cause go down in disruption.

Pompey, Lepidus, and the rest

If in a scheme of things so warped by passion, jealousy and self-seeking, the robust Enobarbus is broken, how shall such weaklings as Pompey and Lepidus survive? ' Fool Lepidus ' is doomed from the start. He must be everybody's friend; and, while the patching up of quarrels is in train, who more useful than this mind-mannered little man, with his never-failing, deprecating tact, his perfect politeness.[1] Cæsar condescends to him with scarcely veiled contempt.

> . . . 'tis time we twain
> Did show ourselves i' the field. . . .

But the ' twain ' are Antony and Cæsar; Lepidus, the ' poor third ' (as Eros calls him later), counts for nothing. The colleagues ' Sir ' each other in this scene, we notice, with suspicious courtesy. There is a touch of mockery in Cæsar's. Later, the generous Antony pays him compensation for one quite undeserved snub. The little man has

---

[1] One sees him, for the play's purposes, physically also, as a little man.

started off the critical debate with Cæsar by a reconciling speech, his only eloquent effort:

> . . . then, noble partners,
> The rather for I earnestly beseech,
> Touch you the sourest points with sweetest terms
> Nor curstness grow to the matter.

and thereafter is so ready—yet never too ready— with cooing interjections, all ignored. Difficulties resolved, he does mildy assert himself; but Cæsar still ignores him, and is departing. Whereupon Antony:

> Let us, Lepidus,
> Not lack your company.
> Noble Antony,
> Not sickness should detain me.

The little man is grateful.

He cannot carry his liquor, and they laugh at him for that. And all but the last we hear of him is in the mocking duet between Agrippa and Enobarbus.[1]

Agrippa.	'Tis a noble Lepidus.
Enobarbus.	A very fine one: O how he loves Cæsar!
Agrippa.	Nay, but how dearly he adores Mark Antony!
Enobarbus.	Cæsar? Why he's the Jupiter of men!
Agrippa.	What's Antony? The god of Jupiter.
Enobarbus.	Spake you of Cæsar? How! the nonpareil!
Agrippa.	O Antony! O thou Arabian bird!
Enobarbus.	Would you praise Cæsar, say ' Cæsar '; go no further.
Agrippa.	Indeed, he plied them both with excellent praises.
Enobarbus.	But he loves Cæsar best: yet he loves Antony: Hoo! hearts, tongues, figures, scribes, bards, poets cannot

---

[1] Shakespeare also throws him into contact with Enobarbus for a brief exchange before the reconciling of Cæsar and Antony begins, and the smoothness and roughness make an illuminating contrast.

228

> Think, speak, cast, write, sing, number—hoo!—
> His love to Antony.   But as for Cæsar;
> Kneel down, kneel down and wonder.

He comes to no heroic end.   Cæsar stows him away somewhere, as one puts a pair of old boots in a cupboard.

> . . . the poor third is up, till death enlarge his confine.

It is a sketch of a mere sketch of a man; but done with what skill and economy, and how effectively placed as relief among the positive forces of the action!   Shakespeare (as dramatist) had some slight affection for the creature too.   For a last speech, when Octavia is tearfully taking leave as she sets forth with her Antony, he gives him the charming

> Let all the number of the stars give light
> To thy fair way.

Should one call Pompey a weakling?   He makes a gallant show; but we suspect from the first that facile optimism:

> I shall do well:
> The people love me and the sea is mine;
> My powers are crescent, and my auguring hope
> Says it will come to the full . . .

And in a moment we are finding him out.   Bad news must be denied; and when it persists, and there is no doubt that the Triumvirs, all three, are to be in the field against him, why,

> . . . let us rear
> The higher our opinion, that our stirring
> Can from the lap of Egypt's widow pluck
> The ne'er lust-wearied Antony.

229

The scene ends with an empty flourish;

> Be't as our gods will have't! It only stands
> Our lives upon to use our strongest hands.

Pompey is full of flourishes; for he seems to be conscious of a certain intellectual hollowness within him, he whistles to keep his followers' courage up, and his own.

He is a great man's son. He must not forget it, for no one else will, and there is a certain debility in this. He makes peace discreetly, is magniloquent, scores a verbal point or so; no one may say he is over-awed. Then comes Menas' offer to cut the throats of his new allies and make him lord of the world; and he answers

> Ah, this thou shouldst have done
> And not have spoke on't. In me 'tis villainy;
> In thee't had been good service. Thou must know
> 'Tis not my profit that does lead mine honour;
> Mine honour, it.

These gallant gentlemen who look to their honour to profit them, and will profit by other men's dishonour! When the Cæsars of the world override them, the world loses little, one must confess. Pompey fades out of the play. To fit him with an appropriate metaphor, he carries too much sail for his keel.

Relays of minor characters, each with a life of its own, help keep the play alive. Shakespeare's fertility in this kind is here at its full; but so forthright is the work that the action is never checked, each character answers its purpose and no more. Nothing very startling about any of them, nothing very memorable as we look back; but this is as it should be, they are accompaniment to the theme, and, at their liveliest, should never distract us from it. Demetrius and Philo, soldiers ingrain, move for a moment in contrast, make their indignant protest against epicene Egypt and Antony in its toils; they have served their purpose, and we see them no more. The soothsayer does his mumbo-jumbo, a peculiar figure; and Egypt and what it stands for will flash back to us when we see him, in Roman surroundings, again. The messengers are conventional figures merely; but Shakespeare gives to the person of each one the weight that belongs to his errand, and so augments the strength of the scene. Menecrates and Menas come out of Plutarch as famous pirates. Menas sustains the character most colourfully (and his admittance to distinguished company may throw a little light upon the Elizabethan conscience in this matter), but Menecrates is needed to offer a sententious check to Pompey's soaring confidence.

> We, ignorant of ourselves,
> Beg often our own harms, which the wise powers
> Deny us for our good; so find we profit
> By losing of our prayers.

A philosophic pirate, indeed; and we may see, if we will, the more pragmatic Menas, chafing, but scornfully silent in the background.

Agrippa and Mæcenas hover after Cæsar to the end, putting in the tactful word—which ripens to flattery, we notice, the minute he is secure in power. Such men, of such a measure, are always forthcoming. Shakespeare once spices their utility with the humour of their hanging back to hear the latest Egyptian scandal from Enobarbus; they are glee-fully shocked by the eight wild boars at a breakfast

231

and the goings on of that royal wench Cleopatra.
Their names apart, there is no history in them, of
course. Ventidius, with good dramatic reason,
dominates a single scene; and Eros, Thidias,
Scarus, Dolabella and the others give vigour and
variety to incident upon incident. They and the
rest of the incidental characters, provide, one might
say, a fluid medium of action with which the
stronger colours of the play may be mixed.

Of Charmian and Iras there is rather more to
be said. They attend upon Cleopatra and she
puts them in the shade; but Shakespeare has
touched them in with distinct and delicate care.
To give them betimes a little importance of their
own we have the scene with the soothsayer with
the irony of its prophecy.

> . . . find me to marry with Octavius Cæsar,
> and companion me with my mistress.

laughs Charmian. And he answers her

> You shall outlive the lady whom you serve.

So she does, by one minute!
Thereafter the two of them decorate the
Egyptian scenes; deft and apt, poised for their
mistress's call. Iras is the more fragile, the
more placid; Charmian, the 'wild bedfellow,'
will be the quicker of her tongue, when a word
may be slipped in. It is an impudent tongue, too;
she has no awe of her betters. Worthless little
trulls, no doubt! But when disaster comes, and
Antony's men, all save one, make their peace with
the conqueror, for these two there is no question.
They also see what lies behind Cæsar's courtesy;

232

and the timid, silent Iras suddenly breaks silence
with

> Finish, good lady; the bright day is done,
> And we are for the dark.

—revealing herself in a majesty of spirit of her own.
Another moment and she is trembling again; one
would think she could hardly carry her share of the
heavy robe and crown.   Her service consummated
by her mistress's kiss, she dies, as the people of
the East can, so they say, by pure denial of life.
Charmian, we know, is of fiercer breed.   Quick,
desperate, agonised, sticking to her task to the
end—when all is over she is at it still, fighting
her queen's battles still, mocking the enemy.   She
laughs in triumph as she too dies.

CYMBELINE

CYMBELINE is said to have been a product, probably the first, of Shakespeare's leisured retirement to Stratford. Professor Ashley Thorndike thinks it was written in emulation of Beaumont and Fletcher's successful *Philaster*. There are signs that it was intended for the ' private ' theatre of the Blackfriars. More than one editor has scented a collaborator; the late Dr. Furness, in particular, put many of the play's weaknesses to this account.

The Folio labels it tragedy, but it is not; it is tragi-comedy rather, or romance. Through treachery and mischance we move to a providentially happy ending. Repentance for wrong done, and then

> Pardon's the word to all.

is the moral outcome, two of the least pardonable characters having conveniently been despatched beyond human pardon's reach. In which digest of charitable wisdom—and the easing of the occasion for it—we may see if we will a certain leisured weariness of mind. The signs of association with the Blackfriars must be looked into carefully when we come to consider the play's staging, if for no other reason than that here was a theatre far liker to our own than the open-air Globe. As for collaboration; we shall not deny Imogen to Shakespeare, nor Iachimo, the one done with such delight, the other, while he sways the plot, with exceeding skill. Here is not the master merely, but the past-master working at his ease. Much besides seems to bear his stamp, from Cloten to that admirable gaoler. Was he as content, in his leisure, to set his stamp on such a counterfeit as the dissembling tyrant Queen? There is a slick professional competence about the writing of her, one may own. And how far is he guilty of the inepter lapses, of which the play is undeniably full?

It is pretty poor criticism (Dr. Furness owns it) to fasten all the faults upon some unknown collaborator and allow one's adored Shakespeare all the praise. Lackeying of that sort leads us first to the minor, then, if we are not careful, into the larger lunacies. Better take shelter behind Johnson, who, like a schoolmaster with cane in hand, sums up his indignation in one tremendous sentence and lets his author—this author, when need be, as well as another—know that he, at any rate, will not ' waste criticism upon unresisting imbecility, upon faults too evident for detection, and too gross for aggravation.' Johnson was spared the dilemmas of modern research. He would not have taken kindly to our armament of the hair sieve. Nor would he ever have subscribed, one feels sure, to the convenience of a whipping-boy, whatever other tribute he might pay to Shakespeare's majesty. Still, even he approves Pope's opinion—for he quotes it—that the apparitions of the Leonatus family and the jingle they speak were ' plainly foisted in afterwards for meer show, and apparently [are] not of Shakespear.'

How much further must we go? The apparitions and their rubbish—

> When once he was mature for man,
> In Britain where was he
> That could stand up his parallel,
> Or fruitful object be
> In eye of Imogen, that best
> Could deem his dignity?

—are not only, one swears, not Shakespeare's, but could hardly have been perpetrated even by the perpetrator of the worst of the rest of the play. One searches for a whipping-boy to the whipping-boy; the prompter, possibly, kept in between rehearsal and performance, thumping the stuff out and thumbing it down between bites and sips of his bread and cheese and ale.

But Furness quotes a round dozen of passages besides, which he declares Shakespeare never, never could have written; and they all, or nearly all, have certainly a very tinny ring. Did the author of *King Lear* and *Antony and Cleopatra* descend to

> Triumphs for nothing and lamenting toys
> Is jollity for apes and grief for boys.

or to

> Th' imperious seas breed monsters, for the dish,
> Poor tributary rivers as sweet fish?

But he also, we notice, will have nothing to do—on Shakespeare's behalf—with

> Golden lads and lasses must
> Like chimney sweepers, come to dust.

and he rejects Belarius altogether on the grounds, mainly, that the old gentleman's demand to be paid twenty years' board and lodging for the children he had abducted touches turpitude's lowest depths. But this surely is to deny even the whipping-boy a sense of pleasantly whimsical humour. It is hard to follow Furness all the way. There are, however, other directions in which we can look for this collaborator or inter-polator; and we may possibly find, besides, a Shakespeare, who, for the moment, is somewhat at odds with himself.

THE NATURE OF THE PLAY

If the play's construction is his unfettered work he is at odds with himself indeed. From the beginning he has been a good craftsman, and particularly skilful in the manœuvring of any two stories into a symmetrical whole. But here the attempt results in a very lop-sided affair. The first scene sees both themes stated: Imogen's marriage to Posthumus, and the strange loss, years before, of her brothers. Then Iachimo's intrigue against her is pursued and completed, most expeditiously; the entire business is done in less than twelve hundred lines, with Cloten and his wooing thrown in. But meanwhile we see nothing, and hear only once, of the young princes. Certainly Imogen cannot set out on her wander-ings and encounter them any sooner than she does; and, once she does, this part of the story—it is the phase of the blending of the two stories, and customarily would be the penultimate phase of the plot as a whole—makes due progress. But what of Posthumus? He is now banished from the scene for the space of another fourteen hundred lines or so. That is bad enough. But when he

does return to it, the only contrivances for his
development are a soliloquy, a mute duel with
Iachimo, a quite undramatic encounter with an
anonymous ' Lord,' a talk with a gaoler, and a
pointless pageant that he sleeps through. This is
far worse. He was never much of a hero, but
here he becomes a bore. The difficulties are
plain. Once his faith in Imogen is destroyed
and he has commanded her murder (and we do
not need both to see him sending the command
and Pisanio receiving it) there is nothing left for
him to do till he returns repentant; and once he
returns he cannot openly encounter any of the
more important characters, or the dramatic effect
of his sudden appearance in the last scene (and to
that, in its elaboration, every thread, obviously,
is to be drawn) will be discounted. But it is
just such difficulties as these that the playwright
learns to surmount. Can we see Shakespeare,
past-master in his craft, making such a mess of a
job? If nothing else showed a strange finger in
the pie, this letting Posthumus slip from the current
of the story, and the clumsiness of the attempt to
restore him to prominence in it, should suffice to.
Nevertheless, Shakespeare's stamp, or an excellent
imitation of it, is on much of the actual writing
hereabouts. One would not even swear him
entire exemption from the apparitions.

> Poor shadows of elysium, hence, and rest
> Upon your never-withering banks of flowers:
> Be not with mortal accidents opprest;
> No care of yours it is; you know 'tis ours.
> Whom best I love I cross; to make my gift
> The more delay'd, delighted. . . .

That, though pedestrian, is, for the occasion, good
enough.

These structural clumsinesses concern the last two-thirds of the play. The passages that Furness gibbets—the most and the worst of them—fall there too; and there we may find, besides, minor banalities of stagecraft, set as a rule in a poverty of writing, the stagecraft and writing both showing a startling change from the opulently thrifty methods that went to the making of *Coriolanus*, *Antony and Cleopatra*, *King Lear*, *Othello*, this play's predecessors.

Are we to debit the mature Shakespeare with the dramatic impotence of Pisanio's soliloquy:

> I heard no letter from my master since
> I wrote him Imogen was slain: 'tis strange:
> Nor hear I from my mistress, who did promise
> To yield me often tidings; neither know I
> What is betid to Cloten, but remain
> Perplex'd in all. The heavens still must work.
> Wherein I am false I am honest; not true, to be true.
> These present wars shall find I love my country,
> Even to the note o' the king, or I'll fall in them.
> All other doubts, by time let them be clear'd:
> Fortune brings in some boats that are not steer'd.

It is poor stuff; the information in it is hardly needed; it does not seem even meant to provide time for a change of scene or costume. Nor does Shakespeare now use to let his minor characters soliloquise to help his plots along.[1] There are two

---

[1] The writing of the rest of this scene is poverty itself (in fact, from Lucius' rescue of Imogen, just before, to the beginning of the long last scene of revelation, there is—except for the character of the gaoler—marked deterioration of writing). The First Lord's

> So please your majesty,
> The Roman legions, all from Gallia drawn,
> Are landed on your coast, with a supply
> Of Roman gentlemen by the senate sent.

about touches bottom. Sheridan's burlesquing in *The Critic* has more life in it.

other such soliloquies: the Queen's rejoicing over Imogen's disappearance, rising to its forcible-feeble climax with

>   . . . gone she is
> To death or to dishonour; and my end
> Can make good use of either: she being down,
> I have the placing of the British crown.

This is nearly as redundant in matter; but villainy has its rights, and premature exultation over the misfortunes of the virtuous is one of them. Though it be Shakespeare at his worst, it may still be Shakespeare. So, more certainly, is the Second Lord's soliloquy, with which Cloten's second scene ends. This probably owes its existence to Imogen's need of a little extra time for getting into bed. But it adds information, and, more importantly, reiterates the sympathy of the Court for her in her trouble. It falls earlier in the play; in the stretch of the action that few will deny to be wholly Shakespeare's.

But, quality of writing and the unimportance of the speakers apart, is there not a curious artlessness about nearly all the soliloquies in the play? They are so frankly informative. Shakespeare's use of the soliloquy is no more subject to rule than are any other of his methods; but his tendency, as his art matures, is both to make it mainly a vehicle for the intimate thought and emotion of his chief characters only, and to let its plot forwarding seem quite incidental to this. *Antony and Cleopatra*, a play of action, contains few soliloquies, and they are not of dominant importance ; Coriolanus, the man of action, is given hardly one; Hamlet, the reflective hero, abounds in them, but they are germane to idea rather than story. Iago's solilo-

240

quies, it may be said, frankly develop the plot. It will be truer to say they forecast it; the dramatic justification for this being that it is, in both senses, a plot hatched in his own brain.[1]   And we notice that once it is well under way he soliloquises no more.

But in *Cymbeline*, what a disintegrating change! Posthumus' soliloquies are reflectively emotional enough.   The first is an outburst of rage; it would not, one supposes, have been any differently framed for Othello or Antony.   The others contain such simply informative passages as

> I am brought hither
> Among the Italian gentry, and to fight
> Against my lady's kingdom. . . .
> I'll disrobe me
> Of these Italian weeds, and suit myself
> As does a Briton peasant. . . .

as the seemingly needless

> . . . I have resumed again
> The part I came in. . . .

And one asks, without being quite sure of the answer, how far is that

> You married ones,
> If each of you should take this course, how many
> Must murder wives much better than themselves,
> For wrying but a little! . . .

meant to be addressed plump to his audience?   But the flow of emotion is generally strong enough to sweep any such obstacles along.

Iachimo passes from the dramatic perfection of

---

[1] Edmund's soliloquies in *King Lear* come into the same category.

the soliloquy in the bedchamber to the feebleness
of his repentant

> Knighthoods and honours, borne
> As I wear mine, are titles but of scorn.
> If that thy gentry, Britain, go before
> This lout as he exceeds our lords, the odds
> Is that we scarce are men and you are gods.

—with which we hesitate to discredit Shakespeare
in any case.

But what of that not merely ingenuously
informative, but so *ex post facto* confidence from
Belarius :

> O Cymbeline! heaven and my conscience knows
> Thou didst unjustly banish me : whereon,
> At three and two years old I stole these babes,
> Thinking to bar thee of succession as
> Thou reft'st me of my lands.   Euriphile,
> Thou wast their nurse, they took thee for their mother,
> And every day do honour to her grave.
> Myself, Belarius, that am Morgan called,
> They take for natural father.

We shall have to search far back in Shakespeare's
work for anything quite so apparently artless, and
may be doubtful of finding it even there.   Furness
would make the collaborator responsible for Belarius.   But what about the long aside—a soliloquy,
in effect—by which Cornelius lets us know that the
Queen is not to be trusted, and that the poison
he has given her is not poison at all?   This is
embedded in the admittedly Shakespearean part
of the play.

The soliloquies apart, when we find Imogen-
Fidele, welcomed by Arviragus-Cadwal with

> I'll make 't my comfort
> He is a man: I'll love him as my brother. . . .

then glancing at him and Guiderius-Polydore and exclaiming

> Would it had been so, that they
> Had been my father's sons.

and when the trick by which Cloten must be dressed in Posthumus' garments (so that Imogen waking by his corpse may mistake it) is not glossed over but emphasised and advertised, here, we feel, is artlessness indeed. But it is obviously a sophisticated, not a native artlessness, the art that rather displays art than conceals it.[1]

A fair amount of the play—both of its design and execution—is pretty certainly not Shakespeare's.[2] Just how much, it is hard to say (though the impossible negative seems always the easier to prove in these matters), for the suspect stuff is often so closely woven into the fabric. It may have come to him planned as a whole and partly written. In which case he worked very thoroughly over what are now the Folio's first two acts. Thereafter he gave attention to what pleased him most, saw Imogen and her brothers and Cloten through to the end, took a fancy to Lucius and gave him reality, did what more he could for Posthumus under the circumstances, generously threw in the First Gaoler, and rescued Iachimo from final futility. This relieves him of responsibility for the poor planning of the whole; he had been able to re-fashion the first part to his liking. But why, then, should he leave so many of the last part's ineptitudes in place? Or did the

[1] For a similar artlessness of method, compare the Prospero-Miranda, Prospero-Caliban scenes in *The Tempest*, by which the story is told.

[2] Both more and less, I myself feel, than Furness allows to be.

243

unknown cling affectionately to them, or even put
them back again after Shakespeare had washed
his hands of the business? We are dabbling now,
of course, in pure ' whipping-boy ' doctrine, and
flaws enough can be found in it. Of the moments
of ' unresisting imbecility ' Shakespeare must be
relieved; careless or conscienceless as he might
sometimes be, critical common sense forbids us to
saddle him with them. But, trying his hand at a
new sort of thing (emulating Beaumont and
Fletcher and their Philaster—why not?—he had
never been above taking a hint), and if, moreover,
he was trying it ' by request ' in hard-won leisure
at Stratford, his grip might easily be looser than
usual. We find him with a firmer one, that
is certain, in *A Winter's Tale* and *The Tempest*.
Allowing, then, for some collaboration, and some
incertitude besides, at what, are we to suppose, is
he aiming, what sort of play is he setting out to
write? And if the sophisticated artlessness is his,
what end is this meant to serve? These are the
practical questions to be answered here.

He has an unlikely story to tell, and in its
unlikelihood lies not only its charm, but largely
its very being; reduce it to reason, you would
wreck it altogether. Now in the theatre there
are two ways of dealing with the inexplicable.
If the audience are to take it seriously, leave it
unexplained. They will be anxious—pathetically
anxious—to believe you; with faith in the dose,
they will swallow a lot. The other plan is to show
one's hand, saying in effect: Ladies and gentlemen,
this is an exhibition of tricks, and what I want you
to enjoy among other things is the skill with which I
hope to perform them. This art, which deliberately

244

displays its art, is very suited to a tragi-comedy, to the telling of a serious story that must yet not be taken too seriously, lest its comedy be swamped by its tragedy and a happy ending become too incongruous. Illusion must by no means be given the go-by; if this does not have its due in the theatre, our emotions will not be stirred. Nor should the audience be overwhelmed by the cleverness of the display; arrogance in an artist antagonises us. This is where the seeming artlessness comes in; it puts us at our ease, it is the equivalent of 'You see there is no deception.' But very nice steering will be needed between the make-believe in earnest and in jest.

Shakespeare sets his course (as his habit is, and here we may safely assume that it is he) in his very first scene. We have the immediately necessary tale of Posthumus and Imogen, and the more extraordinary one of the abducting of the princes is added. And when the First Gentleman brings the Second Gentleman's raised eyebrows down with

> How soe'er 'tis strange. . . .
> Yet is it true, sir.

we of the audience are asked to concur in the acquiescent

> I do well believe you.

For 'this,' Shakespeare and the First Gentleman are telling us, 'is the play you are about to hear; and not only these facts, but their rather leisurely amplifying, and that supererogatory tale of Posthumus' birth, should show you the sort of play it is. There is trouble in the air, but you are not to be too strung up about it. Moreover, the way you are being told it all, the easy fall of this verse, with its light endings and spun-out sentences, should be wooing you into the right mood. And this talk about Cassibelan is to help send you back into a fabulous past in which these romantic things may legitimately happen. So now submit yourselves, please, to the illusion of them.'

The beginning, then—quite properly—inclines to make-believe in earnest, rendering to the theatre its normal due. And the play's story will follow its course, nor may any doubt of its likelihood be hinted; that is a point of dramatic honour. But in half a hundred ways, without actually destroying the illusion, Shakespeare can contrive to prevent us taking it too seriously.

Cornelius lets us know at once that the poison is not poison; for, monster though the Queen is, we must not fear tragedy of that stark sort to be impending. We must be interested in watching for the working out of the trick played upon her, and amused the while that

> She is fool'd
> With a most false effect . . .

There is a subtler aim in the artlessness of Belarius' soliloquy. By accepting its frank familiarity we become, in a sense, Shakespeare's accomplices. In telling us the story so simply he is at the same time saying ' You see what a very simple business this playwriting is; take it, please, no more seriously than I do.' The stressing of the coincidence of the meeting of the sister and her lost brothers has a like effect. We feel, and we are meant to feel, ' What a pretty fairy-tale ! ' The emphasising of the artifice, the ' folly of the fiction,' by which Cloten's corpse comes to be

246

mistaken for Posthumus' does much to mitigate the crude horror of the business, to bring it into the right tragi-comic key. Keep us intrigued by the preparations for the trick, and we shall gain from its accomplishment a half-professional pleasure; we shall be masters of the illusion, not its victims. And throughout the whole elaborate scene of revelation with which the play ends we are most artfully steered between illusion and enjoyment of the ingenuity of the thing. We hold all the clues; the surprises are for Cymbeline, Imogen, Posthumus and the rest, not for us. We soon foresee the end, and our wits are free to fasten on the skill of the approach to it. But there is an unexpected turn or so, to provide excitement; and the situation is kept so fully charged with emotion that our sympathy is securely held.

This art that displays art is a thing very likely to be to the taste of the mature and rather wearied artist. When you are exhausted with hammering great tragic themes into shape it is a relief to find a subject you can play with, and to be safely able to take more interest in the doing than the thing done. For once you can exercise your skill for its own sake. The pretty subject itself seems to invite a certain artlessness of treatment. But the product will have a sophisticated air about it, probably.

THE BLACKFRIARS AND ITS INFLUENCE

Whether the style of the play—out of whatever combination of circumstances this was compacted —owes anything (and, if so, what) to its probable connection with the Blackfriars, it is not much easier to determine; for our knowledge of the stage there, and the degree of its difference from the Globe's, is still much in the realm of guess-work.

Cymbeline must be dated about 1610. It was in 1609 that the King's Men first went to act in these quieter, candle-lit surroundings. They did not desert the Globe, which remained their summer quarters; a successful play would be seen there also. The open-air theatres stayed in use for another thirty years, and the old audiences had still to be catered for. But critical opinion would now come to centre, taste to be dictated at the Blackfriars; and the dramatists attached there would have to consider what sort of work made most effect in these changed conditions. Beaumont and Fletcher may have scored an early hit with *Philaster* [1] and so (if theatre managers of yesterday were as managers of to-day, and possibly they were) set a fashion which would be hastily followed. But sooner or later, a specifically indoor drama must have developed. The change would come slowly, and not very certainly. There would be reaction against it. The elder dramatists might no more take kindly to it than would the old audience when they saw its new effects show up a little pallidly, perhaps, in the sunlight at the Globe. But the shifting from outdoors in made all the difference, finally. Our drama of to-day, with its scenic illusion, its quiet acting, its gains in subtlety and loss in power, was born, not upon the platforms of the inn-yards, but of the patronage and prosperity that produced the private theatre.

[1] They had already written a play or two for the Paul's children and their indoor theatre.

Not that indoor performances were a novelty. The children had always played indoors. Such a man as Lyly had written exclusively for them, and other dramatists gave them plays that might differ little, or not at all, from those provided for their elders. But a boy Tamburlaine could ' holla ' his loudest and yet break no windows; though the plays did not differ, the performances would. The adult companies had played indoors too. *A Midsummer Night's Dream* has a delicacy of fibre and the early *Love's Labour's Lost* a preciosity which may show that Shakespeare devised them for select audiences. When James's Scottish extravagance replaced Elizabeth's English thrift, Court performances were frequent. But the Globe had been the breeding ground of the greater work. *Hamlet, Othello, Lear* and *Macbeth* had come to birth there; and there force and simplicity were cardinal virtues. This was not because a slice of the audience would be uncultured (so it would be at Court), but because the theatre's every condition enhanced such virtues; the daylight, and the actors on their platform, making point-blank unvarnished appeal. Subtleties could be achieved, but they must be lodged in simple and accustomed forms; they were, as we find, thought safest and surest of effect in the comparative intimacy of the soliloquy. Scraps of scenery might come into use; but in daylight there could be nothing like scenic illusion.

What would the confined quiet of the ' private ' theatre bring? The style of the acting of the old plays would change; bad actors would not shout so much, and good actors could develop new delicacies of expression. The plots of new plays

249

might well grow more elaborate and their writing more diffuse, for it would be easier to keep an audience attentive and see that no points were missed. If violence is still the thing, noise will not be. The old clattering battles may gradually go out of favour; but processions will look finer than ever, and apparitions and the like will be twice as effective. Rhetoric will lose hold a little (to regain it when the theatres grow larger and the groundlings come to their own again) and sentiment will become as telling as passion. This would bring softer and slacker versifying, and the impetus to carry through the old powerful speeches will no longer be needed. Humour may be less brisk; the pace of the acting in general will tend to slow down. Mere tendencies, all these, with little consistency to be seen in them for a long while, and recurrent reaction against them.

One speculates upon what might have happened had Shakespeare reached London as a young man, not when he did, but a generation later, to serve his apprenticeship at the Blackfriars instead of at the Theatre, the Rose and the Curtain. As it is he is an old hand when the change comes, and will live out the rest of his life retired, more or less, from the stage. But while he still wrote for it he would remain a most practical playwright. We might look to find in his latest plays signs that he was as sensitive as the youngest to this shift of direction. If *Cymbeline* was written for the Blackfriars it may well owe a few of its idiosyncrasies to that mere fact.

THE PLAY'S FIRST STAGING

Though we do not know how the stage there differed from the Globe's (and there is much about the staging at the Globe which still keeps us guessing), that the two did differ somewhat we may be sure. 'The hall,' Sir Edmund Chambers tells us, 'was 66 ft. from north to south and 46 ft. from east to west. . . . The stage was at one end of the hall.' Not much more than 20 ft. of the whole length, then, would be spared to it. Of this, 8 or 10 ft. would be needed for back stage and passage. That would leave a main stage 10 or 12 ft. in depth, by, perhaps, the full 46 ft. in width. An awkward shape; but about 10 ft. each side would be taken up by the rows of stage stools. The practicable main stage would be, say, 12 ft. by 26. Cramped acting space, after the Globe, even if we deepen it by a foot or so. We do not know the height of the hall; but it could hardly match the Globe's three stories, which gave an upper stage, and room above that for the working of machines, and probably room above that again. On the other hand, if it were ceiled and not too lofty, the descent of deities enthroned would be an effective and fairly easy business, and the present apostrophe to Jupiter, with its

> The marble pavement closes, he is entered
> His radiant roof.

could be exactly illustrated.

While plays had to serve for both theatres, the principles (so to call them) of the Globe staging would be likely to endure, but its practice would need to be adapted to the Blackfriars material

251

conditions; and these—doors, openings, balconies—would have been dictated by the restricted space there and its different disposition. With more breadth than depth available, the inner stage opening might well be widened, both to improve the inner stage itself and to give better access from the main stage. The action upon the inner stage would in any case be more prominent with the main or front stage reduced in size. That was turning already into the 'apron' of its final metamorphosis. But if it has now been brought to a 10 or 12 ft. depth it is to suffer no further in size, nor very much in importance, for another two hundred years to come. The inner stage will be widened still more, and deepened and again deepened as opportunity serves. This, however, will be for the accommodation of scenery, and to give lighting its effect; and for long the actors will confine themselves there as little as may be.

The action of *Cymbeline* evidently makes no demands that the stage at the Globe could not quite well fulfil. But one scene, at least, would be doubly effective at the Blackfriars. It would be played at either house wholly on the inner stage. Imogen is asleep, the taper has been left burning near her. Iachimo comes softly from the trunk, steals about the room, noting all its features on his tablets, stands over her gloating. The dramatic value of all this will depend upon his expression being well seen; and the verse is written for subtle and gentle speaking. How much would not be lost on the removed inner stage of the Globe, and gained in the intimacy of the Blackfriars, where the candlelight too—the effect of it is twice emphasised—would be something more than a symbol.

One other thing about the scene should be noted. Iachimo says:

> I will write all down:
> Such and such pictures; there the window; such
> The adornment of the bed; the arras, figures,
> Why, such and such. . . .

and leaves it at that. Not till two scenes later are we—and Posthumus—given the description of the room, with its tapestry of silk and silver, its chimney

> . . . south the chamber; and the chimney-piece
> Chaste Dian bathing. . . .
>   The roof o' the chamber
> With golden cherubims is fretted: her andirons—
> I had forgot them—were two winking Cupids
> Of silver, each on one foot standing, nicely
> Depending on their brands.

The inference is plain. Whatever changes had been made at the Blackfriars, this scene was not thought to need an individual background; and Shakespeare carefully refrains from calling our attention to—something that is not there! [1]

Belarius' cave, however, is a piece of scenery of some sort. The text makes this clear.

> A goodly day not to keep house, with such
> Whose roof's as low as ours. Stoop, boys; this gate
> Instructs you how to adore the heavens. . . .

A few lines later comes a casual ' We house i' the

[1] Dramatically, as usual, he is the gainer. The Cupids and Chaste Dian and Cleopatra staring us in the face would only have distracted our attention from Iachimo. But it is excellent material for the ' madding ' of Posthumus, and the better for being freshly used.

253

rock,' but there is no definite reference to ' this
our pinching cave ' for thirty-eight lines. It
would be a conventional, decorative piece of
scenery, probably, but very obviously a cave; the
audience could not be left, for a large part of the
scene, to wonder what it was had provoked that
' Stoop, boys . . .' and the sequent moralising.

Of Jupiter we have spoken already; if he could
descend through an actual marble pavement of a
ceiling, so much the better. Posthumus' prison
seems to call for the inner stage. He would lie
down to sleep not too far back from the line of
its opening. Sicilius and the rest, entering ' *as in
an apparition*,' would probably come through curtains (very probably through slits in them) behind
him. ' *They circle Posthumus round as he lies sleeping* '
means, I think, that they stand, not march, round
him.[1] When Jupiter descends, he can hardly
come all the way down. As a god he must hold
the centre of the stage ; and if he did come all the
way he would then obliterate the sleeping Posthumus, who, for decorative reasons (important
when apparitions are in hand), would almost
certainly be in the centre, too. Besides, godhead
is less impressive on the ground; nor does any
one want to lower those machines further than
need be—they are tricky things. He might stay
suspended in mid-air; but he would be terribly
likely to swing about. His best resting-place
would be the upper stage. It is just possible that,
at the Blackfriars, this may not have been the

---

[1] ' With music before them,' read in conjunction with
' after other music,' becomes a careless phrase for music
played before they enter. It cannot imply attendant apparitions performing upon recorders. Cf. p. 267.

254

inconvertible, railed, low-roofed balcony which we commonly imagine for the public theatres. A deep gallery above the inner stage, not more than 8 or 10 ft. up, with its centre open, or able to open, to the ceiling, would answer this particular purpose very well. No other use, we notice, is made of the upper stage throughout the play; [1] Cloten even serenades Imogen at her door, instead of beneath her window.

The comprehensive last scene asks for the full extent of main and inner stage together, especially if Posthumus' listening ' behind ' is to be made effective. The first gaoler's soliloquy—if he is to speak it on the main stage with the inner stage curtains closing behind him—may have been put in to make time for the shifting of the pallet upon which Posthumus had been lying.[2] For the rest of the action, inner stage, outer stage, and the two doors we know of function normally enough.

THE STYLE OF THE PLAY

With furnishing and costume comes the problem —if we choose to make it one—of the play's anachronisms. But why make it one? No such difficulty exists as in *Antony and Cleopatra*, over the

---

[1] Nor is any use made of it in *A Winter's Tale*; nor, apparently, in *The Tempest*, except upon one occasion, when the stage direction reads, instead of the usual *above*, ' *Prospero on the top* (*invisible*).' One must not base too much upon carelessly written stage-directions; one must remember, too, that stage terminology is not exact. But a systematic study of them in the plays that can be safely held to have been written for the Blackfriars will do much to tell us what the stage there was like; and the knowledge is needed.

[2] But here the question of act division is involved. This is discussed on p. 273.

Rome and Egypt that we have learnt to see, that Shakespeare had not; nor as in *King Lear*, over a Court Fool and a topical Oswald, no longer topical to us, set unconcernedly in a barbarous scene. There one can at least contend—though it is a poor plea—for tragedy and its integrity or history and its verities; but why cultivate an archæological conscience towards *Cymbeline's* Britain and such a story as this? Shakespeare knew as well as we know that war chariots and the god Jupiter did not fit with a Posthumus made Gentleman of the King's Bedchamber, who waves his farewells with hat and glove and handkerchief, with a Cloten who fights duels and plays at bowls, a Belarius who talks of rustling at Court in unpaid-for silks, a Guiderius joking about a tailor, an Imogen disguised in doublet and hose; and—if he had stopped to think about it—that in a Rome over which Augustus Cæsar ruled, Frenchmen, Dutchmen and Spaniards would not be found discussing their country mistresses, or an Iachimo making a bet of ten thousand ducats. We commonly say he was careless about these things; it is a very fertile carelessness that shows here. For from this collection of inconsistencies emerges a quite definite picture all illuminative of the fantasy of the story. In a work of art, for what other consistency should we ask?

The style of the play; this is what, above all, its staging must elucidate, for, far more than with most plays, this is its life. Its contents may be mongrel, but it has a specific style. Set Imogen in her doublet and hose beside Rosalind or Viola and—all difference of character and circumstance allowed for—note the complete change of method;

the verse with its varied pace and stress, complex, parenthetical, a vehicle for a strange mixing of artifice and simplicity, of naked feeling and sententious fancy—the old forthright brilliance has given place to this.

It is style (nor of writing only; for writing is but half, or less, of the dramatic battle) that gives their due complexion to all the actualities of the play. Critics have exclaimed against the blinding of Gloucester in *King Lear*. Upon the face of it, Imogen's discovery of Cloten's headless corpse should be as horrible a business; more so, indeed, for much more is made of it. But, thanks to the style of its contriving, this passes unremarked.[1] The artless artifice of the preparations for the episode, this we have noted already. But much more is done in mitigation. We do not see Cloten killed; no moment of poignancy is allowed him; he vanishes bombasting and making a ridiculous fight of it. The next we see of him is his ridiculous head; and the boyish unconcern of the young savage who has slaughtered him puts us in the mood to make as little of the matter.

> This Cloten was a fool, an empty purse;
> There was no money in't: not Hercules
> Could have knocked out his brains, for he had none. . . .

Then, before the body is brought on, comes the long, tender passage of the mourning over the unconscious Fidele; and our attention is so fixed upon her, Cloten already a memory, that when she wakes beside the dummy corpse it is really not much more to us than a dummy and a pretext

[1] I have not pursued comment much beyond the pages of Furness. The outcry against the blinding of Gloucester is misguided, as I have tried to show elsewhere.

for her aria of agony. The setting of the scene, too, must have helped to rob the business of poignancy. There is one sort of realism to be gained on a bare stage and another in scenic illusion; but before a decoratively conventional cave we shall not take things too literally. The right interpretation of all this will depend upon a style of production and acting fitted to the style of the play.

Not too much emphasis, naturally, is to be placed upon so very parliamentary a war; and we notice that the stage directions for the battle are unusual.

> *Enter Lucius, Iachimo and the Romane army at one doore : and the Britaine army at another : Leonatus Posthumus following like a poore souldier. They march over and goe out. Then enter againe in skirmish Iachimo and Posthumus : he vanquisheth and disarmeth Iachimo, and then leaves him. . . . The Battaile continues, the Britaines fly, Cymbeline is taken. Then enter to his rescue, Bellarius, Guiderius, and Arviragus. . . . Enter Posthumus and seconds the Britaines. They rescue Cymbeline and exeunt. . . . Enter Cymbeline, Belarius, Guiderius, Arviragus, Pisanio and Romane captives. The Captaines present Posthumus to Cymbeline, who delivers him over to a Gaoler.*

Here is action enough, certainly. But why are there none of the accustomed directions for alarums, drums, and trumpets? And why is there such a strangely small allowance of intermediate dialogue to so much and such elaborate business? Belarius and Guiderius colour their thrusting in with a line or so, Iachimo soliloquises shortly between whiles, and Posthumus, the battle being over, is given a speech which might be modelled upon a messen-

ger's in Greek tragedy. But while fighting heroic-
ally as a peasant, and when he is brought a prisoner
to Cymbeline he utters not a word; and Cymbeline
himself stays mute as a fish, nor seems (incidentally) to recognise his son-in-law. Stage
directions make a perilous basis for argument;
and we ought, it may be, to lay these to the
account of some editor preparing the text for
printing—for the rest, there are few enough signs
of the prompt book about it. But, as it stands,
the elaborate pantomime really looks not unlike
an attempt to turn old-fashioned dumb-show to
fresh and quaint account. It is certainly not a
battle by either of the very different patterns of
Antony and Cleopatra or *Coriolanus*, nor is it at all
like the simplified affair we find in *King Lear*.
It has, one would say, a style of its own.

Then there are Jupiter and the apparitions; and
upon them hangs that highly fictitious soothsayer
with his

> The piece of tender air, thy virtuous daughter,
> Which we call ' mollis aer '; and ' mollis aer '
> We term it mulier. . . .

There are, as we noted, the (for Shakespeare)
archaic soliloquies, and such strokes of still more
deliberate artifice in this kind as that by which,
in his scene with Imogen, Iachimo is made to
speak an eight-line aside, which he intends her to
overhear. There is Belarius' ' ingenuous instrument ' sounding ' solemn music ' in that salutary
cave.

Make all the allowance we may for the vagaries
of collaboration, the result still shows strange
divergence from Shakespeare's precedent work. In
our art-jargon of to-day (or is it yesterday already?)

259

the thing is very 'amusing.' At the core of the best of it the strong dramatic pulse beats still, and the craftsman still delights in the ease of his cunning. But it is Shakespeare with a difference.

If the garment of the play's writing is artifice, the costuming of the characters must take account of it. The Mask and its fancies were in vogue at the moment. We should not ascribe too much to that; but look at those drawings by Inigo Jones, then read some of the more decorative passages— Iachimo's, for instance—of this verse and prose; there is a common fancy in both. These figures, though, must stand solidly and upon firm ground in their amorphous world. Shakespeare may play tricks with historic time, but to his own chronology—slips apart—he will be true; to his own natural history, so to speak, as well. He knows, for instance, how to etherealise nature without fantasticating the plain facts of it. When the two brothers find Fidele dead:

> Why, he but sleeps.
> If he be gone he'll make his grave a bed;
> With female fairies will his tomb be haunted,
> And worms will not come to thee. With fairest flowers,
> While summer lasts, and I live here, Fidele,
> I'll sweeten thy sad grave. Thou shalt not lack
> The flower that's like thy face, pale primrose, nor
> The azured harebell, like thy veins; no, nor
> The leaf of eglantine, whom not to slander,
> Out-sweetened not thy breath. . . .

No mannerism of costume, or of speech or behaviour must be let obscure the perfect clarity and simplicity of that.

And cheek by jowl with the jingling twaddle of the apparitions (with which no one is ready to discredit Shakespeare) we find the gaoler and his stark prose (which no one will deny him). The contrast alone makes an effect. In the morning, we must suppose, Posthumus is roused: [1]

Gaoler. Come, sir, are you ready for death?

Posthumus. Over-roasted rather; ready long ago.

Gaoler. Hanging is the word, sir; if you be ready for that, you are well cooked.

Posthumus. So, if I prove a good repast to the spectators, the dish pays the shot.

Gaoler. A heavy reckoning for you, sir. But the comfort is, you shall be called to no more payments, fear no more tavern-bills, which are often the sadness of parting, as the procuring of mirth: you come in faint for want of meat, depart reeling with too much drink; sorry that you have paid too much, and sorry that you are paid too much: purse and brain both empty—the brain the heavier for being too light, the purse too light, being drawn of heaviness: of this contradiction you shall now be quit. O, the charity of a penny cord! It sums up thousands in a trice: you have no true debitor and creditor but it; of what's past, is, and to come, the discharge: your neck, sir, is pen, book and counters; so the acquittance follows.

The elaborate pattern of this, the play upon thought and words, the sententious irony, is as sheer artifice as is the vision itself, the ' ingenuous

[1] We only suppose so because the vision should naturally occupy a night, and a criminal goes to his death at dawn. But, on the face of it, Posthumus is taken to prison, has his nap, sees his vision and is roused for execution, all within the time it takes Cymbeline to tidy himself up after the battle and return to his tent (as the editors have it), or wherever else the last scene may be supposed to take place. Yet another instance of the clumsiness of the penultimate section of the play's action. As to the contrast between the gaoler's plain prose and the decorative mystery of the apparitions, though Shakespeare did not write the jingle some of the other verse may well be his; and he was, one supposes, a consenting party to the main scheme of the scene.

instrument,' or Iachimo's overheard asides. Compare this gaoler with his cousin german Abhorson, in *Measure for Measure*. But he is a figure of crass reality, nevertheless. And further fantastication than Shakespeare has already allowed for the fitting of him into the general scheme will be his ruin. That flash of a phrase which gives him life,

> O, the charity of a penny cord!

is actuality supercharged; there is solid man summed up in it.

The problem is, then, to devise a setting and costuming which will neither eccentrically betray the humanity which is at the heart of the play nor, on the other hand, wall it round with ill-fitting exactitudes. Rome, Britain, the cave near the Severn, Cornelius and his drugs, Cassibelan and his tribute, these are decorative material to be turned to account; but to the play's peculiar account. Lucius must be a figure capable of

> A Roman with a Roman's heart can suffer.

neighboured though he is by Iachimo, described as an Italian always, from whom comes naturally enough such talk of Posthumus as

> I never saw him sad.
> There is a Frenchman his companion, one,
> An eminent Monsieur, that, it seems, much loves
> A Gallian girl at home. . . .

Cloten and Cymbeline and the Queen must be as at home in serenading and talk of knighthood and the distilling of perfumes as in argument over Mulmutius. There is no great difficulty about it once we realise that it is a problem of fancy, not

of research; and how and why it was that Shakespeare saw his Princess Imogen, first with

> All of her that is out of door most rich. . . .

then in

> A riding-suit, no costlier than would fit
> A franklin's housewife.

then dressed in

> . . . doublet, hat, hose, all
> That answer to them. . . .

(a figure quite intimately familiar to his audience,
that's to say), and yet gave her for her bed-time
prayer:

> To your protection I commend me, gods,
> From fairies and the tempters of the night
> Guard me, beseech ye!

—why he wished both to bring her as close to us
as he could, at the same time transporting her, not
to a distant world of historic fact, but into a time-
less picture-book. He has, when he needs it, his
measure of accuracy for depicting the past, though
it is not ours. The Rome of *Julius Cæsar*, *Antony
and Cleopatra* and *Coriolanus* is integrated by a very
definite purpose; and it is quite other than the
one which dictates these allusions to Sinon and
Æneas, Gallia and the Pannonians, scattered as if
from a pepper-pot, with (three several times)
fairies thrown in besides.[1]

We can divine, though dimly, one or two details
of the play's first costuming. Posthumus, when he

[1] It is needless to point out, surely, that by dressing the
play in present-day clothes we shall *not* be reproducing the
effect of the first performances. Cloten is no more to be
seen in Piccadilly to-day than he was in the streets of Lud's-
town. We only add another anachronism, which the text
does not provide for.

263

returns with the Roman army, wears distinctive
'Italian weeds,' over which he can slip (apparently) the disguise of a ' poor ' British soldier. In
this he fights Iachimo, who does not recognise
him. He then slips it off again (he is allowed
but a few seconds for either change) for the
encounter with the British Lord, who for his part
does not recognise him as an enemy. Were the
Italian weeds, then, not so very distinctive? But
neither does Cymbeline recognise him when he is
'presented' as a prisoner.[1] Possibly he is meant
to wear some sort of visored helmet. Everything hereabouts is pretty slipshod, be the blame
Shakespeare's or another's, and the audience
must borrow a blind eye from Cymbeline and
Iachimo.

And if ' Italian weeds,' had not those mute
guests of Philario's, the Dutchman and the
Spaniard, also some such distinguishing marks
about them? Either they had or, with the
Frenchman, an explanatory line or two, now lost,
must have been allotted to each. Who was to
know, otherwise, what they were? It would be
a slight, amusing touch or so; an unusual hat or
ruff, a peculiar doublet, a strange pair of breeches,
possibly. It is no great matter; another sign,
though, of the decorative bias of the play.[2]

[1] The stage direction is precise: ' *The Captains present
Posthumus to Cymbeline, who delivers him over to a Gaoler.*' If he
were recognisable the situation is too obvious not to have
been enlarged upon—even by the here suspected whipping-
boy!

[2] Cf. *The Parlement of Pratlers*, 1593, reissued by the Fan-
frolico Press, 1928.

John. God speed, Taylor.
Taylor. Welcome, sir.

If the scenic embryo of the cave is to be made the excuse for a full-fledged family of pictures of Britain and Rome, the designer of them must go warily to work. Just because he will not be flying so fully in the face of this play's stagecraft, he will be insidiously led into one temptation after another. He can fairly safely make, for Cymbeline's Court and Philario's house, the battle-field, Posthumus' prison, a tent, for the royal headquarters, a similar provision to that the cave makes for Imogen's adventures; a decorative background, that is to say, which will be in purpose no more than furniture for the action. If he goes further towards realism or illusion he will soon find himself at odds with his theme. We may now have no such elaborate painting by words and their music of this forest and its cave as forbids us to transpose the moonlit wood of *A Midsummer Night's Dream* into any other medium, nor such magic invoked as will make the best paint-and-canvas versions of *King Lear's* heath or *Macbeth's* Inverness redundant and commonplace; but realism and illusion will as surely

---

John. How many elles of sattin must I buy to make me a doublet?

Taylor. Four elles and a quarter, sir.

John. And how much velvet for my breeches?

Taylor. If you will have them made after the Spanish fashion you must have three elles and a halfe.

John. How much broad cloath must I have to make me a cloake after the Romane fashion, or a riding cloake after the Dutch maner?

Taylor. You must have little lesse than five elles and a halfe, to make one large enough for you with a coxcombado of the same cloth.

Philario, perhaps, wore a ' cloake after the Romane fashion.'

damnify the artifice in which the idiosyncrasy of this action lies. Conventional decoration may do; yet against too much of that, even, the figures of the actors will be blurred. Actors are human; they cannot conform to arbitrary design. Artifice of scene must be measured to the artifice of the play; it should remain, simply and modestly, in the shadow of it, moreover.

Nor, as we have seen, must a designer discount the description of Imogen's bedchamber, with which Iachimo whips his victim into a frenzy, by having painted us a plain picture of it in another medium first. Nor had he better bring Jupiter into a very practicable prison. Nor should he too positively define any whereabouts which the play's text leaves vague. Nor, of course, must he, whatever else he does, let any need for the shifting of his scenery obstruct the easy march of the action.

THE MUSIC

Cloten's aubade will be sung by a man or boy, and most probably to the accompaniment of a consort of viols.[1] But before its ' wonderful sweet

---

[1] It might well have been sung by the actor of Arviragus. He, we find later, is ready enough to sing the dirge over Fidele, while Guiderius' excuse for not joining him in singing it is so palpable and overcharged that we may well set it down to domestic difficulties supervening—and the whipping-boy.

> For notes of sorrow, out of tune, are worse
> Than priests and fanes that lie.

This (it sticks fast in Furness' throat) is indeed just such a pretentious piece of nonsense as a fourth-rate writer would proudly devise for the disguising of a little difficulty—making it, in the event, ten times more noticeable.

266

aire' we have 'First a verye excellent good conceyted thing,' some piece for the consort alone. A glance at the Folio text shows us why; Imogen otherwise will have but a column and a half of it in which to change from her night attire back to her princess's robes (she had had just a column of dialogue—though possibly an act pause besides—in which to prepare for bed; but undressing is a quicker business). The consort will be employed again for the *solemn musick* that comes from Belarius' 'ingenuous instrument,' and again to accompany the apparitions.

No cornets, we notice, are sounded when Cymbeline receives the Roman ambassador in state; we have already discussed the absence of drums, trumpets or alarums from the battle. This may in each case be editorial omission—or it may not.

THE PLAY'S CONSTRUCTION

The scene dividing in the Folio has not been consistently done. The editor apparently set out to mark a fresh scene at every clearance of the stage. But upon the very first page he tripped; for the two gentlemen, seeing the Queen, Imogen and Posthumus approach, will only disappear as they appear.[1] He trips again (in the other direction) when Philario and Iachimo 'exeunt' and Posthumus returns for his soliloquy,

[1] But it is, of course, possible that this effect, a commonplace upon the stage at the Globe, could not be so well contrived in the smaller space at the Blackfriars, and that therefore, to give the three important characters the full sweep of their 'entrance,' the two Gentlemen had to disappear first.

267

Is there no way for men to be, but women
Must be half-workers? . . .

and again when Guiderius and Cloten *Fight and
exeunt*. Here, in both cases, is a cleared stage,
and he gives us no scene division. Can one follow
the process of his mind? If the staging was as
we have been imagining, he has the cave before
him, and he comes to think of ' scene ' in this other
sense. But he is far from fixed in the notion; for
a while back, when Imogen entered the cave,
leaving just such a cleared stage with just such an
entrance to follow, he had marked a fresh scene.
In the other case he may have had the furniture
of Philario's house in his mind's eye.

There are signs in the text itself that the opening
or shutting of the inner stage, the drawing of its
curtains, is meant to mark change of place, and,
what is more important, that it is only done to
that end. The scheme—if it is a scheme—does
not work out with absolute consistency, but it is
worth attention.[1] From the first scene till after
Pisanio's account to Imogen of Posthumus' sailing,
when she is sent for by the Queen, there is no
change of place implied (nor lapse of time[2]).
Now we have both; for we are taken to Rome
with Posthumus already arrived there, and this

---

[1] The so-called ' alternation theory,' hard pressed by
Brodmeier and Allbright as a comprehensive rule of Elizabethan stagecraft, and (as that) pretty thoroughly exploded,
has been applied, much modified, by Professor Thorndike
to this very play and to *Antony and Cleopatra* (*Shakespeare's
Theatre*, pp. 121–5). But his arrangement, and his explanation of it, differ in some significant ways from that which
follows.

[2] The half-hour allowed Pisanio in which to see Posthumus
aboard is filled up by Cloten's first scene.

scene can best be played (though of course it need not be) with the inner stage revealed; the Dutchman and Spaniard, at any rate, will better serve such purpose as they do serve seated and in the background. We then come back to Cymbeline's Court, and, once there, neither change of place nor lapse of time is implied (nor is any furniture required; so the action can go forward on the front stage) till after Cloten's second scene and the Lord's soliloquy. By 'place,' of course, we need never understand anything more definite than a particular scene's action indicates.

The bedchamber scene now occupies the inner stage; of this there is no doubt at all. The next scene contains the aubade, and would, as certainly, be played on the outer stage. It gives ample time for the removal of the bed and Iachimo's chest, and for the re-setting of Philario's furniture, if the inner stage is to be used again for his house at Rome. There is not quite the same need for this; but certainly Philario and Posthumus *sound* like men sitting waiting (from the play's point of view) for Iachimo. There is also an interval of time to account for.

If the inner stage has been used again (furniture and all) for Philario's house there might now supposedly be some difficulty, for the next scene's first stage direction begins, ' *Enter in state, Cymbeline . . .*,' and we at once envisage the conventional throne set on the inner stage. But the direction continues :

> . . . *Cymbeline, Queene, Cloten and Lords at one doore, and at another, Caius Lucius and attendants.*

269

So that apparent difficulty is surmounted, whether purposely or by chance.[1]

There is now no change of place nor use for anything but the front stage till the introducing of Belarius, Guiderius and Arviragus discloses the cave—and the inner stage, of course. And if this ' place ' that the sight of the cave suggests is a little more generalised as forest than the ' place ' we have called Cymbeline's Court, which, in turn, was as much more generalised than Philario's house and Imogen's bedchamber, then an hypothetical plan of shifting from outer to inner stage or back only to mark change of place (and secondarily, it may be, lapse of time) works out well enough. For, Belarius and his boys departed, Pisanio and Imogen arrive.[2] They ignore the existence of the cave, as they have no use for it, but it remains in our eye as a symbol of the forest. Incidentally, the reminder that Imogen in her trouble is near her lost brothers will both sharpen and sweeten that dramatic effect.

We then return to the Court and the front stage;

[1] It could equally have been surmounted by Posthumus re-entering for his

> Is there no way for men to be, but women
> Must be half-workers? . . .

soliloquy upon the outer stage; this, indeed, he may be meant to do in any case. Moreover, the act-division, if this implied a pause, would have surmounted it. We come to that question later.

[2] Rowe, re-editing the play eighty years later, quite disregards the Folio's ' Scena Quarta ' and brings them on in this same scene, which he, the first, has labelled ' A Forest with a Cave.' He sees scenes broadly in terms of scenery; just about as broadly, rather more logically, than this editor of the Folio sees them.

then again to the forest and the cave for a long stretch of action, which is broken only by that seemingly futile fifteen-line Roman irruption of two Senators and the two Tribunes. We may observe that Imogen, after two nights wandering, is still in front of the cave. So we should put it, sitting in an 'illusionary' theatre; and then, perhaps, start to argue that she might have wandered round and round. But it was long enough before audiences granted scenery such autonomy. She was in the forest before, and here she still is; that is all the sight of the cave would testify at the Blackfriars—or the Globe.

But why are we presented (upon the front stage; and the cave will be hidden) with the paltry little episode of the Senators and Tribunes? One reason is that it will not do to let the Roman invasion lapse for too long from the story; the arrival of Lucius and his legions must be prepared for. Another is that an impression of the passing of time must be given us, between Imogen's welcome to the cave and the setting out for the morning's hunt. There is Cloten's soliloquy to serve the purpose; but if this is to be spoken with the cave in sight—as it probably should be, to 'place' him in the forest—it may not be sufficient. Here, then, would seem to be change of place employed to mark lapse of time.[1]

We probably see no more of the cave once Lucius has led the weeping Imogen away. Belarius

[1] Would not the act-division, which falls after the Senators' scene, serve? One would suppose so. Then, if this is an authentic part of the play, the little scene is upon that count redundant, and it certainly has no merits of its own. But an editor might well place an act division here to reinforce the effect of a passage of time. For the whole question see p. 273.

and the young princes could play their next scene before it. The question is, have they not been too identified with it for us not to remark, then, *their* never remarking that Cloten's body and Fidele's have vanished? With scenery still embryonic, it is upon nice points of this sort that good stagecraft would depend.

The panoramic process of the battle will pass upon the main stage (would pass more slickly if the two doors faced each other or even were askew instead of being flat in the wall). This will give ample time for the making of the inner stage into Posthumus' prison; and, after, there will be just enough, as we have seen, to clear it, so that the elaborate finale, with every character involved, can have all the space and freedom which main stage and inner stage together will afford.

There is, as we said, nothing very logical in this stagecraft. Its aim would seem to be to create impressions, definitely of a change of place, more vaguely sometimes of a lapse of time, without prompting the audience to ask how they have been created; but (if we divine it rightly) it may show us roughly what the use and wont was at the Blackfriars (and possibly for the Jacobean stage generally) in these matters, and how the old Elizabethan freedom very slowly, almost imperceptibly, contracted. For some time to come it shrinks no further. Rowe, editing the play little less than a century later, and interpreting it, as his wont was, in terms of his own theatre, does not find such stagecraft at all strange to him. He accepts the Folio's act division; and his localising of scenes involves very little change. He gives us

A Palace, Rome, A forest with a cave, A (convenient) *field between the British and Roman camps,* deduces for the finale a *Cymbeline's tent,* has a fancy for *A magnificent bedchamber;* and all this, in effect, coincides with the main stage, inner stage alternation which we have been working out.[1] Later editors, blindly turning the Folio's ' scenes ' into scenery, with their *A garden of Cymbeline's Palace, A public place, A room in Cymbeline's Palace, Another room, Before Cymbeline's Palace, An ante-chamber adjoining Imogen's apartments,* and so on and so forth, make, of course, a hash of the whole matter. The producer to-day is naturally not to be exempt from direct study of the text, and he may well prefer a closer adherence to the ways of the stage of the play's origin, when he can divine them. But if he is for something more of scenery, Rowe marks for him the limits to which he may safely go.

The Question of Act-Division

As to act-division; have we the Folio editor working by rule of thumb without warrant of what had been done in performance (that is one question), did he reproduce what had been done (that is another), did he work with a careful eye to the play's dramatic structure (that is a third), or was its very being incarnate from the beginning in these five acts? It is dangerous to dogmatise. Let us put down the pros and cons as they occur.

For what, dramatically, do the five acts of the Folio stand? The first is preparatory, and its end leaves us expectant of Iachimo's trick; in the second the trick is consummated, and for a climax and a finish

[1] I should add, perhaps, that it was worked out with no reference at all to Rowe.

we are shown its effect upon Posthumus; the third act prepares the Roman invasion, shows us Imogen falsely accused and brings her to an encounter with her unknown brothers, but it actually ends upon the anticlimax of the senators' talk with the Tribunes; the fourth act is short and has little in it but the episode of Cloten's death and Imogen's mistaking of his body (it, also, ends expectantly with the battle beginning); in the fifth act we have the rather clumsy unfolding of the battle to its issue, the spectacle in the prison, the very lengthy (it is by eighty lines the longest scene in the play) and skilful elucidation of the end. This is a fairly well proportioned arrangement; each act has its own chief interest (the last an adventitious spectacle thrown in) and bears a just relation to the whole. There is nothing inevitable about it; one could probably contrive as significant an arrangement in three acts or in four, and quite certainly shift the lines of division a little without greatly prejudicing the general effect. But this would naturally be so in a play fitted to a stage which still encourages fluidity of action; granted division, if there is a best way, there can hardly fail to be several second-best.

As to principles involved, if there were any; it is plain that act-division is not used to mark lapse of time nor change of place (is not in this play, certainly, when it so easily might be, and when scene-division, in the sense of a shifting from inner stage to centre, quite possibly is) and that while one may prefer to begin a fresh act upon a note of revived interest, the effectiveness of its end matters little. An act seems to exist in virtue of its content and of its relation to the play's scheme

274

as a whole. But, with a twofold story to be told, the content must be mixed (one part of it may be dominant, of course) and the relation to the whole can hardly be exact. The Folio's authority apart, then, it will not be very easy to know an act—so to speak—when one sees it.

As to the benefit of this act-division in performance; there is no check in the interest or march of the action between first act and second, though a pause here, as we noted, might conveniently give Imogen more time to get into bed; the third act does definitely and emphatically begin a new interest, but a pause after it robs the poor little scene between the Senators and the Tribunes of one reason for its existence. The fifth act's beginning brings Posthumus back; except for this, it could be as well begun a scene or even two scenes earlier. There is no check to the march of the story here, and its themes by now are blended.

The producer of to-day must marshal these considerations and any others that occur to him, and come to his own conclusions. The play is not passionate and precipitate in mood like *Romeo and Juliet*, nor such a simple and neatly woven affair as the *Merchant of Venice*; it will not suffer from interruption as these must do. There are, on the other hand, no dramatically effective pauses provided (nor, if we do provide them, can the audience employ them very profitably in thinking over the likelihood of the play's story); and as the tension of the action is on the slack side already, it certainly does not need more relaxing. Four prolonged intervals will be too many. Division by subject will provide two. Iachimo's plot is worked out by the end of the Folio's Act II; Imogen's flight and her adventures by the cave have a unity of their own; [1] the Folio's fifth act, with the repentant Posthumus to set it going, makes a good last division.

The Last Scene

The finer phases of the play's construction are to be seen in the swift forwarding of the first part of the story, in the subtle composition of Iachimo's three scenes (best studied in relation to him) and in the elaboration of the finale.

This last has not lacked praise. Steevens summed up its merits in one of those excellently comprehensive eighteenth-century phrases, calling it ' a catastrophe which is intricate without confusion, and not more rich in ornament than in nature '; and Barrett Wendell tells us that ' into four hundred and eighty-five lines Shakespeare has crowded some two dozen situations, any one of which would probably have been strong enough to carry a whole act.' [2] It is at any rate so important a piece of the play's economy that the producer must analyse it with care and see that its every twist and turn is given value.

A final, and often a fairly elaborate, unravelling of confusions is, of course, a commonplace of Elizabethan stagecraft. Compare this one to the endings of *Measure for Measure, Romeo and Juliet*

[1] And possibly its Scena Tertia and Scena Quarta are better tagged to this than prefixed to the last division.

[2] I quote from the footnotes of the Furness Variorum. Thorndike, on the other hand, seeing in it Shakespeare's effort to beat the young Beaumont and Fletcher at their own game, is critical and calls it ' a dénouement . . . so ingeniously intricate that it is ineffective on the stage. . . .' But was it—and will it be—upon Shakespeare's stage?

and *Othello*. It is far more elaborate in workmanship, but it hardly differs in kind. *Romeo and Juliet* ends upon anticlimax, no more is to be done and we have nothing left to learn; in *Othello*, the disclosures feed his agony, which dominates everything; in *Measure for Measure* we share the plot's secret with the Duke, but we are kept uncertain what the end will be. But here we surmise a happy ending. Our interest must be kept alive, therefore, by the strategy of its bringing about, and—the dramatic decencies observed—the more frankly we are shown how the thing is done, the better. That aspect of the scene is of a piece with the general artifice of the play's method; but something much better than mechanical skill is now put to use. Not only is the tangle of the story straightened, the characters are brought into harmony, and we, too, are reconciled to faith in their happiness.

For the scene to be effective one rule must be observed in its acting; it is a fundamental rule in all acting, strangely liable to neglect. Each actor must resolutely sustain his part through his long intervals of listening. The action is kept alive by a series of surprises—there are eighteen of them; each character in turn provides one, or is made its particular victim—and it must be *kept* alive, not saved from extinction in a series of jerks. We, who are not surprised, find our interest in watching for each turn to come, and the producer must see that each figure in the group has its point of vantage. As it is the last scene of the play each character is well known to us, and can be effective, therefore, even in silence.

The main action is preluded by the knighting of

Belarius and the two boys, by the doctor bringing
the news of the Queen's death, and the disclosure
of her villainies. Cymbeline certainly takes this
very calmly, with his ' How ended she '; ' Prithee,
say'; and his 'Proceed.'[1] But the plain fact
is that this Goneril-like lady has never been in
place in the play, and her dismissal from it is as
awkward. He seems to relapse with thankfulness
upon

> Mine eyes
> Were not in fault, for she was beautiful,
> Mine ears that heard her flattery, nor my heart
> That thought her like her seeming; it had been vicious
> To have mistrusted her.

There is the authentic note again; we are back
among golden unrealities.

The scheme of the scene begins to work with the
entrance of Lucius, Iachimo and the other Roman
prisoners; Posthumus and Imogen are among
them, disguised, unknown to each other and to the
rest.[2] The first chord struck comes from a certain
calm savagery in Cymbeline, an answering stoicism
in Lucius; this gives a firm foundation to build
on. Sentiment and emotion must not come too
soon; if the pendulum is to swing to harmony and

---

[1] Nor can we acquit him of tactlessness in his prompt
remark to Cornelius that

> . . . death
> Will seize the doctor too.

[2] ' *Leonatus behind* ' says the Folio's stage direction. His
chief disguise now is the ' Italian weeds,' and these would
hardly conceal him from Imogen. He may have some helmet
or head-dress he can throw off. But guards keep the
prisoners from mingling; and, generally speaking, there is
much goodwill in these disguises.

278

peace it must be held back for a start at the other extreme. The more effective too, in quick contrast, will be Lucius' bringing forward of the fragile Fidele and his plea for the lad to be spared, the gentle Fidele who can in an instant 'look himself' into Cymbeline's graces. The transparent

> I have surely seen him;
> His favour is familiar to me. . . .

is in the true key of the play's artifice. Yet Fidele can—it is another quick contrast—the next instant coldly turn his back on his benefactor, to that noble Roman's indignation and surprise. But we know that Imogen knows she has time enough in which to save him; and Cymbeline, plainly, is looking for an excuse to spare him. These grace-notes enrich the theme and soften its present asperity.

Then comes the puzzle of her picking upon Iachimo, and the little mystification of her walk aside with Cymbeline—which is indeed mere excuse for the dramatist to let Belarius and the brothers, on the one hand, recognise their Fidele, Pisanio, on the other, learn that Imogen is safe; artifice unashamed, but they are thus made livelier lookers-on. Then the truth—or enough of it—is wormed from Iachimo.[1] The spider must

[1] Critics dispute as to whether, and why, Iachimo is purposely embroidering his story. It is the sort of dispute that the nineteenth-century idolaters of Shakespeare particularly rejoiced in, demonstrating the master's supersubtlety by their own (doubtless to-day we err as far in other directions). But will any audience now remember the play's early scenes in such inessential detail as to be able to check his equivocations? Surely it simply is that Iachimo is 'making a story of it,' the 'Italian brain' operating as tortuously as ever, and to no purpose now. That, at any rate, is the obvious effect made; and it is a very good one.

unweave his web; and the Italian brain, operating so tortuously, sets British Cymbeline stamping with impatience: will this damned foreigner never come to the point?

But it is not, of course, upon Cymbeline chiefly that we are meant to mark the cumulative effect of the long-drawn-out confession; upon Posthumus rather, there in the background, ready for death, roused to the hearing of these horrors, mocked by this scoundrel's iterated praise of him, only so slowly seizing on the full truth; when he does, though, breaking all bounds in his agony of remorse.[1] And Imogen? The long ordeal of the telling of the story sets her before us in sharp contrast to anxious father and agonised husband both. She stands listening stonily, almost indifferently one would say. True, her good name will be cleared; but Posthumus is dead. When she heard that her life would be spared (Fidele's life, truly; Imogen's would be safe enough, but it is the surface effect which counts here) and that any boon should be hers for the asking, she had only dully responded with

> I humbly thank your highness.

When she sees the ring, it is, she says,

> . . . a thing
> Bitter to me as death.

She stands gazing dumbly at this enigmatically evil Iachimo, till Cymbeline has to urge her with

> On, speak to him.

---

[1] Iachimo does not know he is there (*Enter . . . Leonatus behind*), though in reality there was no reason he should not. This, again, is artifice.

280

Very clearly, coldly and quietly the few words
come:

> My boon is that this gentleman may render
> Of whom he had this ring.

And thereafter she stays silent. These two figures
make the centre of the dramatic picture. The
floridly gesticulating Italian, wounded and weak,
his gesture wounded too, pitiful, a little ridiculous. And Imogen, dead at heart, white and
still, gazing wide-eyed, and wondering that such
wickedness can be.

Even when Posthumus is raised from the dead
before her eyes she cannot of a sudden turn joyful,
the ice will not break so easily. The torrent of
his ecstatic self-reproach would indeed take some
stemming. He is still the manly egotist. But she,
when she can swear she is in her senses, thinks only
of him, of calming and comforting him, forgets her
disguise, but finds so inarticulate a tongue with
her

> Peace, my lord! Hear, hear—

that, his rage unspent, he turns and strikes little
Fidele to the ground. To avoid anticlimax,
Pisanio is ready (and his earlier aside has brought
him under our eye) with his

> O, gentlemen, help!
> Mine and your mistress! O, my lord Posthumus,
> You ne'er killed Imogen till now. Help, help!
> Mine honoured lady!

And so, recovered after a few tense moments from
her swoon, Imogen also stands revealed.

Consider the dramatic achievement. The
double disclosure itself is the simplest part of it,
and could well be done in half a dozen different

ways. But it is given emotional value by the slow crescendo which leads up—till the strain becomes intolerable—to Posthumus' outburst. This, when it comes, violently reverses the situation's appeal; the shock is not mere shock, it contains fresh stimulus both to interest and emotion. Our eyes have been chiefly on Imogen; she thinks Posthumus is dead, and, though we suffer with her, we know better. Now, of a sudden, our eyes are on Posthumus; he thinks Imogen is dead, and we know better. What matters far more, though, is that his outburst restores him a little to our sympathy. His moralising soliloquies will have left us cold. When a man has behaved like a wicked fool he had better not be too philosophic in repentance. Posthumus, stamping and bellowing in his despair and calling for the street dogs to be set on him, is a far more attractive figure than Posthumus reasoning out retribution with the gods.

This is the scene's dramatic pinnacle. Surmounted, and the anticlimax saved, now, by an admirable little device, the theme is resolved into its key of semi-comedy again. Imogen, waking from her swoon, finds ' old-dog ' Pisanio fussing over her; and in a flash we have

> O, get thee from my sight.
> Thou gavest me poison: dangerous fellow, hence!
> Breathe not where princes are.
> > The tune of Imogen!

cries Cymbeline. It is indeed. Doublet and hose despite, the timid Fidele has vanished in the princess, very much her royal self again.

Now twenty lines are given to quite subsidiary talk about the poison. Why? So that Posthumus

may be left standing apart, silent and shamed.[1]
He will not face her in his unworthiness. She is
watching; she understands. And in a minute,
dropping her royalty, she goes to him and puts her
arms round his neck. It is a fragile embrace; but
the man, it seems, would fall if she did not hold
him. They stand there as it might be two
wrestlers with the fortune of their love. And what
she says is one of those odd humorous things which
make reconciliation easy, and with which Shakespeare knew so well how to temper feelings too
secret and too sacred for fine words. She is half-
laughing, half-crying in her joy!

> Why did you throw your wedded lady from you?
> Think that you are upon a lock, and now
> Throw me again.

This is her forgiveness; he is man enough to take
it, and his amending is pledged with

> Hang there like fruit, my soul,
> Till the tree die.[2]

Now the second theme, the discovery of the
two princes, must be worked out; and we are
brought to it by another twenty thrifty lines,
which are chiefly given to Pisanio for his account
of the crapulous Cloten's vanishing into the forest,

[1] Or to speak by the card, the poison-story is needed for
the symmetry of the plot; the dramatist turns this to account
for the more vital business of illuminating character.

[2] Dowden is the first to give us ' lock ' in place of the
Folio's ' rock,' and no one, envisaging the business of the
scene, can doubt that he is right. This single minute or so,
felt and acted as it should be, makes the play's production
worth while. And one likes to think of the dying Tennyson,
the play in his hand opened at this very passage, one among
those he loved best.

and are capped by the little calmly-loosed thunder-
clap of Guiderius'

> Let me end the story:
> I slew him there.

—young prince and young savage in a sentence!

From now to the end the scene runs a stabler
course. Guiderius has again tuned it to dramatic
pitch and holds it there in his terse defiance
of his unknown father; the due dash of humour
added, too:

> I have spoke it, and I did it.

Cymbeline. He was a prince.
Guiderius. A most uncivil one. The wrongs he did me
Were nothing prince-like; for he did provoke me
With language that would make me spurn the sea,
If it could so roar to me. I cut off's head;
And am right glad he is not standing here
To tell this tale of mine.

Then Belarius brings his weight into the contest,
speaking, so to say, bass to the young man's tenor;
Arviragus, when the chance comes, adding his
alto, now tremulously, now bravely, he the only
one of the three to be abashed by these regalities.
The simile is permissible, for the verse takes on a
regular rhythm and full-toned harmonies. The
sententious contrast between

> . . . the art of the Court,
> As hard to keep as leave, whose top to climb
> Is certain falling, or so slippery that
> The fear's as bad as falling. . . .

and the life of honest freedom in the pinching
cave is here brought to visible issue. They con-
front each other, the noble mountaineers and the
none too noble Cymbeline. Needless to say,
Belarius' simple eloquence—not untinged, how-

ever, with very courtly respect—carries all before it.

The princes restored to their true father, it only remains to have Posthumus recognised as

> The forlorn soldier, that so nobly fought. . . .

This rounds in the story; and the moral scheme is completed by his forgiveness of Iachimo, which prompts Cymbeline in turn to spare his prisoners:

> Pardon's the word to all.[1]

One may own perhaps to a little impatience with the postscriptal Soothsayer, and the re-reading (surely once is enough!) of Jupiter's missive. We can call the whipping-boy to account if we will. These fifty lines are, in a strict view, dramatically redundant, and, at such a moment, dangerously so; this cannot be denied. Even so, there is a quaintness about the business which makes it a not unfitting finish to a charmingly incongruous play. It does not help to hold us spellbound in excitement to the end. But must we always insist on excitement in the theatre? Let the producer consider whether something—not too much—cannot be done to give the rococo symbolism of

> The lofty cedar, royal Cymbeline. . . .

and of

> . . . the Roman eagle
> From south to west on wing soaring aloft. . . .

---

[1] As Ruggles notes (I quote from the Furness Variorum), if Posthumus had not spared Iachimo when he had him down, there could have been no disclosure of his villainy. But this is perhaps to consider things a little too closely.

a significant setting.

> Laud we the gods;
> And let our crooked smokes climb to their nostrils
> From our blest altars.   Publish we this peace
> To all our subjects.   Set we forward: let
> A Roman and a British ensign wave
> Friendly together: so through Lud's-town march,
> And in the temple of great Jupiter
> Our peace we'll ratify. . . .

There need no stage directions here, at any rate, to show us Cymbeline and Lucius, Posthumus, Imogen and her brothers, Belarius, Iachimo and the rest setting out in elaborate procession; the play dissolving into pageantry.

THE VERSE AND ITS SPEAKING

The verse flows with amazing ease, and often seems the very natural rhythm of speech; yet it is set to music, in its kind, as certainly as if it were staved and barred—time, tone and all are dictated to a sensitive ear.   The first scene sees it in full swing;   The first lengthy speech is the story of Posthumus:

> I cannot delve him to the root: his father
> Was called Sicilius, who did join his honour
> Against the Romans with Cassibelan,
> But had his titles by Tenantius, whom
> He served with glory and admired success;
> So gained the sur-addition Leonatus:
> And had, beside this gentleman in question,
> Two other sons, who in the wars o' the time
> Died with their swords in hand; for which their father,
> Then old and fond of issue, took such sorrow
> That he quit being; and his gentle lady,
> Big of this gentleman, our theme, deceased
> As he was born. . . .

286

Straightforward narrative; not so mellifluous that the sound can slip in at the ear and leave the sense outside; masculine, with a few firmly finished lines, but a proportion of feminine endings to save the whole thing from sounding too clarion; the carried-over sentences give it speed; one rich unusual phrase at the beginning—

> I cannot delve him to the root:

—arrests attention; while the limpidity of

> . . . for which their father,
> Then old and fond of issue, took such sorrow
> That he quit being. . . .

(with the need to linger ever so slightly over the doubled consonants and sibilants) runs a fine little thread of sentiment all unobtrusively into the speech and out again.[1]

For a still more straightforward passage, take Belarius' soliloquy:

> How hard it is to hide the sparks of nature!
> These boys know little they are sons to the king;
> Nor Cymbeline dreams that they are alive,
> They think they are mine: and though trained up thus meanly,
> I' the cave wherein they bow, their thoughts do hit
> The roofs of palaces, and nature prompts them
> In simple and low things to prince it much
> Beyond the trick of others. . . .

The three first lines, each a completed phrase, gain our attention, the feminine ending of the first and (for variety) the similar ' little ' coming before the

---

[1] From a speaker's point of view, it makes, of course, little difference whether a doubled consonant falls in one word or connects two. Needless to say, the symbol ' th ' as in ' the ' and ' that ' is not included in the term.

cæsura of the second make easy speaking, while the dominating ' dreams ' in the third gives force —just enough; and after this, carried-over sentences and half-elided syllables send the speech familiarly on its way.

The verse throughout is very rich in texture; and if sometimes it seems over-rich, this suits it to the frank artifice of the play, and the actors may allow themselves a certain slight sophistication of style for its delivery. Shakespeare in fact—the wheel come full circle—seems almost to be cultivating a new Euphuism. It has no close likeness to the old; by the difference, indeed, we may measure something of the distance he has travelled in twenty years of playwriting.[1] It is a Euphuism of imagination rather than expression. This will often be simple enough; it is the thought or emotion behind that may be too far-fetched for the occasion or the speaker. What she means is made plain, but would Imogen, we ask, even if it took her so long to break the seals of Posthumus' letter, excogitate meanwhile to such effect as this?

> Good wax, thy leave. Blest be
> You bees that make these locks of counsel! Lovers

---

[1] But the degree of likeness will depend upon how much of Cymbeline we allow to be Shakespeare's. Biron's

> Light seeking light doth light of light beguile:
> So, ere you find where light in darkness lies,
> Your light grows dark by losing of your eyes.

has, for instance, a more than distant likeness to Arviragus'

> Nobly he yokes
> A smiling with a sigh, as if the sigh
> Was that it was for not being such a smile;
> The smile mocking the sigh. . . .

But then Furness—and others of his opinion, supposedly—will allow Shakespeare none of this.

> And men in dangerous bonds pray not alike:
> Though forfeitors you cast in prison, yet
> You clasp young Cupid's tables.

Would Posthumus, still full of faith in Imogen, regreeting Iachimo, cap his tribute to her as one of the fairest ladies he had looked upon with

> And therewithal the best, or let her beauty
> Look through a casement to allure false hearts,
> And be false with them.

And would Cloten at any time be found reflecting

> I know her women are about her: what
> If I do line one of their hands? 'Tis gold
> Which buys admittance; oft it doth; yea, and makes
> Diana's rangers false themselves, yield up
> Their deer to the stand o' the stealer; and 'tis gold
> Which makes the true man kill'd and saves the thief;
> Nay, sometimes hangs both thief and true man; what
> Can it not do and undo?

Cloten's sentiments, no doubt; but 'Diana's rangers' are hardly within his intellectual range.[1] Is Pisanio so confirmed a moraliser that, even though Imogen be stupent with horror at the accusation of adultery, he (and his author) must keep her standing there while he informs us that

> . . . 'tis slander,
> Whose edge is sharper than the sword, whose tongue
> Outvenoms all the worms of Nile, whose breath
> Rides on the posting winds and doth belie—
> All corners of the world—kings, queens and states,
> Maids, matrons, nay, the secrets of the grave
> This viperous slander enters.

---

[1] Furness refuses Shakespeare's responsibility for the lines, and argues that Cloten is too much of an ass to have such ideas. Cloten is by no means pure ass; a diseased vanity is his trouble; with Caius Lucius he puts up a by no means despicable show of the bluff, blunt Englishman.

ii. 20

And if he does stop to think of the peril it will be
to her complexion to wander disguised through the
forest, is this how he will warn her of it?

> . . . nay, you must
> Forget that rarest treasure of your cheek,
> Exposing it—but, oh, the harder heart!
> Alack, no remedy!—to the greedy touch
> Of common-kissing Titan. . . .

These are, indeed, sheer lapses from dramatic
integrity. They are not the worst to be found in
the play; but we cannot, as with the worst, simply
deny them all to Shakespeare. They are the
failures, the spoiled specimens of a method which
is half-successful in such effects of antithesis and
conceit of thought as Posthumus' later

> . . . so I'll die
> For thee, O Imogen, even for whom my life
> Is, every breath, a death.

as Imogen's rather schoolma'amish (but Iachimo
at the moment is certainly making her feel most
uncomfortable)

> . . . pray you,
> Since doubting things go ill often hurts more
> Than to be sure they do—for certainties
> Either are past remedies, or, timely knowing
> The remedy then born—discover to me
> What both you spur and stop.

It is, however, only the parenthesis that overloads
this and robs it of spontaneity.

For complete success in making the formal anti-
thetical phrase do dramatic service take the
Queen's description of Imogen:

> . . . she's a lady
> So tender of rebukes that words are strokes
> And strokes death to her.

For a clever woman's bitter-sweet summing up of her foe, what could be better? Take Pisanio's reproachful

> O, my master,
> Thy mind to her is now as low as were
> Thy fortunes. . . .

Brooding indignation does gather itself into just such epitome. We shall not even find his description of the departing Posthumus, standing on deck,

> Still waving, as the fits and stirs of 's mind
> Could best express how slow his soul sail'd on,
> How swift his ship.

out of keeping. It is in the key of the scene; and Imogen, we feel, thrilled through with love and faith, might move a stone to eloquence.

And coming to Iachimo, how else should the subtle, tricky Italian express himself but in paradox and over-wrought metaphor? The device of the asides, that are meant to be overheard while Imogen re-reads the letter he has brought her, is pure artifice. But it seems no more the dramatist's than Iachimo's, touches, on that stage, the limits of convention, but by no means exceeds them; and the high-coloured, harlequin phrases are all Iachimo's own.

> What, are men mad? Hath nature given them eyes
> To see this vaulted arch and the rich crop
> Of sea and land, which can distinguish 'twixt
> The fiery orbs above and the twinned stones
> Upon the numbered beach, and can we not
> Partition make with spectacles so precious
> 'Twixt fair and foul?

Imogen.   What makes your admiration?
Iachimo. It cannot be i' the eye; for apes and monkeys,
'Twixt two such shes, would chatter this way and

Contemn with mows the other: nor i' the judgment;
For idiots, in this case of favour, would
Be wisely definite; nor i' the appetite;
Sluttery, to such neat excellence opposed,
Should make desire vomit emptiness,
Not so allured to feed.

Imogen. What is the matter, trow?

Iachimo. The cloyed will—
That satiate yet unsatisfied desire, that tub
Both filled and running—ravening first the lamb
Longs after for the garbage.

Imogen. What, dear sir,
Thus raps you? Are you well?

Iachimo. Thanks, madam, well.

This is the new Euphuism *in excelsis*. For yet another taste of it, here is his outburst to her some fifty lines later.

O dearest soul, your cause doth strike my heart
With pity that doth make me sick! A lady
So fair, and fastened to an empery,
Would make the great'st king double, to be partner'd
With tomboys hired with that self-exhibition,
Which your own coffers yield! with diseased ventures,
That play with all infirmities for gold,
Which rottenness can lend nature, such boiled stuff
As well might poison poison.

But the mature dramatist has turned decorative flourishes to strict dramatic account. Belarius and his cave and his bluff talk stand for rustic honesty; here, at the other end of the scale, is this degenerate Italian, come to Cymbeline's Court

. . . to mart
As in a Romish stew, and to expound
His beastly mind. . . .

and he presents us, in his arrogance, with an approach to a travesty of himself, which is also a travesty of the very medium in which he exists.

292

A subtle and a daring piece of craftsmanship, germane to this hybrid tragi-comedy. Instead of opposing the heroic and the comic, Shakespeare blends the two. But the integrity of the character must be preserved; it would not do for Iachimo to become even half-conscious of what a figure he cuts in the eyes of the gods—and in ours. And it is this that is achieved by the modulating of the medium itself. Artifice is its norm throughout the play; but the range is wide. Iachimo's mean of expression lies at the florid end, and itself ranges from the polished prose by which he asserts himself among his fellows in Rome (made here and there a little plainer to suit the blunt Englishman's understanding), from the argute, sensuous verse of the soliloquy over the sleeping Imogen (the man himself, this), from the elaborate, parenthetical repentance at the last, even to the high-coloured complexity of these speeches, in which, as we said, he is meant to seem to us not only pretentious and false, but—all unconsciously, and that he may not rank as too tragic a villain—just a trifle ridiculous.

For simpler and subtler examples of this moulding of verse and its conventions to the expression of character, we can turn to Imogen, and notably to the scene in which she learns from Pisanio what is Posthumus' doom for her. The verse is full of metaphor; but it is all (or nearly all; we have noted a peccant passage or so) directly dramatic, prompted by the occasion, by the very properties of the scene.

> Come, here's my heart,
> (Something's afore't—soft, soft! we'll no defence)
> Obedient as the scabbard! What is here?
> The scriptures of the loyal Leonatus,

All turn'd to heresy? Away, away,
Corrupters of my faith! You shall no more
Be stomachers to my heart. Thus may poor fools
Believe false teachers: though those that are betrayed
Do feel the treason sharply, yet the traitor
Stands in worse case of woe. . . .

We are conscious neither of the metaphor nor of the structure of the verse, only of its music. The fusion of substance into form is complete.

Even when the prompting is not immediate, it is but at one remove.

False to his bed! What is it to be false?
To lie in watch there, and to think on him?
To weep 'twixt clock and clock? If sleep charge nature,
To break it with a fearful dream of him,
And cry myself awake? That's false to 's bed, is it?

We have seen her lying so, glad to have tired herself by hours of reading to the point of sleep. She has dressed for her journey in the

. . . riding suit, no costlier than would fit
A franklin's housewife.

There will, then, be sufficient strangeness in the now unroyal look of her to sharpen for us, to strengthen by its touch of incongruity (though we shall not guess why) the image of

Poor I am stale, a garment out of fashion;
And, for I am richer than to hang by the walls,
I must be ripp'd . . .

That it is a princess speaking who has stooped to her subject, to a marriage at once made desolate and homeless, is vividly implicit in

When thou sees't him
A little witness my obedience. Look!
I draw the sword myself: take it, and hit

> The innocent mansion of my love, my heart;
> Fear not; 'tis empty of all things but grief:
> Thy master is not there, who was indeed
> The riches of it. . . .

These are the subtler strokes. But the simplest actualities are given a place. They talk of the tired horses, of the doublet, hat and hose she is to wear; and the talk is matched with action. The language is ordinary, and the brief sentences would often disintegrate the verse if the rhythm were not kept regular. But this triple combination, of simple speech, short sentence and regular rhythm, gives an effect of familiar strength. Imogen is speaking:

> Thou toldst me, when we came from horse, the place
> Was near at hand: ne'er long'd my mother so
> To see me first, as I have now. Pisanio! man!
> Where is Posthumus? What is in thy mind
> That makes thee stare thus? Wherefore breaks that sigh
> From the inward of thee? One but painted thus
> Would be interpreted a thing perplexed
> Beyond self-explication: put thyself
> Into a 'haviour of less fear, ere wildness
> Vanquish my staider senses. What's the matter? . . .

Two lines that can be strictly scanned; the third has 'Pisanio! man!' for its two last beats, each word being one; five more regular lines, only the sense and the sentences breaking their regularity; two lines with feminine endings to ease the rhythm and a long sentence running through them to give them, for the finish, continuity and strength.

The technique of the scene's writing can so be analysed through speech after speech. But the art of it is not calculated; it shows us a Shakespeare so at one with his medium that he manipulates it as easily, as instinctively as he expects his actors, in their turn, to move and speak. Too easily, if anything; tension will slacken, ideas tangle, and with emotional pressure lacking, the verse will hang loose. But it is still a very far cry from this easy freedom that has succeeded the decorative contrivings of the earlier plays, the ordered march of the rhetoric of the Histories, and the tragic passion in which he fired verse as in a furnace— it is still a far cry from this to the flaccidities of a Massinger or Shirley, or of Fletcher at his worst. Dryden, in the end, had good reason to bring some discipline to bear. Whatever Shakespeare's metrical wilfulness, his verse will be pregnant with drama; and in this, this only, will be found the significance of its vagaries. Verse was his supreme dramatic resource. We may well expect to find it, in its full development of craftsmanship, alive with purpose, a very inventory for the acting of the play; and to find it so in this play more than another, for romantic substance is malleable into many delicate effects.

Its dictation can be minute. Can anyone miss the indrawn gasping sob with which

> . . . To break it with a fearful dream of him
> And cry myself awake? That's false to 's bed, is it?

finishes? Or not hear how the expanding vowels and doubled consonants conspire to give Pisanio's long-bottled-up

> Hence, vile instrument!
> Thou shalt not damn my hand.

just the explosiveness it should have? Or not find the Imogen that, once disillusioned about Post-humus, has little faith left for anyone or anything, that will suspect Pisanio of murdering him and poisoning her, in the quick exchange of

Imogen.   But speak.
Pisanio.   Then, madam.
    I thought you would not back again.
Imogen.   Most like,
    Bringing me here to kill me!

and in that contemptuous, bitter, Iachimo-poisoned

    Some Roman courtezan!

The play abounds in such matter for her. In the first scene her attitude to her father (and her private opinion of his weakly tyrant's temper), the quality of her love for her husband, the dead blow that his banishment is to her, the uncompromising dignity with which she suffers it, are all summed up for us in five lines.

Imogen.   I beseech you, sir,
    Harm not yourself with your vexation:
    I am senseless of your wrath; a touch more rare
    Subdues all pangs, all fears.
Cymbeline.   Past grace? obedience?
Imogen. Past hope and in despair; that way, past grace.

And when, twenty lines later, news comes as she stands there with the Queen, of Cloten's flourishing attack on the departing Posthumus:

    Your son's my father's friend; he takes his part.
    To draw upon an exile! O, brave sir!
    I would they were in Afric both together,
    Myself by with a needle, that I might prick
    The goer-back. Why came you from your master?

That is another view of her: the scornful girl, flashing artless indignation at her stepmother. Note the daintily vixenish 'Afric . . . needle . . .

prick,' with slick syllables joining them; then the sudden imperious turn upon Pisanio. Tune, time, attitude, movement, what amount of stage direction could make them plainer?

Effect after effect will be found lodged in the simple cadence of the verse. Take these few more lines from Cymbeline's rating of his daughter,

> . . . That mightst have had the sole son of my
> queen!
> *Imogen.* O blessed, that I might not! I chose an eagle,
> And did avoid a puttock.
> *Cymbeline.* Thou took'st a beggar; wouldst have made my
> throne
> A seat for baseness.
> *Imogen.*   No, I rather added
> A lustre to it
> *Cymbeline.*   O, thou vile one!
> *Imogen.*   Sir. . . .

Shrill puerile scolding in the monosyllables of the first line; the blend in Imogen of pugnacity and respect shown by one overflowing line, the next truncated; Cymbeline's anger then gathering and deepening in weightier words, the last three regular lines giving strength, the shortening sentences adding violence to the quarrel—till, after the full stop of that ' Sir!'', Imogen resolves it into a calmer, but still very positive

> It is your fault that I have loved Posthumus;
> You bred him as my playfellow. . . .

Half the effect of Cloten's first scene lies in the peculiar pattern given to the action of it by the Second Lord's strange succession of asides. Cloten is crossing the stage, returning to his apartments from the frustrated duel, the First Lord fawning on him. The Second Lord follows, five paces or so behind, commenting on the conversation he can just overhear. There will be a very slight midway pause; then the walk continues. Within reach of the door Cloten turns and sees the Second Lord for the first time, catches him, probably, in the midst of his final mocking aside, suspects nothing though—for who would dare to laugh at him? Then follows

Cloten.   You'll go with us.
First Lord.   I'll attend your lordship.
Cloten.   Nay, come, let's go together.
Second Lord. Well, my lord.

and the three depart; the Second Lord constrained to congé too. A scene of no great importance; it serves to introduce Cloten, and to fill up the ' half-hour ' needed for Posthumus' embarking. But its odd perambulation gives it comic distinction; the passing across the stage hints at the passing of time; the slipping-in of the asides keeps it moving and denies it solid emphasis.

There is, naturally, less flexibility in the writing of the prose scenes. Iachimo's provoking of the wager is remarkable rather for the way in which the close-knit, unrelaxing sentences are made to suggest a certain intellectual power in the man. Posthumus is no fool; he can to a point play up to him. But early in the scene, and in the midst of the prose, has come his heartfelt tribute to his Imogen:

She holds her virtue still and I my mind

—and, of itself, the sudden melody of the single line of verse proclaims the honest romantic fellow, tempting prey to a sensualist cynic. We seem to

299

see Iachimo stalking him in the stealthy prose line that follows pat:

> You must not so far prefer her 'fore ours of Italy.

In the verse scenes, on the other hand, a sudden line of free rhythm may be used to ease the strain of a situation; as when Imogen accepts Iachimo's apology for his experimental libelling of Post-humus with a

> All's well, sir: take my power i' the court for yours.

The limpid flow of the line does, indeed, far more than this; it speaks—its sense apart—of the nobly innocent nature, ready to be twice deceived. We hear the self-same tune when Arviragus welcomes her to the cave:

> The night to the owl and morn to the lark less welcome.

In the very tune there is generous frank affection, flowing from a nature like her own.

The free rhythm of long, simply worded lines makes its best effect in the pastoral scenes. It fits with pathos and gentle humour; not with wit, wit asks for the discipline of stricter scanning or of prose. When Imogen, disguised as Fidele, has been discovered in the cave:

> Good masters, harm me not.
> Before I entered here I called; and thought
> To have begged or bought what I have took; good troth,
> I have stolen nought; nor would not, though I had found
> Gold strewed i' the floor. Here's money for my meat:
> I would have left it on the board so soon
> As I had made my meal, and parted,
> With prayers for the provider.

the form and colour of the lines redouble their meaning; the timid half-line for a beginning, the appeal of the long, evenly stressed, all but monosyllabled sentence, the apologetic hiatus that ends the last line but one,—it is all a painting in sound of helpless indomitable Imogen.[1]

More regular verse, thriftily worded, simply phrased, and of a fine virile swing, is to be found when it is wanted; as it is for Imogen's flashing response to Iachimo's first crude attempt upon her.

> . . . What ho, Pisanio!
> The king my father shall be made acquainted
> Of thy assault: if he shall think it fit
> A saucy stranger in his court to mart
> As in a Romish stew, and to expound
> His beastly mind to us, he hath a court
> He little cares for, and a daughter who
> He not respects at all.

And it is instructive to compare Imogen's out-breaking horror and grief, when she wakes to find the headless body beside her, with Juliet's when the Nurse brings her, as she thinks, the news of Romeo's death. Between that

> I am not I, if there be such an ' I,'
> Or those eyes shut that make thee answer ' I ' . . .

and

> Damn'd Pisanio
> Hath with his forged letters—damn'd Pisanio—
> From this most bravest vessel of the world
> Struck the main-top. O Posthumus! alas,
> Where is thy head? where's that? Ah me, where's that?
> Pisanio might have kill'd thee at the heart,
> And left this head on. How should this be? Pisanio!
> 'Tis he and Cloten: malice and lucre in them
> Have laid this woe here. O, 'tis pregnant, pregnant!
> The drug he gave me, which he said was precious
> And cordial to me, have I not found it
> Murderous to the senses. . .?

---

[1] Early editors merely surmised a word missing from the penultimate line, and filled in the gap with a ' thence ' or ' hence.' A banal solution.

what a gulf! From purely verbal effect, a dervish-whirling feat of elocution, we have passed to a subtly elaborate use of parenthesis and reiteration, which gives us, as nearly naturally as need be, her anguish and the reeling agonies of her mind, yet never destroys the integrity of the verse nor breaks from the mood of the play.

There are, as always, those pregnant phrases and passages, in which all that is most significant in a character or the turn of an event will seem to be packed, or by which a whole scene may suddenly be keyed to a strange nobility.

We have Iachimo's self-portrait reflected from his very painting of Posthumus, unfaithful, slavering,

> . . . with lips as common as the stairs
> That mount the Capitol. . . .
> . . . by-peeping in an eye
> Base and illustrous as the smoky light
> That's fed with stinking tallow.

There is the painting of the candle-lit silence of Imogen's bedroom, of the night and its passing. It ranks among Shakespeare's masterpieces of mere writing; from that

> The crickets sing, and man's o'er-laboured sense
> Repairs itself by rest. . . .

to the

> Swift, swift, you dragons of the night, that dawning
> May bare the raven's eye! I lodge in fear;
> Though this a heavenly angel, hell is here.
> One, two, three! Time! Time!

There is the description of the dead Fidele:

Guiderius. . . . How found you him?
Arviragus. Stark as you see:
> Thus smiling, as some fly had tickled slumber,

302

> Not as death's dart, being laugh'd at; his right cheek
> Reposing on a cushion.

Guiderius.   Where?

Arviragus.   O' the floor;
> His arms thus leagued: I thought he slept, and put
> My clouted brogues from off my feet, whose rudeness
> Answer'd my steps too loud.

There are a dozen other such luminous passages, and more.

Finally it is worth noting how full of concrete imagery the verse is. This would be so. The mood of the play is not introspective, but romantic, concerned with things as they seem, and with emotion little purged by thought. The expression of it will rightly be picturesque.[1]

THE CHARACTERS

In the best of these, and in these (one must qualify it) at their best, we find the unfailing Shakespeare. Imogen is the life of the play; it would be a pedestrian affair without her. Posthumus, in execution as in quality, is only half a hero, a torso of the study of a man, but he is justly viewed. Iachimo is excellently done. If the last part of the story had more use for him, and if he did not suffer such a dull wordy declension from his brilliant beginning, he might rank as a masterpiece

---

[1] The actual text of the play is unusually troublesome, but I do not propose to discuss all the minor difficulties here. They are complicated, and, in some cases, so much matter for bibliographers that it would not be for me to venture an opinion. In the *Cymbeline* volume of The Player's Shakespeare I noted such readings as I preferred; and I am still ready to stand by most, but not all of them.

in his kind. Cloten has blood and bones, is by no means a mere stage figure of fun. He is, indeed, an uncommon if not unique item in the Shakespearean catalogue, a comic character drawn with a savagely serious pen. Nor are Guiderius and Arviragus mere romantic fictions, for all their provenance from that paste-board cave. Guiderius, in particular, exists in his own right, stands firmly on his feet. He is, in a double sense, set against Cloten, true heir against usurper, noble barbarian beside degenerate debauchee. And as the bestial truth beneath the comic mask turns convention into character with the one, so it is with Guiderius once he is set in motion; copy-book maxims will by no means contain him. Caius Lucius, little as we see of him, stands clear cut as a soldier and a gentleman; and as an instance of temperance in character made interesting—nothing is harder to do. There is vigour enough in Belarius and enough stability in Pisanio to beget belief in them while they are on the scene. But, apart from their use to the story, they have little life in them, and Cymbeline and his Queen have less.

The Queen is indeed worth some study as a failure. She is given fairly prominent place. She has to dominate husband and son, be double-faced to Imogen, cajole Pisanio, she is even allowed a most masculinely impressive address to the Roman envoy. She soliloquises; no advantage is denied her. But never is she co-ordinate into a human being. How account for it? For one thing, her wickedness proves of singularly little effect. Imogen is not taken in by her, nor are Pisanio and Cornelius. Pisanio does metaphorically swallow the 'poison-cordial' as Imogen does actually;

but the episode is so obviously—and very clumsily
—contrived for the sake of the sensational waking
beside the headless corpse that it can hardly reflect
much dramatic credit upon the poor lady. It
really looks as if Shakespeare, committed to the
story and not interested enough to re-model this
part of it, had said to her, as he sat down to write
scene after scene: Well, come alive if you can.
And when with her fifth scene it becomes clear that
—very excusably under such treatment—she cannot, he finishes her off, the quality of her last
couplet telling us pretty plainly what he thinks
of her and her wicked-stepmother banalities:

> . . . and my end
> Can make good use of either: she being down
> I have the placing of the British crown.[1]

Most unfair treatment; but dramatists do sometimes behave so to their unsatisfactory offspring.

Iachimo

It is cursory criticism that will see in Iachimo
a shadow of the master-villain with the ' Italian
brain.' He is made of quite other stuff than
Iago, and it is very solid stuff too. He is most
objectively viewed (a corollary of the picturesque figurative method of the play's writing, a
corrective, for Shakespeare, to its romantic spirit,
would seem to be a colder detachment from the
characters—Imogen excepted—than usual), and he
and his villainy are nicely suited to the story and
its ending; for from the first there is something
fantastic about the fellow, and no tragically-potent
scoundrel, we should be sure, will ever come out

---

[1] She has, to be quite accurate, still another, a broken one.

of a trunk.   He is wicked for the pure pleasure of
it, for the sake of the sport; there could hardly be
a more hazardous speculation than the adventure
in seduction into which he incontinently plunges.
At the bottom of the business is his vanity.   The
very first note struck from him—and Shakespeare,
we know, will mean it to be a leading note—is of
that grudging envy which vanity chiefly breeds.
He is speaking of Posthumus:

> Believe it, sir, I have seen him in Britain: He was then
> of a crescent note; expected to prove so worthy as since he
> hath been allowed the name of: but I could then have
> looked on him without the help of admiration, though the
> catalogue of his endowments had been tabled by his side and
> I to peruse him by items.

No woman, he is confident, can resist him (though
his opinion of women is so low that the compliment
he pays himself is a poor one), and when Imogen
does, he has his trick in store; he will do anything
but own himself beaten.   He is a sensualist and
something of an æsthete.   He has a quick and
sensitive mind.   He can size up another man's
weaknesses, and play on them with artistic skill.

Posthumus proves fairly easy quarry.   For there
will be, one fears—though he may mask it with
good manners—just such a slight complacency
about him as a life-diet of praise and nothing but
praise is likely to produce; it does not, at any rate,
give one over-much interest in other people's points
of view.   Even this banishment, his first misfortune, is a kind of tribute to his conquering charm.
His lessons are all to learn.   He is a little patron-
ising, too; the more British, and the blinder for
that.

In some such terms, while he leaves him to

change greetings with the Frenchman, and the two of them fight their old battles over, Iachimo will be summing up the stranger. Then he goes delicately to work. His first approach:

Can we with manners ask what was the difference?

the Frenchman must respond to. Posthumus does not like the look of this fellow, insinuating himself into the conversation, hinting, is he ('with manners' indeed!) that they are ill-mannered to leave him out of it. Forced to speak to him, he can give him, at any rate, a straight snub.

Iachimo. That lady [Posthumus' so vaunted mistress] is not now living, or this gentleman's opinion by this worn out.
Posthumus. She holds her virtue still, and I my mind.

But it takes more than a line of blank verse, however conclusive its cadence, to defeat Iachimo. Adroitly:

You must not so far prefer her before ours of Italy.

And as Posthumus, after all, is a guest here, the ironic appeal to his courtesy cannot be ignored. With his response to it (which is a little crude, perhaps, but he has small turn for irony)

Being so far provoked as I was in France . . .

Iachimo has him in hand, and he begins to play him.

It is an amusing, if unequal contest. On the one side, delicate dialectic, ironic humour, the salty cynical mind. On the other, Posthumus does his blunt, blundering best, encounters at every point; but with only his plain British common-sense and simple pride in his Imogen for weapons, he has much ado even to keep his touchy British temper.

Iachimo's tactics are to lead his man on to challenge *him* to make good his boast that with 'five times so much conversation' he'll 'get ground' even of this paragon among ladies and 'make her go back even to the yielding.' Patently, that will be the better position to be in; and we mark him feeling for the steps to it, every faculty alert. In this finesse lies the interest of the scene. It is Posthumus' moral sense that he plays upon (better sometimes to attack a man at what he thinks his strongest point than at one he knows to be weak); and how artfully he moves from the disarming tribute of

I make my wager rather against your confidence than her reputation. . . .

—which is a seeming retreat from the cynical

You may wear her in title yours; but, you know, strange fowl light upon neighbouring ponds. . . .

—through the designedly preposterous

. . . commend me to the court where your lady is, with no more advantage than the opportunity of a second conference, and I will bring from thence that honour of hers which you imagine so reserved.

to the provocative, brutal

If you buy ladies' flesh at a million a dram, you cannot preserve it from tainting. . . .

Posthumus is duly shocked by this last:

This is but a custom of your tongue; you bear a graver purpose, I hope.

is his comment. Yet somehow or other—he

would be infinitely at a loss to say how—within a minute more, for all Philario can do, the outrageous wager is laid. What notion he has of what he is after, poor muddlehead, must lie in

My mistress exceeds in goodness the hugeness of your unworthy thinking: I dare you to this match: here's my ring.

Imogen shall show the world, so she shall, and this contemptible foreigner in particular, what an English lady is.

It is, we may say, if we take a detached view of the business, a thing that no man in his senses could ever be brought to do. Better not be too sure of that; is there any conceivable folly that some man has not at some time committed? But Shakespeare, it must be remembered, is not approaching his dramatic problem by that way. He has chosen a story; his task is to make the events of it look likely. He need not even make them seem so in calm retrospect; the best of audiences will be content to be convinced at the time. The facts he must take for granted (if he does, so shall we); and it is in the characters themselves, in the why and wherefore of the things they do, nor in that only, but in the processes by which men's minds, shot with vanity or passion, work and can be made to work, oftenest to their own confusion, that we are to be interested. Too fine a study for the theatre, it will sometimes prove to be; and much pre-occupation with it goes with dangerously dwindling regard—or capacity!—for the enlivening of plain-as-a-pikestaff issues. But Shakespeare's art has been consistently developed towards this end, the popular borrowed story and his own businesslike sense of the stage serving to

keep the balance roughly true. He had always the
soliloquy to turn from a confidential talk about the
plot into a mirror of a mind's working; and once
the whole action of a play and every means he
could command were bent to show us how the
acid of Iago's guile eat into Othello's heart.
Iachimo's is a pettier game, and there is but a
scene or so in which to play it. It can be the
more subtly, and must be the more cleverly played
for that. One might even suspect that Shakespeare was attracted by its very difficulties. Put
the problem thus : here were a hundred and
eighty lines (he could not allow himself much more)
with which to introduce Iachimo and let him
persuade Posthumus to this preposterous wager,
and persuade us that he *had* persuaded him. The
thing asked some doing. But, absorbed by that
curious combat of disparate minds, we shall admit
when the scene ends that it has been done.

But what possesses Iachimo, we ask, who can
turn Posthumus round his finger, to make such a
crassly blundering approach to Imogen that he
comes within an ace of being thrown neck and
crop from the Court? The answer is an index
to the man, and shows no more inconsistency in
him than goes to make him a living character,
not, as he might have been—as the Queen is—
a mere joint in the mechanism of the plot. It is
an illuminating inconsistency. He has a keen eye
for a man's weaknesses; they are food for his
cynicism and a sop to his vanity. But the ways
of such honest innocence as Imogen's are without
the range of his understanding. For, even if we
must acknowledge it, we cannot understand what
we do not believe in.

310

At a first sight of her he guesses she will be no good game for a seducer. Still, he has his trick of the trunk in reserve, so why not try? He makes the classic opening moves; marvels at her beauty, cryptically deplores the lucky husband's gross unworthiness—overdoes this somewhat, to her puzzled amusement.

We must, by the way, make liberal allowance in this scene for the exigencies of dramatic time; its effects, in fact, may be said to disregard time altogether. We shall not question Iachimo's rising to these deliberate ecstasies within a minute of his arrival (though note the touch of the comic in them that discounts any incongruity there may seem to be); nor will it trouble our sense of likelihood that within ten more he should have played out his first game and lost it. Mere haste is not meant to be his error. The scene is framed to another pattern, as a conspectus of the assault upon Imogen; the effect would be poorer strung out in terms of time. But, while the verse and its modulations provide colour and excitement, the business of the scene and the shifting of the subjects of its talk give the checks and suspensions and slackenings that the use of time would give.

Iachimo's next move is to rid himself of the watchful Pisanio, who leaves them most unwillingly, not liking the look of the stranger at all. Then, alone with her, he stands deliberately mute, as oddly so as he was oddly eloquent a moment since, till she must break the silence with

> Continues well my lord? His health, beseech you?
> Well, madam!

he answers, putting a chapter of considerate mystery into the two words! She tries again:

311

> Is he disposed to mirth?   I hope he is.

He sees the opening and swiftly takes it:

> Exceeding pleasant; none a stranger there,
> So merry and so gamesome; he is call'd
> The Briton reveller.

This is not quite what she expects, nor, even in her generous love, can be too glad of.

> When he was here,
> He did incline to sadness, and oft-times
> Not knowing why.
>
>   I never saw him sad. . . .

Deftly now he gets to work, picking at the fabric of her faith with a fascinatingly evil skill.   Imogen is, after all, not a woman of the world.   Rome, seen from the shelter of her British Court, is Babylon.   The picture of the Frenchman, mocked at for faithfulness to his 'Gallian girl at home' by a Posthumus

> . . . who knows
> By history, report, or his own proof,
> What woman is, yea, what she cannot choose
> But must be. . . .

—by Posthumus, who thought far otherwise of women here, and of her (here is not there, though), a little sears her mind.

Note that they are his own convictions which Iachimo lends to Posthumus; thus they sound the more credible as he vents them; this is the accepted technique of slander.   But though he does excellently for a while, with his obvious wish to be quite just to Posthumus, with his flair for that unusual mingling in Imogen of humility and pride (two strengths that love and sacrifice have turned into a weakness he can play upon), with his pity of her that shames and angers her at once (he is bringing her, he must feel sure, into a very likely mood), the one warped factor in his combination— is himself. In slandering Posthumus he paints himself to her, all unaware. For who but he is now

> . . . by-peeping with an eye
> Base and illustrous as the smoky light
> That's fed with stinking tallow. . . .

—at Imogen!—oblivious of him yet, her grieved mind far away.   It is he, who thinks he knows

> What woman is, yea, what she cannot choose
> But must be. . . .

that can mirror himself—to Imogen!—in the significance of those

> . . . diseased ventures
> That play with all infirmities for gold,
> Which rottenness can lend nature! such boil'd stuff
> As well might poison poison. . . .

can, when at last she does turn to him, make confident attempt—upon Imogen!—with

> Should he make me
> Live like Diana's priest, betwixt cold sheets,
> While he is vaulting variable ramps
> In your despite, upon your purse?   Revenge it.
> I dedicate myself to your sweet pleasure,
> More noble than that runagate to your bed,
> And will contrive fast to your affection
> Still close as sure. . . .
> Let me my service tender on your lips.

Where indeed is the Iachimo, subtle, dexterous, shrewd, that could turn Posthumus round his finger? Vanished in this slavering, lascivious fool!

313

Chastity—and married chastity, that larger virtue—is the chief theme of the play. Imogen is its exemplar. Iachimo and Cloten, the clever fellow and the blockhead, are alike blind in lust. In the story Shakespeare borrowed the villain relies only on his trick, makes no attempt at all on the wife's virtue.[1] But Iachimo's insensate blunder (Cloten's bestiality too) is most germane to the play he evolves from it.

He makes, does Iachimo, a most brilliant recovery, nevertheless; winning her forgiveness out of hand with his ingenious

> O happy Leonatus! I may say
> The credit that thy lady hath of thee
> Deserves thy trust, and thy most perfect goodness
> Her assured credit. . . .

and the rest of the dithyramb. If we feel that she now is a bit of a fool to be taken in by him—well, he is a foreigner, it must be remembered, and all foreigners are eccentric; he had shown himself so upon the moment, in those strange extollings of her beauty. Besides, to hear Posthumus praised, when no one here dares praise him any longer! Even that

> He sits 'mongst men like a descended god:
> He hath a kind of honour sets him off,
> More than a mortal seeming. . . .

will not sound over extravagant to her. Iachimo, once he can rein in that satyr-demon of his, knows how to win her.

His sensuality is dominant again in the soliloquy

[1] This is true also of 'Westward for Smelts,' the other possible source.

in her bedchamber.   But the night's lonely silence brings it to an æsthetic fineness.   Here is Iachimo, his stallion vanity quiescent, the artist in life.   Yet from

> Cytherea,
> How bravely thou becom'st thy bed! fresh lily!
> And whiter than the sheets. . . .

he must still pass to

> That I might touch!
> But kiss; one kiss! . . .

and risk his whole enterprise on the chance that she will wake as he kisses her:

> Rubies unparagon'd
> How dearly they do't! [1] . . .

But, his lickerishness appeased, he can refine it again to

> 'Tis her breathing that
> Perfumes the chamber thus: the flame o' the taper
> Bows towards her, and would under-peep her lids
> To see the enclosed lights, now canopied
> Under these windows, white and azure-laced
> With blue of heaven's own tinct.

---

[1] The text, surely, leaves us in no doubt that he kisses her. Most editors will not have this at any price, their sensibilities being offended by the notion of it, and they find ingenious reasons why he should not—he would never risk waking her—and still more ingenious (mis)interpretations, since they must then have them, of the manifest ' How dearly they do't.' But a kiss is no more likely to wake her than is the stealing of the bracelet, even if Shakespeare were one to trouble about such trifles. And our sensibilities are meant to be offended. The sight of the fellow smacking his own lips that have just polluted hers should veritably make us squirm.

—which are arguably the most purely beautiful lines in the play.

By now we have the figure fully drawn in, and coloured too. Iachimo, then, is the sensual æsthete, the a-moral man. And this scene is, among other things, an exercise in the perversion of the sense of beauty. As we watch him weaving his evil web around her, making his damning inventory, even to the mole upon her breast,

> Cinque-spotted, like the crimson drops
> I' the bottom of a cowslip. . . .

we should be made to feel him only the wickeder for his seeing the while how beautiful in her purity she is. But Shakespeare, we may note, does not weaken the character by cant.

> Though this a heavenly angel, hell is here.

A modern villain would hardly be so simple-minded.

Back in Rome, with men to encounter, Iachimo is his masterful self again. A bracelet, after all, is not irrefragable evidence; he will need to have his wits well about him. Shakespeare sees that he has; the 'madding' of the victim into belief in his betrayal is as skilfully contrived as was his bringing to the point of the wager (and it presents the dramatist with no easier a problem).

Posthumus, chafed by his exile, wears, while he waits, that positively confident front which may so often mask, not a doubt, but the fear of one. He greets Iachimo with stiffly tolerant good nature, even rallies him, rather frostily, upon his failure. Behind that too there may be lurking the shadow of the shadow of a doubt. Iachimo, as before,

watches his man, keeps a cryptic countenance, lets
Posthumus make what he will of

>   Your lady
> Is one of the fairest that I have looked upon.

and waits to be questioned. Posthumus cannot
question him; that would be to admit a doubt.
He holds to his raillery:

> Sparkles this stone as it was wont? or is't not
> Too dull for your good wearing?

Iachimo counters it by assuring him coolly and
categorically that

>   . . . the ring is won.
> *Posthumus*. The stone's too hard to come by.
> *Iachimo*.   Not a whit,
>   Your lady being so easy.
> *Posthumus*.   Make not, sir,
>   Your loss your sport: I hope you know that we
>   Must not continue friends.

So far, so good. Here is the quarry lured from
behind his humorous defence, pricked to the beginnings of anger. Then, with a yet more categorical

>   . . . But I now
>   Profess myself the winner of her honour,
>   Together with your ring, and not the wronger
>   Of her or you, having proceeded but
>   By both your wills.

Iachimo brings him to the direct grim challenge of

>   If you can mak't apparent
>   That you have tasted her in bed, my hand
>   And ring is yours: if not, the foul opinion
>   You had of her pure honour gains or loses
>   Your sword or mine, or masterless leaves both
>   To who shall find them.

—and to make it, we note, Posthumus must needs

bring from the far back of his consciousness the
brutal image of that 'tasted her in bed.' It will
stay staring at him now, and Iachimo knows
better than to disturb it by a word. For his
part, he will avoid all mention of Imogen for
awhile. Distrust shall be left to work. So he
launches into his elaborate, choice description of
the bedchamber, which the exile knows so well,
making the lost joy of it yet more vivid to him,
quickening his senses to render them the more
vulnerable, smirching the picture with just one
lewd parenthesis, one drop of irritant poison to
the compound; yet for all his hardihood making
so reticent a case of it that Posthumus, though
puzzled, is reassured. But to feel reassured is to
feel that you have needed assurance. And, having
brought him to this state of sensitive, unbalanced
discomfort, he produces the bracelet.

The bracelet is good evidence, and far better
than Iachimo has till this moment known, for he
did not know Posthumus had given it her. But
how quick he is to seize the advantage, and to
better it!

Posthumus.   . . . is it that
          Which I left with her?
Iachimo.   Sir—I thank her—that.
          She stripped it from her arm; I see her yet;
          Her pretty action did outsell her gift
          And yet enrich'd it too. . . .

(Posthumus sees her yet; and writhes)

                    . . . she gave it me
          And said she prized it once.

Even so, a bracelet—this bracelet, even!—ranged
with things of its own kind, inanimate things, put

318

plump down on a table, might be matter for reason, for argument. Iachimo makes better use of it than that.

> . . . I beg but leave to air this jewel; see!
> And now 'tis up again.

Held for a horrid moment in the husband's face, and then returned so caressingly to his bosom, it seems a living thing. Posthumus makes one clutch at reason:

> May be she plucked it off
> To send it me.

But Iachimo is ready for this, has led him, indeed, into the trap of it.

> She writes so to you, doth she?

Whereupon, without more warning, this hero and his brittle faith collapse.

He is but half a hero; and while things went so smoothly with him, while he was Cymbeline's favourite,

> . . . most praised, most loved,
> A sample to the youngest, to the more mature
> A glass that feated him.

what chance had he to store up resistant virtues? And exile has been hard on him. Still, it is a pretty ignominious collapse. Soothed by Philario, he makes yet one more clutch at commonsense. The bracelet was stolen. Iachimo has his oath in reserve:

> By Jupiter, I had it from her arm.

nor is he perjured swearing it; and with this the wretched Posthumus is utterly undone.

Hark you, he swears; by Jupiter, he swears.
'Tis true:—nay, keep the ring—'tis true: I am sure
She would not lose it: her attendants are
All sworn and honourable:—they induced to steal it
And by a stranger!

They, who are nothing to him, may be trusted;
she, who is all the world, no! An admirable
stroke! Iachimo has won. He contemplates
in quiet detachment this moral fool demoralised.
Such a short step is it from the boast of 'her pure
honour' to

Never talk on't;
She hath been colted by him.

Partly to seal his victory, partly, one supposes,
for the simple pleasure of seeing the human animal
suffer, he goes on:

If you seek
For further satisfying, under her breast—
Worthy the pressing—lies a mole, right proud
Of that most delicate lodging: by my life,
I kiss'd it, and it gave me present hunger
To feed again, though full.

—to discover (interesting phenomenon!) that the
victim now asks to be tortured:

No swearing.
If you will swear you have not done 't you lie,
And I will kill thee if thou dost deny
Thous't made me cuckold.

—with which, and a little more raging, he breaks
from them in impotent fury. The shocked Philario
gazes after him:

Quite besides
The government of patience! you have won:
Let's follow him and pervert the present wrath
He hath against himself.

With all my heart!

The artist in Iachimo must be conscious of a fine piece of work done; and he feels, for the moment, quite good-natured.

It has been worth while, perhaps, to subject these three scenes to such close analysis, for this is how their actors must work at them, and their artistry ranks high even among Shakespeare's mature achievements of the kind.

Cloten

Cloten (pronounced Clotten to rhyme—most appropriately—with rotten, by warrant of the pun 'I have sent Cloten's clotpole down the stream,' which is reinforced by several spellings in the Folio) is far from being a merely comic character. His aspect is amusing; without that much mitigation, the truth about him (and Shakespeare does not shirk it) would be intolerable in such a play—in any play! He stands in the character-scheme contrasted with Iachimo; scoundrels both, the coarse numskull beside the clever hedonist, but each, as we saw, the other's complement in lechery—with Imogen, but for providence, their victim. He is a booby; even so, less booby than brute, and debased brute at that.

The first we hear of him is as

> . . . a thing
> Too bad for bad report. . . .

We see him with one sycophant companion, and another mocking him, all but to his face. It is harsh, unsavoured mirth, though; and we shall hardly laugh at him, unless as harshly. For to laugh at a man is to be at least in the way of forgiving him; and Cloten, gibbeted for vermin from the start, is turned round and round till all the foulness under his folly can be seen, to be slaughtered like vermin at last. Shakespeare was to evolve a little later a more picturesque and far more pardonable monster. But this civilised Caliban!

He is not pure poltroon. He challenges Posthumus (pretty confident, no doubt, that the 'gentlemen at hand' will part them) and fights the hefty young Guiderius (who is only armed, it would seem, with hunting knife and club [1]). He has as much courage, that's to say, as will go to make a bully.

> Would there had been some hurt done!

—but not, of course, to him. He is lit up for us in that line; and shortly by two more. Never was there a more patient man in loss, his ironic flatterer tells him. He is

> . . . the most coldest that ever turned up ace.
> *Cloten.* It would make any man cold to lose.
> *First Lord.* But not every man patient after the noble temper of your lordship. You are most hot and furious when you win.
> *Cloten.* Winning will put any man in courage.

It will never enter his thick head that he is being laughed at. Cockered and coached by his mother, and thanks to his tailor, he makes some sort of figure at court, woos Imogen, assails her with 'musics' in the morning, being told this will 'penetrate,' orders the musicians about, we notice, as if they were dogs. The music not penetrating sufficiently, he must bribe her ladies, he thinks;

[1] 'With his own sword,' says Guiderius. . . . 'I have ta'en his head from him.'

his own idea, this. He goes about it with true
delicacy:

> There's gold for you;
> Sell me your good report.

When she does at last give him a word he manages
to start with

> Good morrow, fairest sister: your sweet hand.

But soon he is hectoring her too. He is not in love
with her, needless to say. She is 'this foolish
Imogen'; when he has got her he will 'have gold
enough,' that is all. He makes not a little noise
at the reception of the Roman envoy. Critics have
objected that Cymbeline would never admit such
a blockhead to his counsels. Bless their innocence!
At such courts as Cymbeline's any loud-voiced
bully who is in royal favour, given chance to say

> Come, there's no more tribute to be paid . . .

and damn the consequences, will have his cheering
backers. What's Rome to them? But when the
fighting comes it will be one of them that Posthumus
finds

> Still going? This a lord! . . .
> To-day how many would have given their honour
> To have saved their carcasses! took heel to do't,
> And yet died too. . . .

Yet Cloten rises to a sort of dignity when he
bids farewell to Lucius with

> Your hand, my lord.
> Receive it friendly; but from this time forth
> I wear it as your enemy.

Even Cloten, we are tempted to say, can show himself at his country's call to be a soldier and a gentleman.

323

One of Shakespeare's touches of grim mischief, this; for he has not done with him. Imogen fled and in disgrace, the gallant gentleman scents the opportunity for another sort of wooing of her. He will pursue her, dressed (the story demands it) in the very garments Posthumus wore at their leave-taking, those that she said she held, the meanest of them—that insult particularly rankles!—in more respect than his 'noble and natural person'; and

With that suit upon my back, will I ravish her; first kill him and, in her eyes, there shall she see my valour, which will then be a torment to her contempt. He on the ground . . . and when my lust hath dined . . . to the Court I'll knock her back, foot her home again.. . . .

'When my lust hath dined. . . .'! Shakespeare can, on occasion, lodge a fair amount of meaning within four words, give us the marrow of a man in them too. This is Cloten with the comic mask lifted, the soldier and gentleman shed, the beast showing. A Cloten hardly in his right mind, one would suppose—even *his* right mind. He does, a little later, when he recapitulates the programme, seem to realise that her father

. . . may haply be a little angry for my so rough usage, but my mother, having power of his testiness, shall turn all into my commendations. . . .

A Cloten merely weaving these Alnaschar fancies for his private delight, is he? By no means. War is beginning; his fine defiance of the Romans and the Court's applause of it have swollen his vanity yet higher; he and his kind, surely, are to have things their own way now; his appetites are whetted. The Clotens of the world, in Shakespeare's age, or Cymbeline's, or any other, ask

324

no more than opportunity. Scarcely a comic character!

Posthumus

Iachimo's victim we have already studied; is there more to be said for Imogen's husband? It will be hard for any dramatic hero to stand up, first to such praise as is lavished upon Posthumus before we see him (though when we do he is not given much time or chance to disillusion us), next against the discredit of two scenes of befoolment, then against banishment from the action for something like a dozen scenes more. Nor in his absence are we let catch any lustrous reflections of him. Were he coming back, Othello-like, to do his murdering for himself, we might thrill to him a little. He is a victim both to the story and to the plan of its telling. Even when he reappears there is no weaving him into the inner thread of the action. He cannot, as we saw, openly encounter any of its prime movers without prejudicing the elaborate revelations saved up for the last scene. He can only soliloquise, have a dumb-show fight with Iachimo, a didactic talk with an anonymous ' Lord ' who has nothing to say in return, a bout of wit with a gaoler who has much the best of it; worst of all, he becomes the unconscious centre of that jingling pageant of his deceased relatives—a most misguided attempt to restore interest in him, for we nourish a grudge against him for it. One can detect, nevertheless, unworked veins of interest in the man. He is among those who live (the benefits of their natural happy egoism apart), rather by credulity than faith, and not at all by judgment, whose moral balance, then, is easily

325

upset, hard to recover, no broad base being there
to rest it on. No wisdom in him, nor ever likely
to be much; but, in its place, some humility of
heart.

> And sweetest, fairest,
> As I my poor self did exchange for you
> To your so infinite loss. . . .

That is not spoken to Imogen the princess, but to
the woman; he knows himself, for all men's praise
of him, coarse clay beside her. We like him too
for his boyish boastfulness of her perfections—it is
its very innocence that sets the cynic Iachimo compassing his downfall—and can find something
pitiful in the as boyishly passionate disillusion-
ment of

> Could I find out
> The woman's part in me! For there's no motion
> That tends to vice in man but I affirm
> It is the woman's part: be it lying, note it
> The woman's; flattering, hers; deceiving, hers;
> Lust and rank thoughts, hers, hers; revenges, hers.
> Ambitions, covetings, change of prides, disdain,
> Nice longing, slanders, mutability,
> All faults that may be named, nay, that hell knows
> Why, hers in part or all, but rather, all;
> For even to vice
> They are not constant, but are changing still
> One vice but of a minute old for one
> Not half so old as that. . . .

Whoever has not at some time felt the better for
such an outburst (no inconvenient plot of a play
pending to translate it into action) let him laugh
at poor Posthumus.

But there is matter of more interest in his remorse.
It overwhelms him before ever he has learnt that
Imogen is guiltless, and here is the drift of it:

326

> You married ones,
> If each of you should take this course, how many
> Must murder wives much better than themselves
> For wrying but a little . . .
>   Gods! if you
> Should have ta'en vengeance on my faults, I never
> Had lived to put on this; so had you saved
> The noble Imogen to repent, and struck
> Me, wretch, more worth your vengeance.

Neither Othello nor Leontes, those other exemplars of the jealous husband repentant, reach this point of view. It belongs to the humility of heart which, we may like to think, was what Imogen found to love in him. And it is the same humility and generosity—for the accepting of forgiveness makes as much call on generosity as offering it, and more— that takes him back to her with no wordy repentance, no closer promise of amendment than his

> Hang there like fruit, my soul,
> Till the tree die.

He finds his new faith in her, and in himself, in her forgiveness of him. She understands; and so should we.

Guiderius and Arviragus

They are dowered with some of the best poetry in the play; but there is more to them than this.[1] They stand, of course, for products, the very choicest, of the simple life. What would they have come to be at Court; with Imogen for a sister, it is true, but with Cloten for a step-brother besides? As it is, they skip ruddy and skin-clad from their cave, exhorted by the good Belarius:

[1] Burdened with some few vapidities besides—of the worst of which, though, we have argued, Shakespeare can hardly have been guilty.

327

> Stoop, boys: this gate
> Instructs you how to adore the heavens, and bows you
> To a morning's holy office: the gates of monarchs
> Are arch'd so high that giants may jet through
> And keep their impious turbans on, without
> Good morrow to the sun. Hail, thou fair heaven!
> We house i' the rock, yet use thee not so hardly
> As prouder livers do.

Guiderius.   Hail, heaven!
Arviragus.   Hail, heaven!

Nor does he let any other occasion, great or small, pass unimproved. Luckily for their characters (dramatically speaking at any rate) they are at once set in opposition to this sort of thing; it is the simplest dramatic recipe for giving a scene life. But it is not till Guiderius, in particular, comes into action on his own account (this shows the authentic dramatist, too) that he effectively reveals himself. Himself, and another aspect of the simple life at once. Cloten, we shall agree, gets no more than his deserts. But when Guiderius appears, swinging his head as a gardener might a turnip:

> This Cloten was a fool, an empty purse;
> There was no money in 't: not Hercules
> Could have knock'd out his brains, for he had none:
> Yet I not doing this, the fool had borne
> My head as I do his.

—departing a moment later with

> I'll throw 't into the creek
> Behind our rock, and let it to the sea,
> And tell the fishes he's the Queen's son, Cloten:
> That's all I reck.

—here is simplicity with a vengeance, we feel. And young Arviragus' only comment is

> Would I had done 't—
> So the revenge alone pursued me! Polydore,
> I love thee brotherly—but envy much
> Thou hast robb'd me of this deed.

328

The slaughter-house side of the business is miti-
gated as much as may be, by more sententious talk
from Belarius, by the contrasting fancy of the dirge
over Fidele, by the palpable artifice of the whole
affair. But Shakespeare keeps the values of his
picture true. Beside the tailored brute the noble
savage is as sharply drawn; and, at the salient
moment, made no merely flattering figure. There
is another side to the simple life.

Imogen

When Shakespeare imagined Imogen (for she is
to be counted his, if anything in the play can be) he
had but lately achieved Cleopatra. And whether
meant to be or no, they make companion pictures
of wantonness and chastity; and, of women, are
the fullest and maturest that he drew. Chastity,
faith, fidelity strike the ideal chord in *Cymbeline;*
and Imogen is their exemplar.

But a pleasantly human paragon! She has
married without her father's consent (a grave
matter that in Shakespeare's time), has been a
clandestine wife for some while, what is more,
under Cymbeline's very nose—which shows, for a
start, some ability in deception.[1] Doubtless her

[1] Furness falls into the (for him) amazing error of suppos-
ing that the marriage had not been consummated, that it is
in the nature of a ' troth-plight.' But, apart from repeated
' husbands,' this is to ignore Posthumus' specific

> Me of my lawful pleasure she restrained
> And pray'd me oft forbearance; did it with
> A pudency so rosy. . . .

And as to the still threatened marriage with Cloten (another
difficulty he makes) the Second Lord speaks definitely enough of
> . . . that horrid act
> Of the divorce he 'ld make.

Relationship and situation are made amply clear.

329

stepmother is a tyrant and worse, and the prospect
of Cloten as a husband would justify much; but
her father has excuse for his anger. And she does
not—before his courtiers too!—yield him very great
respect, granted that he inspires very little. We
find her answering him, indeed, with something
uncomfortably near to condescending irony, an
invidious weapon to be wielded by the young
against the old.

> I beseech you, Sir,
> Harm not yourself with your vexation:
> I am senseless of your wrath. . . .

She has retorts, calm and conclusive, for his every
splutter; she is not, from the parent's point of
view, an easy young lady to manage.

It is, of course, her innate truthfulness and, even
more, her inextinguishable sense of realities which
are to blame; couple these with as inextinguishable a courage, and we have the first flush of the
effect she is meant to make upon us. Her first
words are to tell us that she is not for a moment
taken in by her stepmother's ready smiles. She
has nothing save her courage with which to meet
her father's powerful wrath; but that is enough,
and somehow, somewhere Posthumus will be
restored to her. And, princess to the marrow
though she be, her

> Would I were
> A neat-herd's daughter, and my Leonatus
> Our neighbour shepherd's son.

is no mere flourish of a phrase. She has not con-
descended to Posthumus.

> . . . he is
> A man worth any woman . . .

330

she says. What more is there to say? She is
princess most in her utter unself-consciousness.
Pisanio is her servant, and she orders him about
sharply enough.[1] But, as she trusts him, why
should she not show him how fathom-deep she is
in love? When he comes back to tell her of the
ship's sailing:

> Thou should'st have made him
> As little as a crow, or less, ere left
> To after-eye him.
> Madam, so I did.

(stolid, honest, categorical Pisanio!)

> I would have broke mine eye-strings, crack'd them, but
> To look upon him, till the diminution
> Of space had pointed him sharp as my needle:
> Nay, followed him till he had melted from
> The smallness of a gnat to air; and then
> Have turned mine eye and wept. But, good Pisanio,
> When shall we hear from him?
> Be assured, Madam,
> With his next vantage.

(Much solid heartening comfort in Pisanio! And
how, by the way, Shakespeare does love that word
' air '!) Imogen speaks half to herself now; her
thoughts aboard the ship.

> I did not take my leave of him, but had
> Most pretty things to say: ere I could tell him
> How I would think on him, at certain hours

---

[1] More properly he is Posthumus' servant left with her for
a faithful watchdog. The Queen's repeated reference to him
as hers—in particular the

> This hath been
> Your faithful servant . . .

has something of irony in it. For he has obviously helped
the two of them to conceal the marriage and hoodwink the
Court.

331

Such thoughts or such; or I could make him swear
The shes of Italy should not betray
Mine interest and his honour; or have charged him
At the sixth hour of morn, at noon, at midnight
To encounter me with orisons, for then
I am in heaven for him; or ere I could
Give him that parting kiss which I had set
Betwixt two charming words, comes in my father,
And like the tyrannous breathing of the north,
Shakes all our buds from growing.

The long-drawn-out sentence, fading to an end,
paints the flagging of her spirits from that intense

I would have broke my eye-strings, crack'd them . . .

to the loneliness of the prospect she faces. The
fresh simplicity of it all; the little joke about the
' shes of Italy ' (which is to come back upon her in
poisoned earnest, as such jokes will); the wifely
sanctity of the

. . . for then
I am in heaven for him;

—such strokes complete the statement of her;
gallant, generous, royal, innocent, unguarded. To
round it in:

Enter a lady.

The queen, Madam,
Desires your highness' company.

—and the girl-wife stiffens to princess again.
Would she for one moment tolerate Iachimo,
credit his excuse for his outrage upon her, or accept
his apology? There are the claims of the borrowed
story; and once again Shakespeare—artfully, tact-
fully, and by what he leaves out or suggests far
more than by what he puts in—brings them to tally
with the character he is creating.

This queer foreigner comes from Posthumus.

332

That in itself will frank him past much eccentricity of behaviour. But though she makes remorseful amends for her harsh misjudgment of him her courtesy turns cool, even to wariness. And it is her pathetically pretty fancy to have the plate and jewels near her for a while, only because

> . . . My lord hath interest in them. . . .

—to do even so much for him !—that serves to bring the fatal necessary trunk into her bedchamber.

Her attitude throughout the scene is quietly eloquent of her miseries. And when Iachimo, spreading his net, baits her with a little pity, her quick proud resentment speaks of other pitying eyes, which follow her now about the court, to which she'll turn as proud a front; even as the wistful

> My lord, I fear
> Has forgot Britain.

with its unspoken, questioning echo ' is forget-ting me?' tells of happy humilities of love left starving, comfortless, to wear down to secret self-distrust.

We see her braving the worst of her afflictions, her wooing by the wretched Cloten; the high-mettled courage that she showed her father is edged here with a sharper scorn—the object of it so contemptible! But the strain of the misery is telling on her; that final, gratuitously defiant fling at the Queen, for answer to Cloten's

> I will inform your father.
> > Your mother too!
> She's my good lady, and will conceive, I hope,
> But the worst of me. . . .

savours of desperation.

The godsend, then, of the news that Posthumus
has returned, is at Milford Haven, expects her there!

> O, for a horse with wings! Hear'st thou, Pisanio?
> He is at Milford Haven: read and tell me
> How far 'tis hither. If one of mean affairs
> May plod it in a week, why may not I
> Glide thither in a day? Then, true Pisanio—
> Who long'st like me to see thy lord; who long'st—
> O, let me 'bate—but not like me—yet long'st
> But in a fainter kind. O, not like me;
> For mine's beyond beyond: say, and speak thick,—
> Love's counsellor should fill the bores of hearing,
> To the smothering of the sense—how far it is
> To this same blessed Milford.

In a moment all the stored suffering and doubt
convert into oblivious joy, and she is at the height,
again, of her old confident vitality. The lines are
yet another example of the raising of simple,
seemingly natural speech to poetic power, and of
Shakespeare's maturest craft in this kind.[1] The
whole scene is finely contrived. For Imogen
clouds have vanished; but the glum taciturn figure
of Pisanio is to remind us that they are gathering
more blackly than she can imagine. She appeals
to him:

>   Prithee, speak;
> How many score of miles may we well ride
> 'Twixt hour and hour?
> *Pisanio.*   One score 'twixt sun and sun,
> Madam 's enough for you and too much too.
> *Imogen.* Why, one that rode to 's execution, man,
> Could never go so slow. . . .

---

[1] And some of us—nineteenth-century playgoers—can
remember Ellen Terry speaking and acting them, and seeming, for those few moments, to fill the Lyceum Theatre with
dancing sunbeams. There was the fine achievement, too,
of Irving's Iachimo—with its angular grace and intellectual
art.

As it is to hers, he knows—and we know—that
she is going, the joke is a grimly good one. She
enjoys it!

> But this is foolery.
> Go, bid my woman feign a sickness, say
> She'll home to her father; and provide me, presently,
> A riding suit no costlier than would fit
> A franklin's housewife.

Reluctantly he departs to obey her; and off she flies
to make herself ready. This is the last we are to
see of the princess, of the imperious Imogen.

The sight of her in the drab riding-suit will
speak of changing and diminishing fortune; she is
adventuring into a strange unprivileged world,
made the stranger, the more ominous by Pisanio's
silence as the two of them go on their way. At
last she wins the truth from him; and rather,
we note, by pleading than command—she is
conscious already of her declension. He hands
her the fatal letter.

But she is very Imogen in her meeting of the
blow. She risked all when she loved Posthumus
and married him. Her trust has brought her to
this. It never occurs to her to try to escape the
reaping of what she has sown. That she is innocent is beside the point. When she gave herself
she made no reservation that it should be for as
long as he loved her, or treated her well, or as it
might suit with her self-respect. So, 'When thou
sees't him,' she tells Pisanio,

> A little witness my obedience. Look!
> I draw the sword myself: take it, and hit
> The innocent mansion of my love, my heart.
> Fear not; 'tis empty of all things but grief;
> Thy master is not there, who was indeed
> The riches of it. . . .

CYMBELINE

We have had just a flash, though, of her shrewd unilluded temper:

> Iachimo,
> Thou didst accuse him of incontinency;
> Thou then look'dst like a villain; now, methinks,
> Thy favour's good enough. Some jay of Italy,
> Whose mother was her painting, hath betray'd him.

She knows (she thinks) the fate of such a handsome hero, finding another Court to flatter him. *She* fell a victim to him. She is wrong; it is the mud of Iachimo's flinging that has stuck, as mud will; shrewdness, wounded, does thus go astray. We hear the transcendent Imogen again in

> And thou, Posthumus, thou that didst set up
> My disobedience 'gainst the king, my father,
> And make me put into contempt the suits
> Of princely fellows, shalt hereafter find
> It is no act of common passage, but
> A strain of rareness: and I grieve myself
> To think, when thou shalt be disedged by her
> That now thou tirest on, how thy memory
> Will then be pang'd by me. . . .

—for in such perception and detachment lies greatness of soul. Her grief it is that is stressed; grief that such faith as hers, such love as theirs, should be thus brought to ruin.

> All good seeming
> By thy revolt, O husband, shall be thought
> Put on for villany. . . .

It is love and faith itself—all that she knew of good in an evil world—which stand betrayed.[1]

[1] A touch of this nobility was left to Posthumus too. He speaks, his letter to Pisanio says, ' not out of weak surmises, but from proof as strong as my grief.' The word can, of course, be used in the mere sense of injury. But Imogen certainly does not so use it, and we may read the deeper meaning into it here as well.

But while she may grieve nobly, meek mournfulness is no part of her nature, nor has she much patience with Pisanio's remorse.

> The lamb entreats the butcher; where's thy knife?
> Thou art too slow to do thy master's bidding,
> When I desire it too.

Pisanio.   O, gracious lady,
Since I received command to do this business
I have not slept one wink.

Imogen.   Do 't, and to bed then.

He means to spare her and save her, has some hope of the future. She hardly believes him (what should she believe in now!) or cares to be saved. But her native pride (at least she will never return to the father she has defied), her courage, and the instinctive hope that dwells in her youth (though she admits none of Posthumus, nor indeed any, yet she will act as if she did) all conspire to set her on the path he opens to her.   Stoically:

> . . . this attempt
> I am soldier to, and will abide it with
> A prince's courage.

—with the old dignity that her drab garmenting cannot disguise; with a new quietude.   When they part, her answer to his

> . . . may the gods
> Direct you to the best.
>   Amen: I thank thee.

—in the four words (if an actress can speak them) is an Imogen white from the fire.

We shall hardly know her as Fidele; the tiny fragile figure, once so commanding in her Court brocades and lately buckramed in her riding gown. Nor is this all the change.   Her utter helplessness, as she wanders lost in the forest, breeds a new humour in her; a sense, half comic, half pathetic, of what is ridiculous in her plight, of fellowship with the wretched, in their follies, even in their sins, a whelming sense of the pitifulness of things and of poor humanity astray.

> I see a man's life is a tedious one:
> I have tired myself, and for two nights together
> Have made the ground my bed. . . .

It needs no more than that and an empty stomach to make one very tolerant. Even Posthumus' wronging of her rouses no bitterness in her now:

>   My dear lord!
> Thou art one o' the false ones. . . .

—only a wistful, still loving, regret.

The conventional disguise, the sententious tone of the play (doubly sententious in these scenes around the cave) are turned to good account for this latter phase of the picturing of Imogen. They help her steer the nice course between comedy and tragedy that the story demands. As she enters the cave:

> Best draw my sword; and if mine enemy
> But fear the sword like me he'll scarcely look on 't.
> Such a foe, good heavens!

That ever-useful joke at once blunts the tragic edge of the business. The marvel of her meeting with her brothers is dramatically subdued by the matching of such frank artifice as Arviragus'

> I'll love him as my brother,
> And such a welcome as I'ld give to him
> After long absence—such is yours; most welcome!

338

with her

> Would it had been so, that they
> Had been my father's sons. . . .

It must be kept subdued, not only for the sake of the elaborate finale of revelations, but because a fresh emotional interest here, which involved Imogen, would discount the intensity of the climactic moment of her waking beside Posthumus' supposed corpse. This itself we find very subtly prepared for; producer and actors must carefully note how.

She is wooed from the worst of her sorrow by such brotherly love. Once again—far more effectively here indeed—the sense of indeterminate time gives atmosphere to the picture. For ' two nights together ' she has made the ground her bed; that is long enough to leave her starving, and there is no more point in the exactitude. But we are not to calculate that she reaches the cave one afternoon and is found seemingly dead in it the morning after. We are simply to see her gratefully happy with these good companions, the cruelties of the Court fading to oblivion, while she busies herself with homely duties :

Belarius.   Pray be not sick,
> For you must be our housewife.
Imogen.   Well or ill,
> I am bound to you
Belarius.   And shalt be ever.
>   (*She goes into the cave.*
> This youth, howe'er distressed, appears he hath had
> Good ancestors.
Arviragus.   How angel-like he sings !
Guiderius. But his neat cookery ! he cut our roots in characters,
> And sauced our broths, as Juno had been sick,
> And he her dieter.

An idyllic interlude, with its idyllic sequel in

the speaking of the dirge over the dead boy. For if Imogen is to survive to happiness, Fidele is dead. The three good companions are to meet again, but never in this wondrous world—which will fade for them (as imaginings of it do for us) into the commonplace; even as

> Golden lads and girls all must,
> As chimney sweepers, come to dust.

With the dirge and the departure of Belarius and the boys their idyllic life ends too—they pass to war and its realities. And Imogen returns to consciousness to fancy herself upon her lonely desperate journey again—

> Yes, sir, to Milford Haven; which is the way?—
> I thank you—by yond bush? Pray, how far thither?
> 'Ods pittikins! can it be six mile yet?—
> I have gone all night. . . .

—with the friendly comfort of the cave become a dream. Her last waking words had been the smiling

> Well or ill,
> I am bound to you.

and by the contrast the horror of the waking is redoubled.

But now that we have reached this most effective situation, we must own it, and the whole business of it, to be, from one point of view at least, dramatically inexcusable. It is a fraud on Imogen; and we are accomplices in it. We have watched the playwright's plotting, been amused by his ingenuity. We shall even be a little conscious as we watch, in this sophisticated play, of the big bravura chance to be given to the actress. But Imogen herself is put, quite needlessly, quite heartlessly, on exhibition. How shall we sympathise with such futile suffering? And surely it is a vicious art that can so make sport of its creatures.[1]

All this is true. But tragi-comedy—in this phase of its development, at least—is a bastard form of art; better not judge it by too strict æsthetic law. Tact can intervene; that reconciling grace which sometimes makes stern principle so pleasant to forswear. And Shakespeare palliates his trick with great dramatic tact; he veils its crudity in beauty (a resource that seldom fails him) and even manages to make it serve for some enriching of his character.

The atmosphere of artifice in which the whole play moves—in these scenes in the forest it is at its densest—helps soften, as we saw, the crudity of the butchered corpse. The long, confused waking (dream, to Imogen's drugged senses, only emerging into dream) tempers the crassness of the horror, too. Such a touch of sheer beauty as

> Good faith,
> I tremble still with fear; but if there be
> Yet left in heaven as small a drop of pity,
> As a wren's eye, fear'd gods, a part of it! . . .

---

[1] Hermione's reported death in *A Winter's Tale* is a somewhat similar fraud; but to this we are not made party. We should not sympathise overmuch with Leontes, in any case. But if we knew that he was suffering needlessly would not the retributive balance of the scene be truer, its dramatic value greater, therefore? This (if so) is sacrificed to the surprise of the living statue at the end. Would it not be better if we were in the secret and our interest set upon the effect of the revelation on Leontes? Once we know the story the practical test is hard to make. But there are more signs than one that Shakespeare never fully 'found himself' in this new form of play. For how seldom do we have to ask, when he is going full swing, whether there could be a more effective way of doing what he wants to do!

will sweeten it.   And from the positive

> A headless man! The garments of Posthumus!
> I know the shape o's leg: this is his hand;
> His foot mercurial. . . .

we are carried very quickly to the agonised climax and as quickly on.   There is no shirking.   Shakespeare, once committed, will have every ounce of his effect.

> Posthumus! O! Alas!
> Where is thy head? where's that? Ah me, where's that?
> Pisanio might have kill'd thee at the heart,
> And left this head on. . . .

is material for as blood-curdling an exhibition as any actress need wish to give.   But—here is the master-stroke—even while she is thus racked, and beyond endurance, Imogen's heart is purging of a deeper pain.   There is no remotest reason for her jumping to

> Pisanio,
> All curses madded Hecuba gave the Greeks,
> And mine to boot, be darted on thee! Thou,
> Conspired with that irregulous devil, Cloten,
> Hast here cut off my lord. . . .

She does not even know of Cloten's attempt to suborn him.   But her suffering—and her sex, if we like—is excuse enough for anything of the sort. And to find that Posthumus, even though she finds him dead, was not after all her reviler and would-be murderer, cleanses and exalts her grief.   Shakespeare does not insist on this.   Imogen, for one thing, is not in a very analytical or explanatory mood.   It is as clear as he needs it to be.   He leaves it to become effective in the acting :

342

> That confirms it home:
> This is Pisanio's deed and Cloten's: O!
> Give colour to my pale cheek with thy blood,
> That we the horrider may seem to those
> Which chance to find us: O, my lord, my lord!

She rallies from delirium; the pictorial phrase is a resolution into the play's proper key; and in the simple ' O, my lord, my lord! '—spoken as it can be spoken—we are to hear, as she faints away, her reconciliation with her dead.

Nevertheless, contrive as he may, it is a pretty damnable practical joke; and Shakespeare, the creator of Imogen, must now pay the price of Shakespeare's the showman's escapade.[1] He does; to whatever else he may yield we shall not find him at this time of day finally playing false to character. A happy ending may be the play's due, but Imogen can make no full recovery from what has been pure poignant tragedy for her. When the kind hands of Roman enemies recover her from her ' bloody pillow ' she stands tongue-tied at first. Lucius has to question and question before she answers his ' What art thou? ' with

> I am nothing: or if not,
> Nothing to be were better.

She is stunned and dazed; what wonder! She will follow whither she is bid:

> But first, an 't please the gods
> I'll hide my master from the flies, as deep
> As these poor pick axes can dig. . . .

The royal Imogen, to whom Posthumus kneeled with his

> My queen! my mistress!

---

[1] Or we may, of course, make the whipping-boy the original culprit, if we prefer.

who could gallantly defy her father and his Queen, and laugh at the brute Cloten and his wooing, has travelled far. 'Happy ending' looks little congruous with the sight of her now.

So Shakespeare finds. He frees her from the action for four full scenes, gives her time, as it were, for recovery; but restored to it, restored to husband and father, united to her brothers, her path fair before her, she is a wounded woman still. Her ring on Iachimo's finger; that only means she may learn how all the evil came to pass, the tale cannot bring her dead back to life; she listens to its verbiage in numb silence. When it does, when by miracle Posthumus stands there before her, the very joy leaves her speechless; she can only cling to him and stammer helplessly. Just for one moment, when she turns upon Pisanio, she rallies to 'the tune of Imogen,' and they know her by it. The 'happy ending' is duly brought about. But Shakespeare gives her little more to say; that little quiet and colourless, almost. He could not in conscience set her—or set any of them—merrymaking.

Lady Martin, who wrote pleasant reminiscences of Miss Helen Faucit's applauded performances of Shakespeare's heroines, ends the study of Imogen with a sentimental picture of a slow decline (the play being over), of her dying—'. . . fading out like an exhalation of the dawn'—surrounded by the rest of the cast in appropriate attitudes of grief and remorse. This is certainly not criticism; and one is apt to smile at such 'Victorian' stuff, and to add 'and nonsense' as one puts the book down. But there is something to be said for acting a part if you want to discover those last few secrets about it

that the author knew but did not see fit to dis-
close. And Lady Martin is essentially right here.
The figure of Imogen is life-like, of a verity that
transcends the play's need; and the blows that
Shakespeare had to deal her were death-blows.
It is something of a simulacrum that survives.
But there is a truth to life in this, too.

No one will rank *Cymbeline* with the greater plays.
It is not conceived greatly, it is full of imper-
fections. But it has merits all its own; and one
turns to it from *Othello*, or *King Lear*, or *Antony and
Cleopatra* as one turns from a masterly painting to,
say, a fine piece of tapestry, from commanding
beauty to more recondite charm.

HARLEY GRANVILLE-BARKER

Prefaces to Shakespeare

Demy 8vo. Each, 9s. net.

SOME OPINIONS OF THE PRESS

(*First Series*)

" Actual guides to production written by one who has been the greatest English producer of our time and who has now added an informed and acute Shakespearean scholarship to his technical qualifications as a man of the theatre."—I. B. in the *Saturday Review*.

" Here is an abundance of illuminating comment from a writer in whom the gift of literary analysis and the experience of practical stage production are most happily combined. . . . Three plays are specially studied, and all with singular insight . . . the analysis in each of dramatic values and of the presentment of character in action is close and illuminating."—Sir Edmund Chambers in *The Year's Work in English Studies*, 1927.

" Perhaps the most remarkable quality of Mr. Granville-Barker's book is the width of its intellectual sympathy; academic and theatrical, ancient and modern, textual and philosophic points of view fall into a scheme of sweet reasonableness which is not less Mr. Granville-Barker's because it is not violently antagonistic to anybody else's. He may dissent from Mr. Bradley on this issue, or on another he may demolish the fallacy of the modern-dress Shakespeareans; but as a rule there is an unforced conviction of irrefutable commonsense in all his findings."
—H. B. C. in the *Manchester Guardian*.

" It is pardonable to regard with caution every book and pamphlet that bears Shakespeare's name. What a blessing, then, to receive a Shakespearean volume that bears also another name which stands above the quibblers and the sycophants and is itself a warrant of balanced knowledge and temperate enthusiasm. . . . The quality that first made them delightful remains—the quality, rare in all dramatic criticism and most rare in criticism of Shakespeare, which gives to the reader a feeling that he is present in a theatre and is engaged under the guidance of a brilliantly perceptive *régisseur*, in an honest voyage of discovery. . . . His purpose throughout is the only reasonable purpose—so to set Shakespeare's work on the stage that an audience may still be affected by it as Shakespeare himself would have had them be affected."—*The Times*.

(Second Series)

" Mr. Granville-Barker . . . even while dealing with the most material details of production, is dealing with questions which Shakespeare himself must have considered in some form. He has the instinctive insight of a fellow-craftsman."—*Oxford Magazine.*

" It is impossible to do justice to this book by a casual reading. It is an aid to study, and it demands study. . . . He makes things mean so much that he shames our careless readings. In his close, sympathetic analysis everything means something. . . . It is the kind of criticism that makes you think. The whole book is thought-compelling."— A. N. M. in *The Manchester Guardian.*

" Most of the books that profess to deal with [the conditions under which Shakespeare's plays were produced] manage to say very little. The best of them all in my opinion is Mr. Harley Granville-Barker's *Prefaces to Shakespeare.* . . . Few of the critics of Shakespeare have been men of the theatre. Granville-Barker is the only one who is actor, producer and dramatist as well as student of the text. That is why what he says is of such value."—*Everyman.*

" Mr. Granville-Barker is not a stage-manager only; he adds to a superbly quick eye for the dramatic action implied in the text a fine ear for the music of the verse and a finely tempered reaction to the infinite shades of Shakespeare's sensibility. There is in his work the marriage of two minds; the man of the theatre and the lover of letters unite to draw out the full-fleshed life from the Folio's pages. The result is Shakespeare, in his habit, as he worked.
" . . . The producer-critic who boldly proclaims this [*Antony and Cleopatra*] to be the ' most business-like of plays,' proves his case by a brilliant survey of how the comings and goings would work out on the Elizabethan platform. Over and over again his realization of the conditions illumines a new point . . . light after light on the spring and reach of the workaday Shakespeare's mind."—I. B. in the *Saturday Review.*

" There is much in this volume, as in the one before, that has little or nothing to do with problems of stage presentation in the strict sense— the analysis of the characters of the plays, for instance, or the subtle investigation of the qualities of the verse. But the sections devoted to the questions of stage arrangement, mounting and decoration are as valuable really to the library student as to the theatrical manager. . . . These character-studies have not only the subtlety to be expected from a commentator who is himself a psychological play-writer of high rank, they have the zest and alertness of a student who enjoys his Shakespeare before thinking of worshipping or criticizing him. . . . No critic has shown more forcibly than he that, as a rule, the tiniest personages in any one of Shakespeare's plays is no figure of a pageant, but breathing flesh and blood."—*The Times Literary Supplement.*

SIDGWICK & JACKSON, LTD.
44 Museum Street, London, W.C.1